THE MUDDIED MIRROR

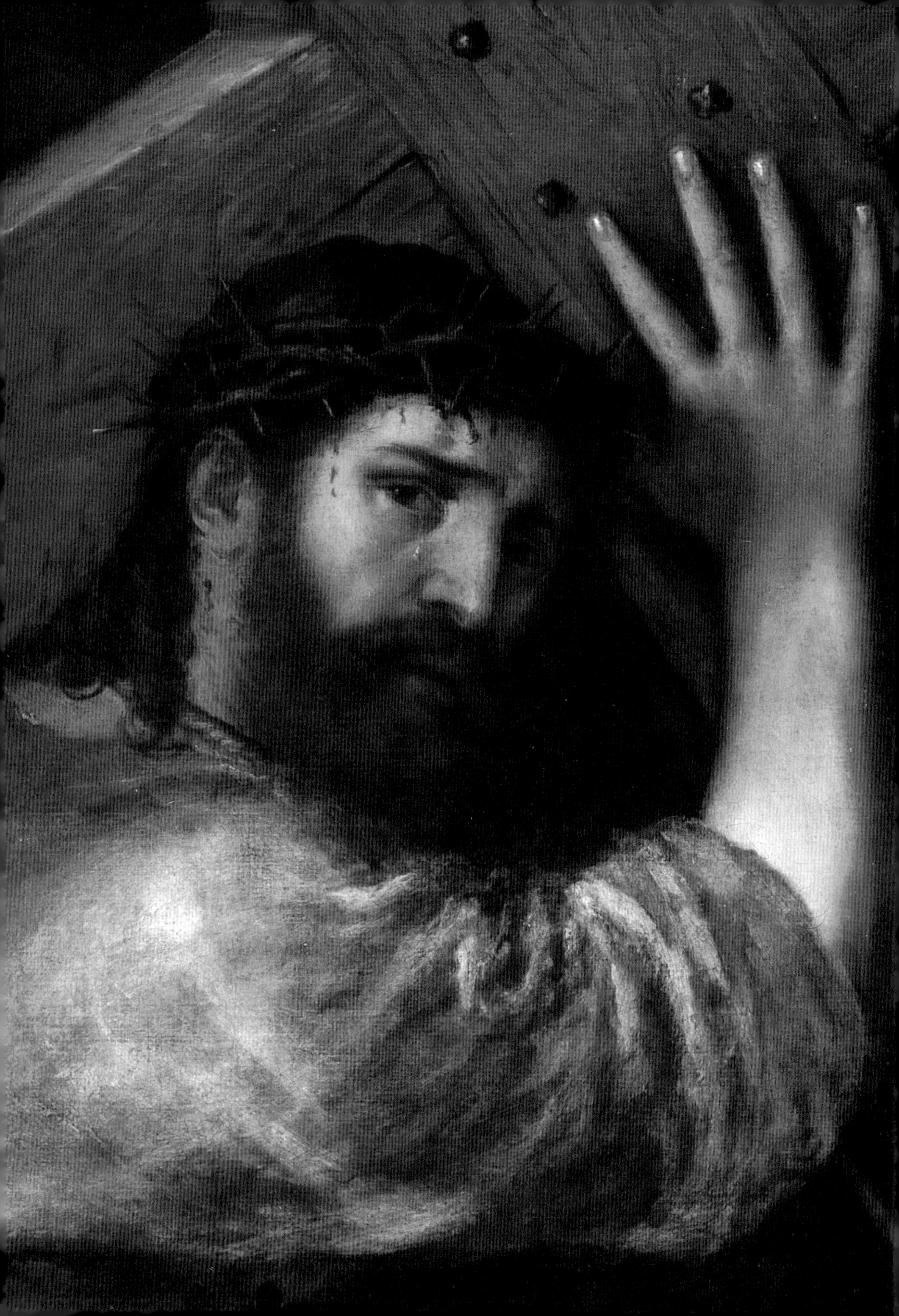

JODI
CRANSTON

THE MUDDIED MIRROR

MATERIALITY AND FIGURATION *in* TITIAN'S LATER PAINTINGS

The Pennsylvania State University Press
University Park, Pennsylvania

Library of Congress Cataloging-in-Publication Data

Cranston, Jodi, 1969–

The muddied mirror : materiality and figuration in Titian's later paintings / Jodi Cranston.

p. cm.

Includes bibliographical references and index.

Summary: "Extends formalism to facture and situates the materiality of Titian's later works within the late sixteenth-century interest in embodiment and violence rather than within the Renaissance ideals of classicizing beauty and perfection"—Provided by publisher.

ISBN 978-0-271-03529-1 (cloth : alk. paper)

1. Titian, ca. 1488–1576—Criticism and interpretation.
2. Painting, Renaissance—Italy.
3. Painting, Italian—16th century.
4. Figurative painting—Italy.
5. Violence in art.
I. Titian, ca. 1488–1576.
II. Title.

ND623.T7C73 2009
759.5—dc22
2009003732

Printed in China by Everbest Printing Co., through Four Colour Imports, Louisville, KY
Published by The Pennsylvania State University Press,
University Park, PA 16802-1003

The Pennsylvania State University Press is a member of the Association of American University Presses.

It is the policy of The Pennsylvania State University Press to use acid-free paper. Publications on uncoated stock satisfy the minimum requirements of American National Standard for Information Sciences—Permanence of Paper for Printed Library Material, ANSI Z39.48–1992.

Design by Jason Harvey

FOR DAVID ROSAND

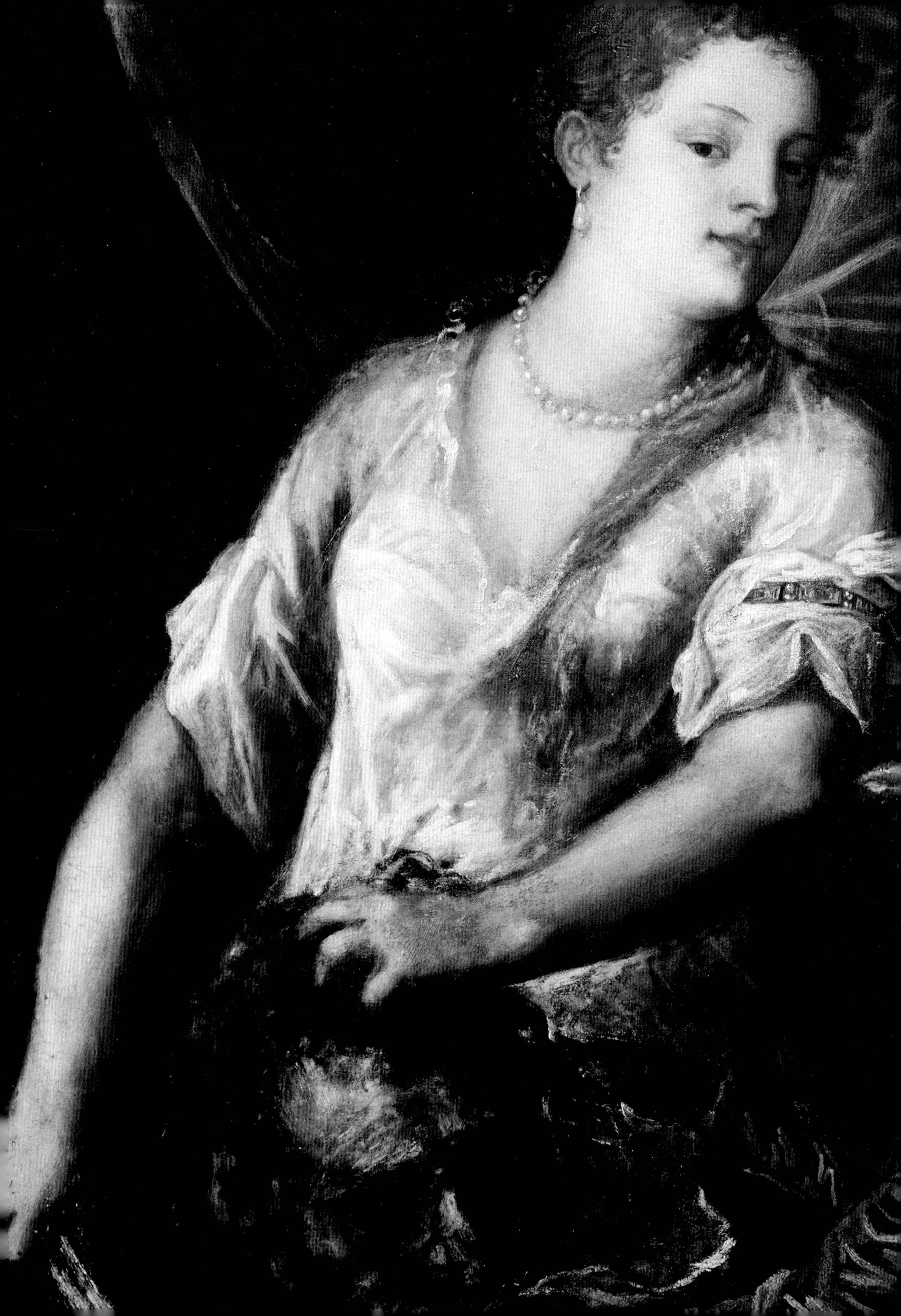

CONTENTS

ILLUSTRATIONS

ACKNOWLEDGMENTS

My work on this book began several years ago, when a group of graduate painting students at Boston University asked me to participate in a discussion of Titian's paintings. Their interest in how the paintings from the last two decades of Titian's life were made and received raised for me the central questions that frame this book. Foremost among these initial and sustained inquiries was the consideration of the relevance of modernist and contemporary theorizations of facture for Renaissance painting. Many early modern art historians and contemporary painters have sparked and shared these interests, and I have benefited greatly from exchanges with these different voices and perspectives. I am grateful to the following colleagues, who stimulated and supported my project through conversation and their scholarly work: Paolo Alei; Mauro Calcagno; Miguel Falomir, who curated the spectacular exhibition on Titian at the Prado in 2003; Kenneth Gouwens, who organized the New England Renaissance Conference in 2003, at which I first presented these ideas; Frederick Ilchman; Caroline Jones, with whom I organized a conference on medium and first discussed this book; Antien Knaap; and Joanna Woods-Marsden, who organized productive RSA sessions in 2004 on Titian, entitled "Titian: Taking Stock," and edited the anthology of those essays.

The most influential scholar for this book has been David Rosand, whose own work on Titian's later paintings inspired and affected my thoughts on the subject. I had the good fortune of being his student and doctoral advisee at Columbia University, and, years later, I am still the lucky recipient of his generosity. His sensitivity and devotion to this material have been apparent in his work for decades and were once again clarified for me when we spent some time together looking at many of the paintings in this book during the Titian exhibition at the Prado in 2003. Looking at him while he looked at those pictures taught me how to see them.

Several institutions supported my research for this book. My earliest consideration of this subject occurred when I received a Junior Fellowship in the Humanities from the Humanities Foundation at Boston University in 2000. Much of the research and writing was supported by a Charles A. Ryskamp Research Fellowship from the American Council of Learned Societies during 2004–5. I am still grateful for these opportunities to read, think, travel, and write without interruption.

Eleanor Goodman at Pennsylvania State University Press patiently shepherded the book through every stage of publication, and I appreciate her openness and responsiveness to the project. The two anonymous readers offered helpful suggestions and criticism and significantly strengthened the book.

I am also grateful to my family for their encouragement and support for this project, but most especially for whatever I undertake.

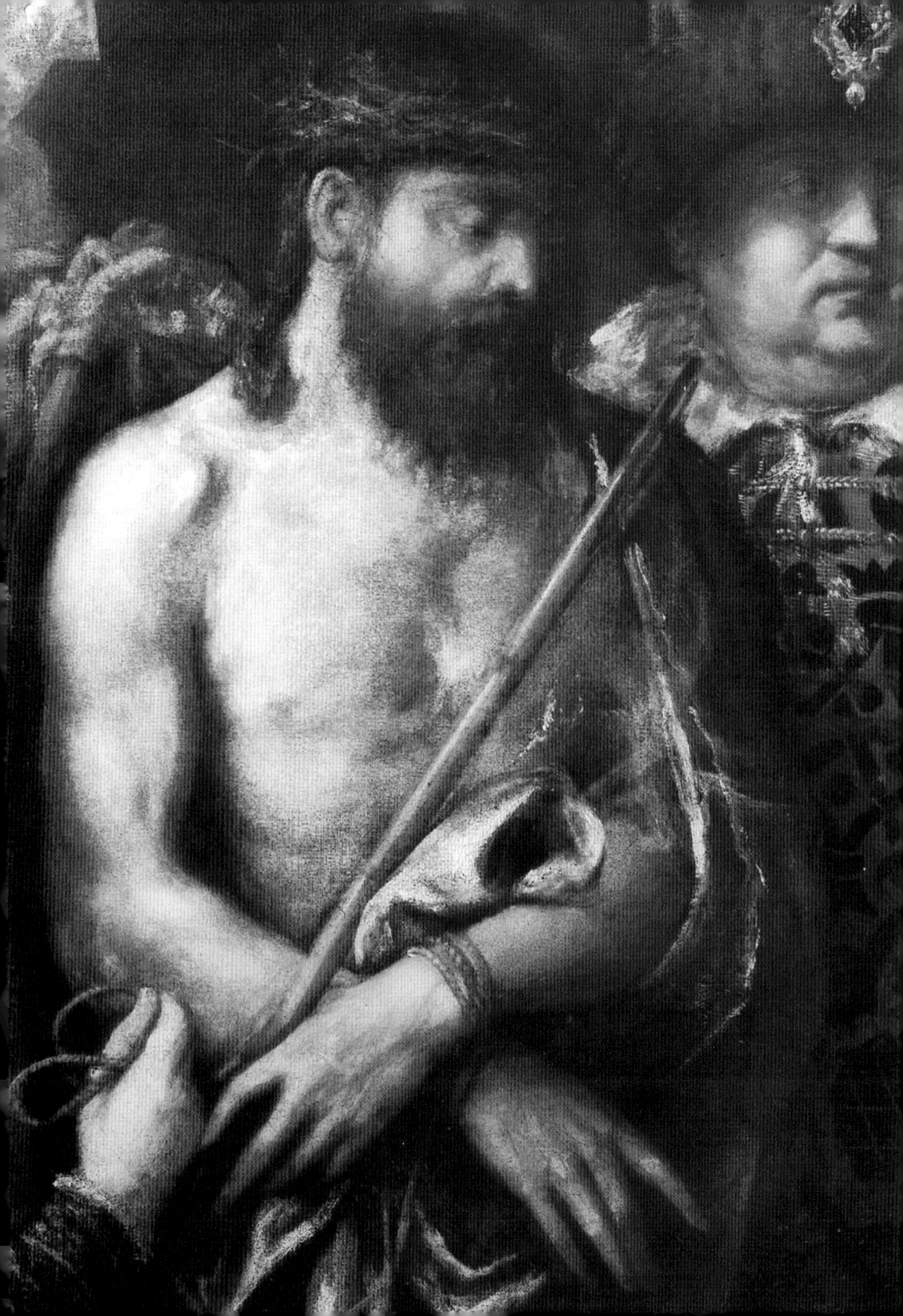

Introduction

THE SUBSTANCE OF RENAISSANCE PAINTING

Painting in the Renaissance was described and practiced as an art that ideally offered notional relief while minimizing the actual depth and thickness on the painted surface. Vasari provides such a definition in his prefatory discussion of the art in his *Lives:* "[Painting] is a plane ['piano'] covered with patches ['campi'] of color on the surface of wood, wall, or canvas, filling up the outlines . . . which, by virtue of good design of the encompassing lines surround the figure."[1] Although Vasari's emphasis on the relief accomplished by good *disegno* reflects the specific ambitions of the Tuscan tradition beginning with Giotto, his definition succinctly articulates the fundamental paradox that structured illusionism in Renaissance painting in general and that cultivated the elevation of painting as a liberal art: painting should suppress surface materiality—the physical materials and the indications of making—in order to affirm the three-dimensionality of the represented object.

In upholding this definition of the art, Renaissance painters and painting theorists believed that they were sustaining and developing a central facet of ancient painting. Without any surviving visual examples, they relied on written descriptions, especially those given by Pliny the Elder in his *Natural History,* that heralded ancient artists for the pleasures and deceits of illusionism in painting. From these ancient accounts of legendary paintings and their frequent Renaissance iterations, early modern readers learned of, among others, Zeuxis's painting of grapes that fooled birds and Parrhasius's painting of a curtain that deceived his fellow painter Zeuxis into trying to lift it.[2] Although never attempting to replicate exactly these inventions, Renaissance painters most certainly emulated this apparent defiance of the physical limitations of painting when developing recessional and spatial devices such as perspective, foreshortening, and *rilievo,* and when celebrating invention over the technical exigencies of the art.[3]

By the mid-sixteenth century, the circumstances of and developments in painting explored and disrupted the tensions and contradictions on which illusionism depended. The ca. 1500 introduction of easel painting created and depended on an intimate viewing situation in which the actual physical limits of the picture were in the viewer's field of vision. The artifice of painting, more than simply entering into the beholder's consciousness, became the rightful subject of the painting. Altering the synonymous relationship between painting and the world, cinquecento pictures indicated poetic interests and ambitions with the appropriation of poetic figures and the representation of things and conditions as they should or could be and not necessarily as they are found through direct experience.[4] The frequent Renaissance utterance that painting makes "that which is not seem to be" ("quello che non è, sia") not only describes the suggestion of three-dimensional relief in painting, but also acknowledges a suggestiveness in painting that oftentimes worked against this fundamental assertion of relief and the imitation of nature.[5] Painters began to draw attention to the precarious and largely undetermined relationship between art and nature through self-conscious manipulations of artistic style, or *maniera,* and artistic license.[6] At the same time, religious reformers interrogated the very nature and function of images, and particularly the often-conflicting relationship between the expectation of mimesis and the affirmation of painting as an object, a material thing incapable of inherence despite convincing illusionism.[7] Perhaps in response to this climate of reform, some painting theorists positively acknowledged the physical work of painting.[8]

Also in the mid-sixteenth century, the later paintings of Titian, with their roughly worked surfaces and evident signs of making, posed a challenge to the predominant Renaissance paradigm of illusionistic painting. Noting the change from Titian's earlier work and the necessary viewing adjustments, Vasari, in his second edition of his *Lives* (1568), writes:

> But it is quite true that his method in these later works is rather different from that of his youth; his early paintings are executed with a certain fineness and incredible diligence and can be viewed both from close up and from afar; these recent works, on the other hand, are dashed off in bold strokes, broadly applied in great patches in such a manner that they cannot be looked at closely but from a distance appear perfect. And this method has been the reason that many, wishing to imitate Titian and so demonstrate their own ability, have only produced clumsy pictures. This happens because they think that such paintings are done without effort, but such is not the case and they delude themselves; for Titian's pictures are often repainted, gone over and retouched repeatedly, so that the work involved is evident. Carried out in this way, the method is judicious, beautiful, and magnificent, because the

pictures seem to come alive and are executed with great skill, hiding the effort that went into them.[9]

Despite Vasari's clear appreciation of these pictures, he stubbornly remains the Tuscan and, following the Horatian trope from poetry, advises adjusting the physical conditions of viewing by standing back in order to view these paintings according to normative expectations of illusionism.[10] At a distance, the surface of painting—or rather, the physical stuff of painting—ceases to be visible and the materials remain subordinated to the mimetic conception. Blobs of paint and exposed canvas cannot be seen and, as Vasari's comments imply, should not be seen. Patrons who received Titian's work after the mid-cinquecento launched similar criticisms of a lack of resemblance and complained that the paintings seemed inferior to their expectations.[11] Pietro Aretino, responding to the rough brushwork and muted palette of his Florentine portrait, joked that the lack of finish and, correspondingly, of flattery might have been resolved with a higher payment.[12] Similar technical observations in his other paintings raised suspicions that the master relied too heavily on studio assistance or showed signs of declining ability and dexterity in old age.[13]

In failing to conform and respond to a well-established mode of painting and viewing, Titian's later paintings raise questions central to the interrelationship between resemblance, illusion, and materiality established since antiquity, but approach these questions in a way that contemporary structures of response and critical discourse could not accommodate or were only beginning to address. One of the central gaps raised by Titian's later paintings was the unresolved and, in the mid-cinquecento, uneasy relationship between the imitation of nature and the artist's personal style.[14] Renaissance theorists acknowledged the variations in *maniera,* but thought of nature in absolute, ideal, and, therefore, vague terms. Understandably, the deviation of Titian's later work from that of contemporary painters and, according to his peers, his own earlier work compromised his apparent commitment to the Renaissance project of painting. Because he did not transform the materials of art into a flawless illusion of relief, Titian's later work could be marshaled to affirm the indirect relationship assumed since antiquity between illusion and materiality. But, as this book suggests, Titian's later work also suggests that painting advances resemblance through other means; through, for example, equivalence in appearance and substance without precise morphological imitation. The physicality of the medium also complicates the longstanding assumption in representational painting that the subject matter dictates and predominates over the means of representation rather than that they affect and change one another.[15] The adjustment of viewing distance allowed these questions to recede and the illusionistic mode of reading Renaissance pictures to persist. In seeking to posit an alternative, historicized approach to Titian's later paintings, this book relies on related critical efforts in modern and contemporary art history to articulate the interplay of facture and representation. The methodologies

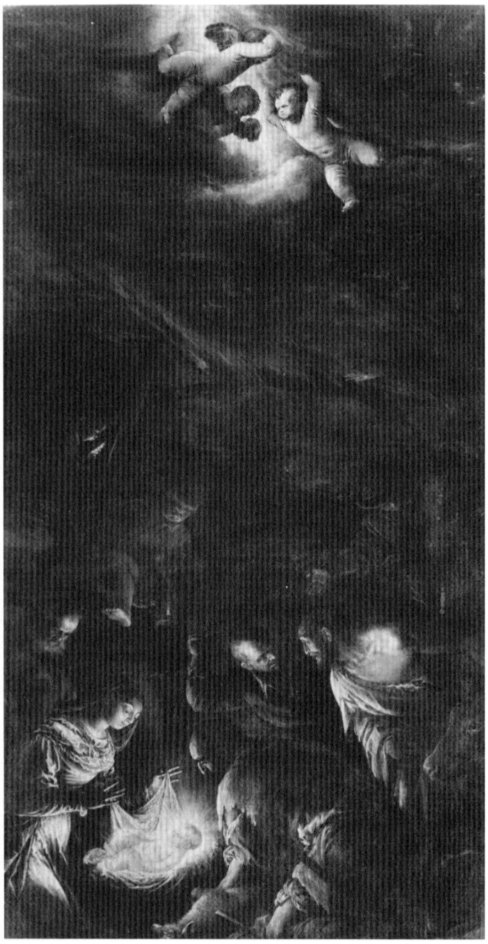

Fig. 1 Jacopo da Bassano, *Adoration of the Shepherds,* San Giorgio Maggiore, Venice

explored in these later texts have been invaluable in directing my attention to how many early modern writers thought in very similar ways, despite their differences in terminology and expectations of illusionism.

The written suggestion that evidently worked paintings might be approached positively and not merely in terms of their aberrance arises in the seicento texts of Marco Boschini, who celebrated and defended the diverse accomplishments of cinquecento Venetian painters in *La carta del navegar pitoresco* (1660) and *Breve instruzione* (1673).[16] Without any investment in the Tuscan tradition of *disegno* and *rilievo,* Boschini appreciated Venetian paintings for their use of color and the manifold ways in which the materials of the art could both represent form and deform those very same forms. His approach to these evidently worked paintings finds its clearest articulation in his descriptions of the experience of viewing a painting not by Titian, the *Adoration of the Shepherds* executed by Titian's contemporary Jacopo da Bassano for the Venetian church of San Giorgio Maggiore (fig. 1).[17] Although awestruck by the entire composition, Boschini focuses his attention in both works on the brilliantly luminous representation of the infant Christ at night and the significance of the loose brushwork in this area of the altarpiece. When closely approaching the depiction of Christ, the viewer finds him "dazzling and incomprehensible, no longer discerning the form or substance, in such a way that, fearful of having inadvertently approached too closely the represented Divinity . . . [the viewer] returns to behold the perfection seen earlier."[18] In the verse account of *La carta,* Boschini concludes from this situation that we cannot touch God with our hands.[19] Boschini finds devotional significance in the looser handling of paint and the absence of contour, relief, and shadow—the form or substance mentioned above—when in close proximity to the painting, playfully manipulating Vasari's resolution of illusion through distance to be indicative of the viewer's relationship with God, of the incomprehensibility of the divine.[20] As much as the visible strokes of paint dissolve the infant body into a radiant patch of light, the stains and splotches, to which Boschini repeatedly refers throughout his rhyming *La carta,* also indicate the physicality that mediates our devotional experience, especially before an altarpiece. Boschini interweaves metaphors of facture and divinity as if to make simultaneous, if not identical, the physical body revealed by light and the materiality of representation, almost dispensing with Vasari's recommended position shifts at the same time that he finds exegetical possibilities in them. Drawing upon the eucharistic function of any representation of Christ's body, Boschini explores how the handling and the substance of paint manifest the liturgical significance and function of the altarpiece.

Boschini's approach to materiality in this one area of the painting demonstrates a formalism extended to technique that informs our approach to Titian's later paintings more generally.[21] Meaning inheres in the form of the infant body, but, as Boschini notes, also in the dissolution or disfiguration of that very form. The brushstrokes—while not exactly treated as an index of the painter's presence, as later viewers have treated the roughly worked paintings of the abstract expressionists—signify more generally as signs of presence through substance; at various moments they imply similar ontological and existential structures of the material trace, such as those of contact, embodiment, temporality, and decay.[22] Boschini suggests this not only in his description of the body of Christ but also in the close connection in his discussion elsewhere of Titian's paintings between brushstrokes and bodily fluids, such as blood and milk, and between his working method and medical procedures.[23] Consequently, in this interpretive paradigm, the operation of the sign is not entirely subsumed by referentiality, which, as exemplified by the incomprehensible and overwhelming presence of the divine in Bassano's painting, affects the presumed transparency and unity of Renaissance figurative painting and its responsiveness to a hermeneutic reading.

In many ways, then, Boschini developed an interpretive approach around the properties and conditions of oil painting that Vasari discussed critically in his *Lives* of Giorgione and Titian and in his and other theorists' descriptions of the technique. The medium of oil paint on canvas introduced physicality to painting, from the varieties of canvas weave employed to the building up of layers of impasto and glazes.[24] Composition involved depth and thickness, even though the earliest experiments in oil paint explored and thematized the refractory properties of such layering in the service of illusion.[25] Oil paint, whether on panel or canvas, allowed the painter to make changes in the process of painting and work directly on the surface.[26] For those more familiar with fresco painting, which required a preparatory drawing and restricted revisions with its quick-drying plaster, the oil medium compromised the standard of planned invention expected for good painting and the fantasy of the original, identifiable intention.[27] Working in oil lengthened the time of painting: the paint, in all of its stages and states, whether fully or partially dry or entirely fluid, could be worked into and onto the canvas, which, when finished, retained the indications of these interactions. Chance and accident played a significant role in how paintings were made, sometimes serving as a spur to further invention and sometimes remaining as the inadvertent creation similar to those described in early modern anecdotes of the image made by chance (plate 13).[28] The proper application of color depended on casualness, or *sprezzatura,* an approach that responded to the amorphousness of color, to how coloring does not always follow the logic of illusionism in application and result.[29] Oil painting, according to Vasari, involved love and diligence, which, despite the slightly pejorative implications, could be taken to recognize its inexactitude of method, resistance to prescriptive discourse, and the potential sweetness and softness of modeling.[30]

Titian's later paintings explore this phenomenology of oil painting by evidently demonstrating the substance of the oil medium and the different stages, even those usually concealed, in figurative painting. The weave of the canvas shows through in some sections of paintings, appearing to reverse the additive process of composition (plate 1);[31] thick impasto gives textural elevations to areas of the canvases (plate 2); glazes appear in areas not expected to have those colors; brushstrokes minimize the sense of notional relief and oftentimes, in their seeming randomness, appear to violate the integrity of the figure and the logic of illusionism (plate 3); the background threatens the self-sufficiency of the figure and, by extension, the Albertian ideal of compositional unity (plates 4 and 5). These paintings appear quite literally to disfigure the Renaissance tradition of figurative painting, as Renaissance and modern critics have suggested through their critical readings of these paintings as unfinished. And this disfiguration, following Boschini's interpretation above, is precisely wherein the significance of these paintings lies. In drawing our attention to the materials of painting in figurative painting, these later works explore the materiality of existence through the physical stuff of painting, and vice versa. Rather than offer the reflected appearance of the visible world, these paintings demonstrate through the technical process the corporeality—the mass, the weight, the density, the thickness, the interior—of the depicted subject. And because the subjects of these later paintings involve the materiality of the body through stories of violence, metamorphosis, and desire, the subject matter also affects our reading of the technical process. The changes undergone by both are read against the background of illusionistic figuration, whether as a generalized ideal or in the specific illusionistic passages in these later paintings.[32]

The interaction between subject matter and technique—and the corresponding connection between subjectivity and disfiguration—reflects and expands mid-cinquecento conceptions of the subjectivity of the artist. The sixteenth-century idea of the irrational artist replaced the controlled, measured creator of the quattrocento imagination and, consequently, the creative process as well as the result were positively received.[33] Contemporaries collected and

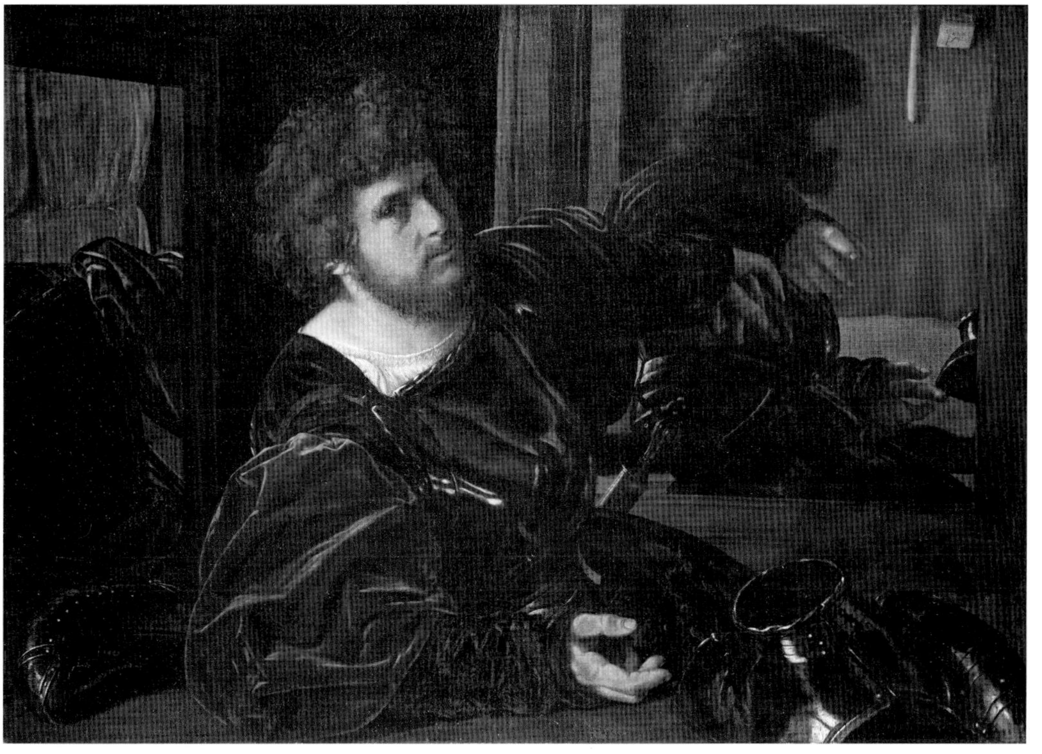

Fig. 2 Giovanni Girolamo Savoldo, *Self-Portrait*, Louvre, Paris

valued preparatory sketches and drawings precisely because they demonstrated through their marks and strokes the creative fury at the moment of invention.[34] The traces of the artist's gesture exemplified the frenzy of divine inspiration, even if those creative energies usually found technical and conceptual resolution in the final painted composition. Other indications of this changing subjectivity include a shift away from earlier, largely metapictorial, motifs of presence: after 1550, painters turned away from thematizing their largely intellectual relationship to their work through the motif of the mirror, through *cartellini* appended to the fictional surface of the painting, or through self-referential gestures in depictions of themselves—all of which suggested the idea, rather than the physical evidence, of their presence (fig. 2).[35] Venetian paintings, in which these devices had appeared most frequently before midcentury and for which drawing remained a relatively minor creative element, demonstrate through their evident brushwork an analogous subjectivity found in those preliminary graphic inventions. Facture in these paintings—as in drawings—posits the artist as a continuing, lingering presence in the artwork; however, perhaps because of the greater finality ascribed to a painting than a drawing, a more nuanced differentiation of subjectivity in these painted Venetian works arose that depended on both the variations in technique and the subject matter. Tintoretto's quick and often thin brushstrokes might have compromised Renaissance notions of thoughtful creative effort, for example, but the material indications of quick engagement in his work—which was predominantly religious—signify the spiritual through the (im)material, at times suggesting the limited human agency in the miraculous or the physical energy of the spiritual world.[36]

Boschini attempts to interpret the varied subjectivities of approach, finding meaning whether in Tintoretto's kinetic speed or Titian's disfiguration over a long period of time.[37] Consider, for example, his well-known recounting of Palma Giovane's experience of Titian's experience of painting in the final years of the latter painter's career:

> Titian blocked in his pictures with a mass of colors, which served as a bed or foundation for what he wished to express, and upon which he would then build. I myself have seen such under-painting, vigorously applied with a loaded brush of pure red ochre, which would serve as the middle ground; then with a stroke of white lead, with the same brush then dipped in red, black, or yellow, he created the light and dark areas of the relief effect. And in this way with four strokes of the brush he was able to suggest a magnificent figure. . . . After having thus established this crucial foundation, he turned the pictures to the wall and left them there, without looking at them, sometimes for several months. When he later returned to them, he scrutinized them as though they were his mortal enemies, in order to discover any faults; and if he did find anything that did not accord with his intentions, like a surgeon treating a patient, he would remove some swelling or excess flesh, set an arm if the bone were out of joint, or adjust a foot if it were misshapen, without the slightest pity for the victim. By thus operating on and re-forming these figures, he brought them to the highest degree of perfection . . . and then, while that picture was drying, he turned to another. And he gradually covered with living flesh those bare bones, going over them repeatedly until all they lacked was breath itself. . . . For the final touches he would blend the transitions from highlights to halftones with his fingers, blending one tint with another, or with a smear of his finger he would apply a dark accent in some corner to strengthen it, or with a dab of red, like a drop of blood, he would enliven some surface—in this way bringing his animated figures to completion. . . . In the final stages he painted more with his fingers than with the brush.[38]

We read about the painter who antagonistically combats his paintings as if enemies and who threatens to destroy and save his creations through the creative process; the elision of surface and subject in the smear of red paint, which almost instantaneously becomes a drop of blood as an indication of violence and creation; the metaphoric potential of brushstrokes to be stains, to be traces of combat between painter and

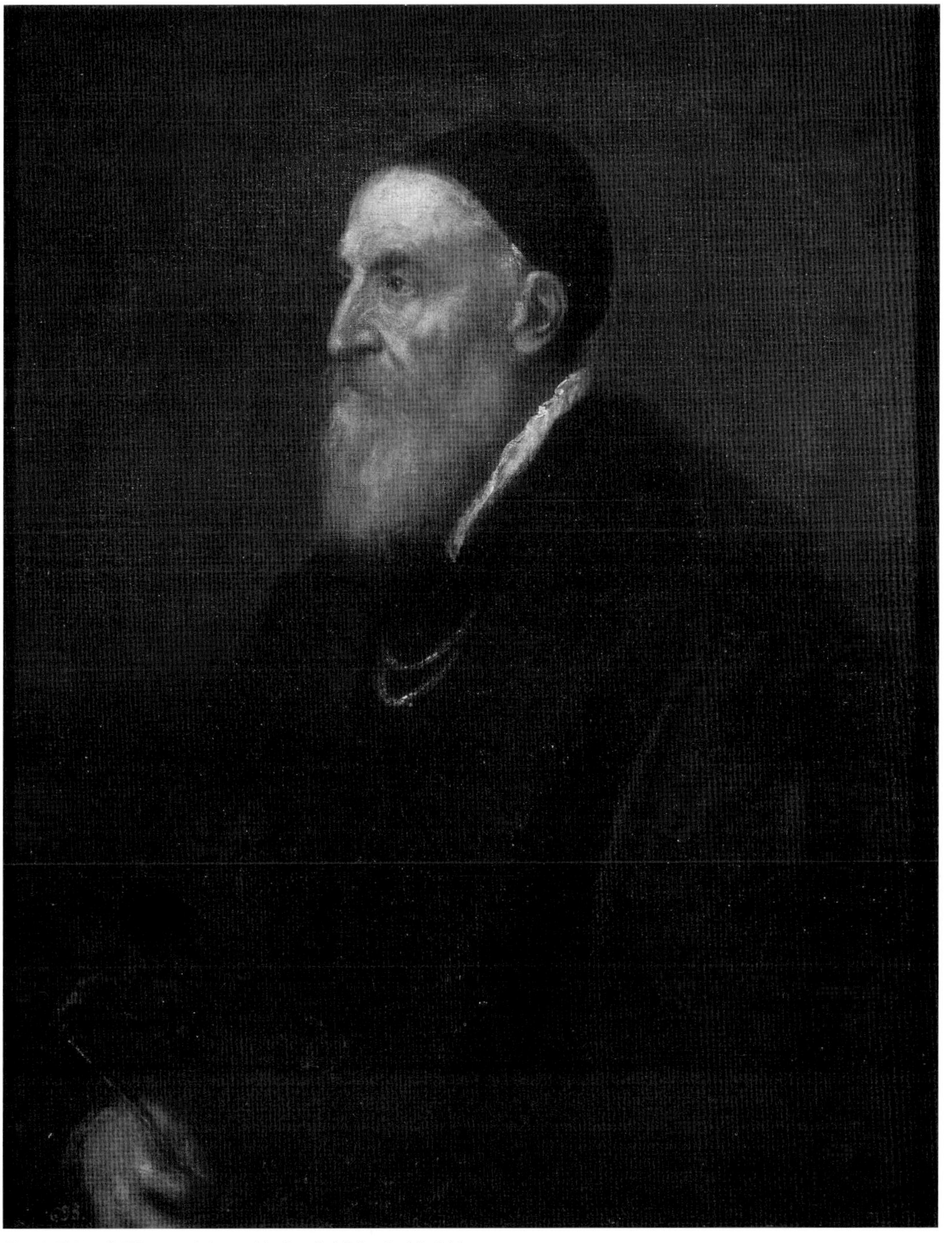

Fig. 3 Titian, *Self-Portrait,* Museo Nacional del Prado, Madrid

painting, and to be painfully dislocating and healing; the inquiry into the inherence of meaning in form and into the relationship between abstraction and mimesis in Boschini's earlier description of Titian's preliminary work as "the promise of the figure made in four strokes [by Titian's hand]."[39]

The passage is striking for its proleptic engagement of modernist tropes, but especially for the connection between gestural mode of painting and heroic masculinity.[40] Perhaps reflective of Boschini's defensive posturing of Venetian painting, his use of this trope participates in the Renaissance discourse of the mastery of artist over materials—as an extension of the superintendency of form over matter—but also interjects into the discourse the disfiguration and physical interaction between artist

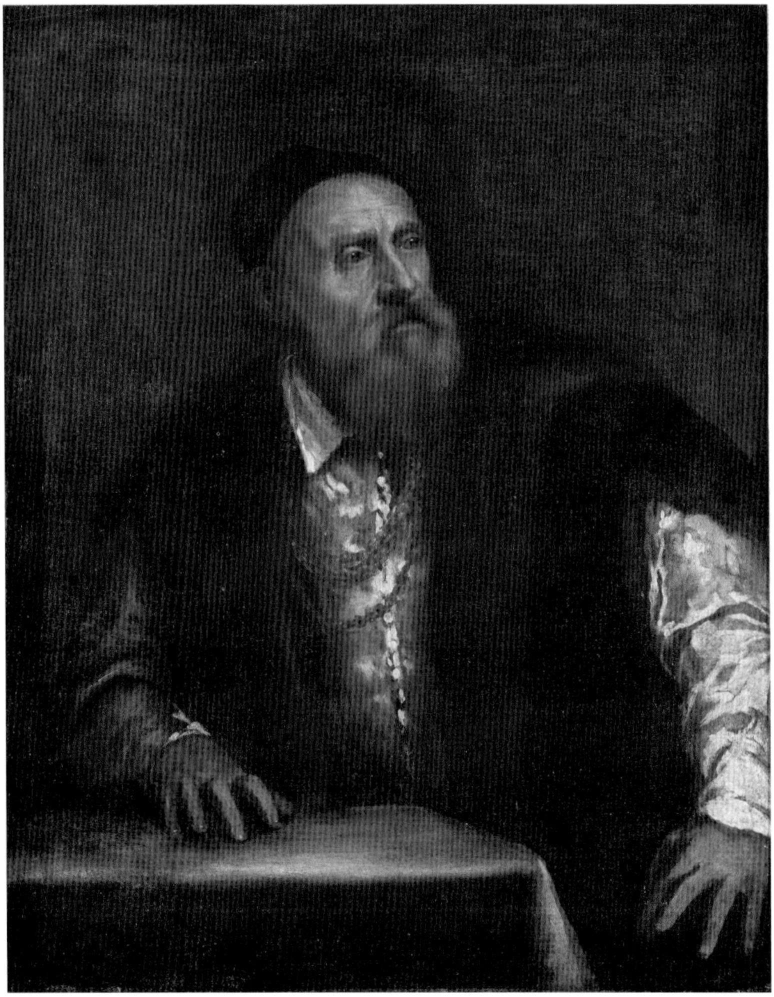

Fig. 4 Titian, *Self-Portrait,* Gemäldegalerie, Staatliche Museen, Berlin

and materials, and not just dominance, which the paintings themselves confirm.[41] The thick blobs of paint and the sections of exposed canvas in Titian's later paintings suggest a radically different conception of medium in which not only the materials, but also the artist himself, function as the medium through the performance of painting. He not only shapes the materials but is shaped by them, in the same way that the canvas support also takes on an unexpected and unprecedented role in shaping paint. In suggesting an active, even violent, interaction between painter, paint, and canvas support, these later paintings present a dynamic of creation and destruction that both reinforces and challenges the Renaissance creation myth of divine mastery with the artist as the authoritative protagonist.[42] His self-portraits reflect as much by depicting himself as the reticent painter who is both the subject of and subject to his own making, whether through the instrument of his quite literally self-directed brush or through the depicted hands made and effaced by his own hands (figs. 3 and 4).[43] In his self-portraits and other later paintings, we find our experience of the artist's subjectivity shifting somewhere in between a transcendent, controlling "I" and a retreating, almost selfless "I" of the accidental mark.[44] This dynamic, which varies from one painting to another and even within a single painting, undermines the predominant interpretive expectation that the medium, artist, and subject matter positively reinforce one another in Renaissance painting, when, as we will see in our consideration of Titian's paintings, they transform and even deform one another.[45]

By involving the circumstances and materials of making in an interpretation of Titian's paintings, this study joins the growing interest among art historians in various aspects of materials and the material objects of Renaissance art. For several decades, technical analyses conducted by conservators have assisted scholars in their knowledge of the rudiments of pictorial composition, of knowing which pigments were used and where, and of how painters applied paint. Recently, more focused histories have emerged that consider the origin, properties, and use of specific pigments in painting and of woods, stones, and metals in sculpture.[46] The consideration of why an artist used certain materials has led in many situations to questions of how these materials were used and, in turn, how the made object was used.[47] Other studies have focused on how the process of making oftentimes finds expression through the represented subject or, similarly, how the work of art elicits an allegorical reading that involves the process of making.[48] Many of these latter narratives explore contemporary tropes of artistic genius in which the artist self-reflexively controls and shapes the materials or, alternatively, how the process of making shapes the artist.[49]

This study considers how paintings that respond to and facilitate a self-reflexive allegorical reading through technique also employ an iconography that undermines the authority of these tropes and that questions the intellectual and self-celebratory model of

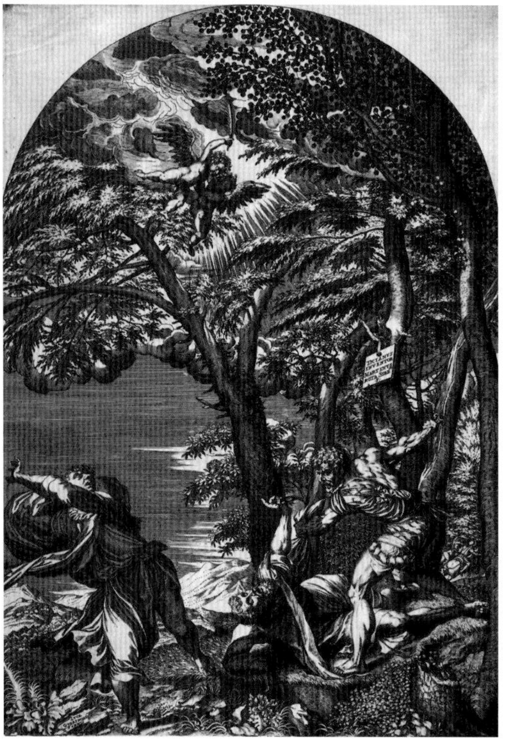

Fig. 5 Martin Rota after Titian, *Martyrdom of Saint Peter Martyr,* after the lost altarpiece for the church of SS. Giovanni e Paolo, British Museum, London

making. Many of these later images by Titian resist hermeneutical reading altogether and instead explore materiality—of the painting and as a subject—through the dissolution of the primacy of figure over ground.[50] The unprecedented role given to the depicted ground, the actual canvas ground, and the compromised figure contributes to and challenges the self-sufficient status of the figure and artist and significantly complicates the role of interpretive approaches dependent on and grounded in ideas of figuration, such as rhetorical theory and iconography. Materiality in all of these later paintings lodges us in the very physical stuff of the world, in the pleasures and dangers of embodiment, and in the situations and conditions that, in their immediate physicality, appear to resist thought and discourse and appear to conflict with the Renaissance ideals that dominate our inherited notion and interpretation of the period.

Not sustaining the idealized beauty and heroic ideal of earlier cinquecento paintings, these later paintings explore violent subject matter and the previously unexplored violent and corporeal dimension of subjects and image types popular in the first decades of the sixteenth century. Coincident with the beginning of Titian's career, these years saw the execution of half-length images of diverse subjects ranging from sensuous women to abbreviated scenes from the Passion of Christ that appealed to the viewer through a direct visual dialogue. Desire and devotion depended on the presence and imaginative participation of beholders to meditate and extend the exchange in their minds.[51] Corporeality and violence, evoked and yet sublimated in these paintings, emerged inconsistently as explicit subjects until the mid-cinquecento, when Titian abandoned the largely rhetorical enactment of cruelty and suffering inherited from antiquity (fig. 5) and directly explored the physicality of horror on and through the surface of the picture (plate 3). Subjects that earlier had offered the opportunity to depict the delights of love in a golden age are transformed into tragic scenes of violence and ominous loss. Compare, for example, his *Three Ages of Man* (fig. 6) with his later *Nymph and Shepherd* (plate 6).[52] Titian might have limited his reliance on *Pathosformel*—those fixed formulae that convey emotions, as termed by Aby Warburg—but he fully developed the irrational, Dionysiac side of the Renaissance embodied by them.[53]

In exploring existential and ontological conditions relating to materiality—and especially the negative implications of corporeality, such as the pure physicality of violence and trauma—these later paintings indicate a largely overlooked dimension of Renaissance culture that shows an interest in the transparency of and deviations from the ideal. Cinquecento painters and sculptors, in pushing the ideal to the extreme of affectation as the century progressed, avoided representations of the materiality of existence, unlike their northern counterparts, who depicted festering flesh.[54] But apparently there was a demand: the rough and low—in subject matter, social class, etc.—found expression in widely disseminated prints.[55] Cinquecento writers, including those close to Titian, satirized the ideals and rules for courtly behavior, mocked learned eloquence through bawdy stories, and emphasized the physicality of human experience through sensuous metaphors and a revival of tragedy.[56] As the less dominant discourse in Italian Renaissance culture, the underside of the ideal received some recognition by those first modern historians of the period, who nonetheless wove a narrative of revival and heroic self-confidence. More recently, historians and interpreters of Italian Renaissance culture have described a more complex and contradictory situation by articulating the anxieties and doubts that coexisted with and even necessitated the polished ideal.[57] This study extends both the conclusions and approaches of these literary,

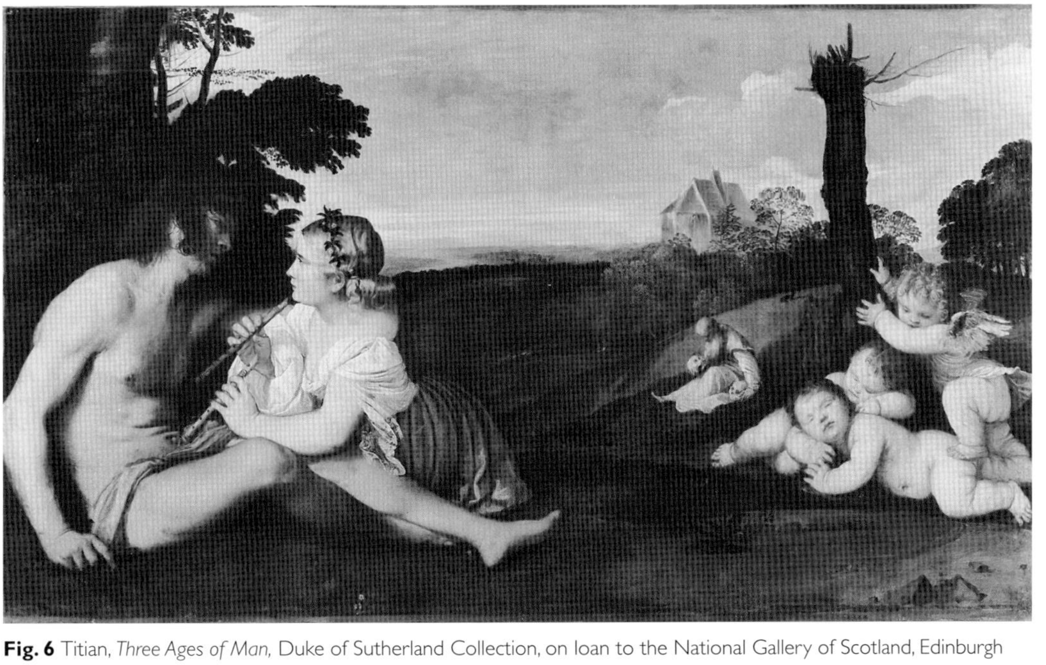

Fig. 6 Titian, *Three Ages of Man,* Duke of Sutherland Collection, on loan to the National Gallery of Scotland, Edinburgh

social, and historical studies to thinking about Titian's later paintings and their reception in the cinquecento.

Although this different sensibility in these accounts establishes a critical, dialectical relationship to the Renaissance ideal, its visual expression extends the structures of viewer involvement theorized and developed for the ideal Renaissance painting and depiction of the ideal. Linear perspective, oriented around the fixed eye of the viewer, was among the earliest Renaissance devices that acknowledged the presence of a beholder outside the frame.[58] Painters also included less analytical motifs, such as a direct address to the viewer through gaze and/or gesture, that immediately involved the beholder in an empathic relationship with the depicted.[59] These inventions aimed to dissolve the idea of the boundary between the worlds of painting and of the viewer at the same time that they reinforced their limits. Many of Titian's earlier paintings employ these empathic motifs to establish precisely this idea of connection. His later paintings extend this intellectual sensibility in viewing to an embodied experience in which beholders feel a physical connection—however ideated or imagined—to the painting through its materiality. We find an indication of Titian's movement along this continuum in his *Venus of Urbino* (1538), in which the sensuous recumbent nude appears to tip toward us due to the unexpected juxtaposition of the

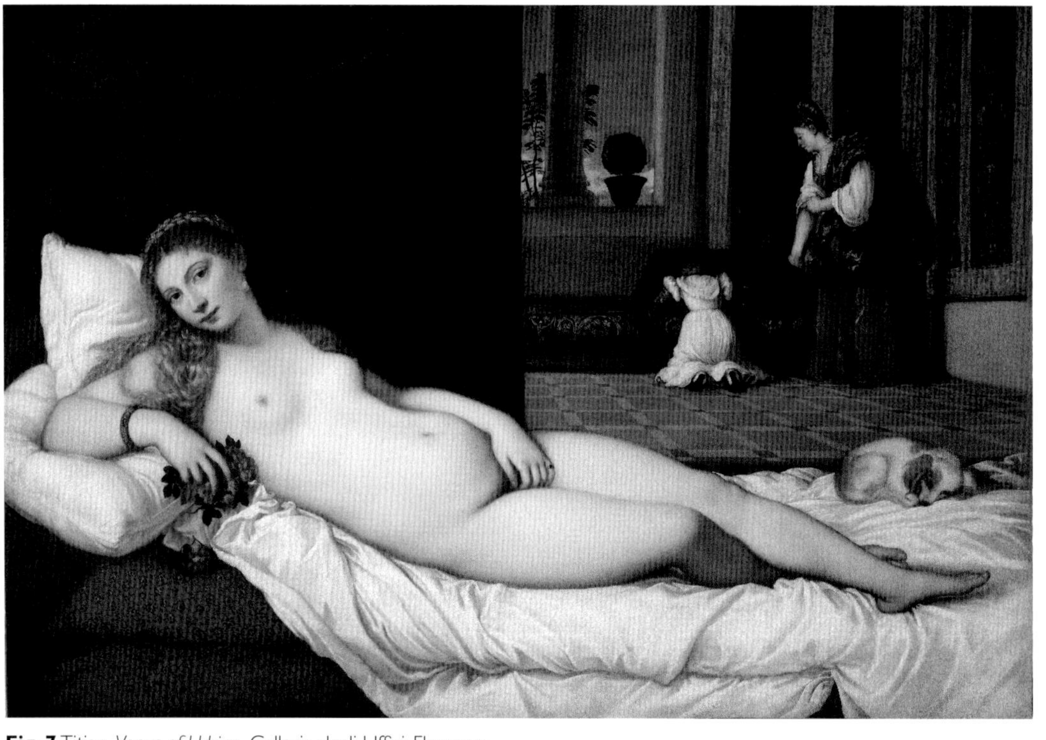

Fig. 7 Titian, *Venus of Urbino*, Galleria degli Uffizi, Florence

flattening curtain and the recessive perspective grid (fig. 7).[60] Our physical access to her remains blocked by the delimiting bed, but the incorporation of the paint into the canvas weave and interplay between the caressed illusionistic roses and the materiality of the printed flowers on the fabric resonate for the interests and direction of Titian's later work. In these paintings, the more obvious layering of paint, the exposure of the canvas support, and the traces of the brushstroke establish a spatial and temporal (kinesthetic) relationship with the beholder that involves the body. Renaissance and modern responses reflect this experience by declaring, as Aretino did, that Titian "has the essence of things in his brush," that he gives us the thing itself, or by suggesting that the viewer feels the depicted body from the inside.[61] Several of the depicted figures in these later paintings visualize precisely this shift away from the fantasy of pure visuality by looking too closely at other figures, as if seeing beyond the visible (plates 3, 6, 11, and 13). The figures themselves—compelled and involved beyond perceptual and communicative necessity—demonstrate how to "look" at these paintings.[62]

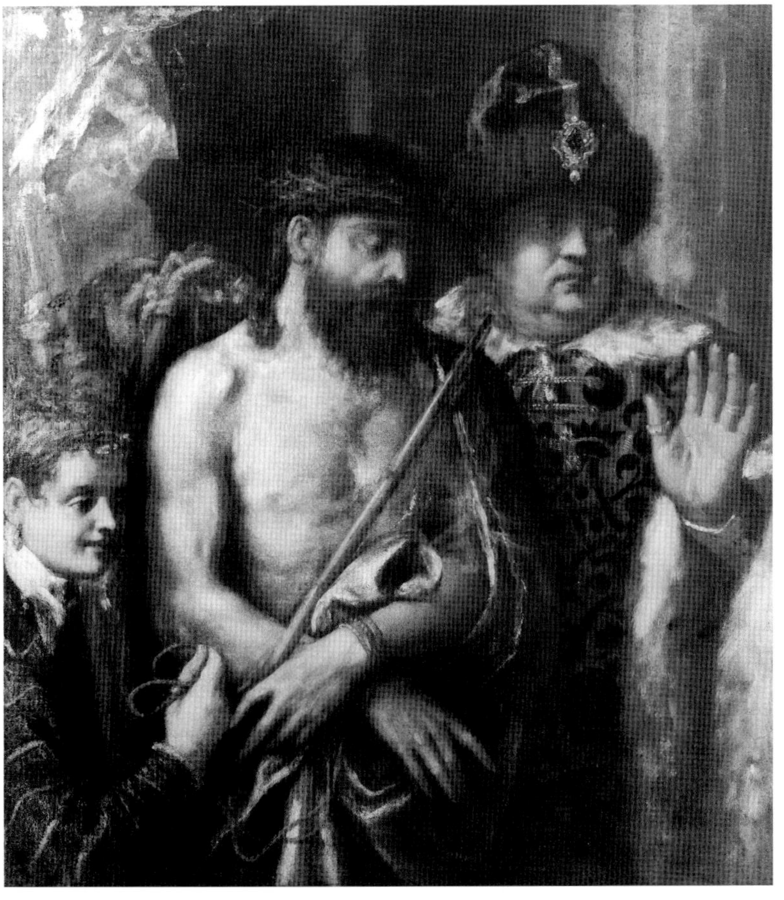

Fig. 8 Titian, *Ecce Homo*, St. Louis Art Museum, St. Louis, Missouri

Early modern viewers acknowledged the potentially phenomenological dimension of painting and sculpture, even if limited to myth, metaphors, and folklore. Beginning with Petrarch, lyric poets developed ancient tropes of the speaking portrait, that image so vivid that it deceptively incites the lover to act as though the beloved is actually present.[63] Equally familiar to Renaissance writers were ancient myths and stories of young men who physically interacted with and reacted to lifelike sculpture. We think, for example, of the Ovidian myth of Pygmalion and Galatea and the story of the unnamed youth who, in his desire, stained the *Cnidian Venus* by Praxiteles.[64] These stories certainly inform more prosaic experiences of artworks, including Leonardo's observation that viewers will assume the depicted poses and motions of the represented bodies.[65] Embodied responses such as these testify to the verisimilitude of the works of art.[66] But they also serve as a foundation for the association of the senses of vision and touch with painting and sculpture, respectively, and for the later cinquecento appreciation of senses other than vision in experiencing the visual arts.[67] Whereas Leonardo in the early cinquecento criticized sculpture as an art that appealed to the tactile sense, Varchi, as an advocate for sculpture, praised the plastic media for precisely this quality;[68] and Marco Boschini later celebrated Titian's paintings and those by contemporary Venetian painters because they appealed to the senses of touch, smell, and taste.[69]

Color, as Boschini and other theorists realized, functions as a sublingual property of painting that arouses the senses more than any other aspect of art.[70] Hardness, softness, heat, cold: all of these conditions and properties found expression through the handling of pigment.[71] In the mid-cinquecento, art theorists and especially religious reformers were keenly aware of the broad appeal of color to the uneducated and of the dangerous effects of the corporeality of vivid hues.[72] Essentially repeating through their criticisms the deeply ingrained division between *disegno* and *colore,* intellect and matter, these writers nonetheless acknowledged through their admonishments the possibility for an embodied experience of painting. Some reformers, perhaps influenced by the positive appraisals of color in Venetian painting, even framed their religious devotion through the corporeality of color.[73]

In spite of the rhetoric of visuality, the early modern body was recognized as a complex, material entity that affected, determined, and effected one's experience of the world. Natural philosophers theorized the operations of the mind in close relationship to those of the body. Humoral fluids in the body, which could vary according to diet, determined personality and disposition.[74] The faculties of common sense and judgment, although located in the brain, were thought to collect information from all of the bodily senses.[75] Discoveries in medicine also affected the conceived relationship between the body, the passions, and perception.[76]

This book considers these issues through a selected group of Titian's later paintings that addresses and thematizes embodiment through pictorial structures, subjects, and genres that, paradoxically, earlier had exemplified, and sometimes allegorized, the intellectual and visual ideals of quattrocento and early cinquecento painting. It focuses on a few paintings, the *Venus with a Mirror* (plate 8), the *Flaying of Marsyas* (plate 3), and a group of later half-length images (plates 1, 9, 14, 15, 18; and fig. 8), which themselves appear to reflect on the intersection of the art of painting and materiality. Not only do the subjects of these images relate to the conflicting conditions of embodiment and of disembodied vision through their depiction of specular desire, of competition between two modes of creation, and of physical sacrifice and spiritual redemption, respectively, but they raise these concerns in somewhat archaic image types that emphasize these very tensions. Titian's reinterpretation of these earlier compositions indicates that, even if these returns exemplify the large workshop practice of making replicas, the painter found creative possibilities in the past—not unlike his fellow Venetian Tintoretto.[77] Titian's sustained interest in the recumbent nude—although without the historical break considered here between the later compositions and their earlier sources—speaks to his inventive engagement with the history of art and to the lessening importance of the imitation of nature as the sole aim of art.[78] The supportive network formed by Titian's other later paintings in the argument of this book suggests that the pictures considered here in detail are not so exceptional as to be without interpretative implications for many of the paintings produced from the early 1550s to Titian's death in 1576.

The book begins with a discussion of one of the paintings, the *Venus with a Mirror* (plate 8), which remained in Titian's studio at the time of his death. As a mythological variant on the "woman at her toilette" type popular in the early sixteenth century, the picture similarly appears to explore themes of desire and possession through vision and specularity. However, the materiality of the mirror reflection—and of the entire painting—deviates from the reflective standard underpinning the image-type, suggesting to some viewers that Titian left the picture unfinished. This first chapter approaches the deviation from a different perspective by asking how this materiality changes the significance of the image-type and, more generally, indicates the role of materiality in early modern framings of desire. Metaphors for love and desire began at midcentury to extend from the illusionistic mirror to include metaphors evoking the physicality of these amorous situations. Vision loses its predominance in later Renaissance dialogues on love, and the less mimetic—or formless—situations of *macchie* in painting theory and of blurriness, clouds, and wind in lyric poetry are suggestive for considering Love's embodiment in this painting.

Chapter 2 considers Titian's *Flaying of Marsyas* (plate 3), a painting that explores the negative aspects of materiality, but through a subject with similar metapictorial relevance. Instead of the pleasures of love, we confront in this later painting the horror of violence done to the body; instead of a subject with a rich heritage of allegorizing mimesis, we find the mythical creative confrontation between Dionysian materiality and Apollonian rationality. The subject bears an obvious relevance to contemporary discussions of the heroic act and art of Renaissance painting as intellectually inspired. But Titian's depiction undermines these assumptions by manipulating a well-established iconography of devotional imagery and of creativity. In asserting the interdependence between making and unmaking, production and destruction, the *Flaying* asserts a changing subjectivity of the artist that conflicts with the predominant Renaissance (and modern) narratives of making as constructive and intentional.

The striking return of both the *Mellon Venus* and the *Flaying* to earlier compositional types might indicate a retrospective turn expected for an older painter.[79] However, as chapter 3 asserts, this archaism emphasizes a broader waning of the humanistic ideal and of the imitation of nature in the history of art, and also challenges the intertwined teleological accounts of biography and stylistic development in art history that lead to the largely pejorative concepts of old-age and "late" style. Rather than focus on a single painting, this chapter considers Titian's return to half-length compositions—including devotional narrative images and some portraits—which, in turn, remind us so clearly of the earlier Renaissance visual traditions from which they deviate (plates 1, 9, 14, 15, and 18; fig. 8). These paintings suggest that painting is no longer conceived or experienced as a kind of friendship or as a self-sufficient totality, as earlier theorists—primarily Alberti—who structured painting according to a rhetorical model claimed; instead, these works advance a more confrontational relationship with the viewer.[80] This dynamic of violence found in Titian's paintings relates to the intersection of violence and materiality in the sister medium of sculpture, specifically in some of the sculpted works of Donatello and Michelangelo—which, not so coincidentally, have elicited similar allegations, in the artists' lifetimes until the present day, of old-age style and the *nonfinito.* Although representative of different visual modes—Florentine sculpture rather than Venetian painting—all of these artworks require viewer involvement that, in its physical immediacy, challenges the concept of the image as appealing primarily to the intellect and draws upon the earlier cultic and mystical associations with bodily presence embedded in these image-types and their sources. Both the return to the earlier history of art and the violent corporeality reflect many of the reformatory prescriptions for the visual arts. Although their specific impact on Titian's work is difficult to discern, many of these religious discussions contribute to a late Renaissance culture of materiality by questioning, and sometimes even asserting, the possibility of inherence in images, reliquaries, and the Eucharist, and by recommending a greater visceral display in painting. This later interest in the vulnerabilities of humanity, found also in contemporary performances of tragedy and publications of martyrologies, offers a significant counterpoint to the recovered, restored, and idealized body so central to discussions of Renaissance art.

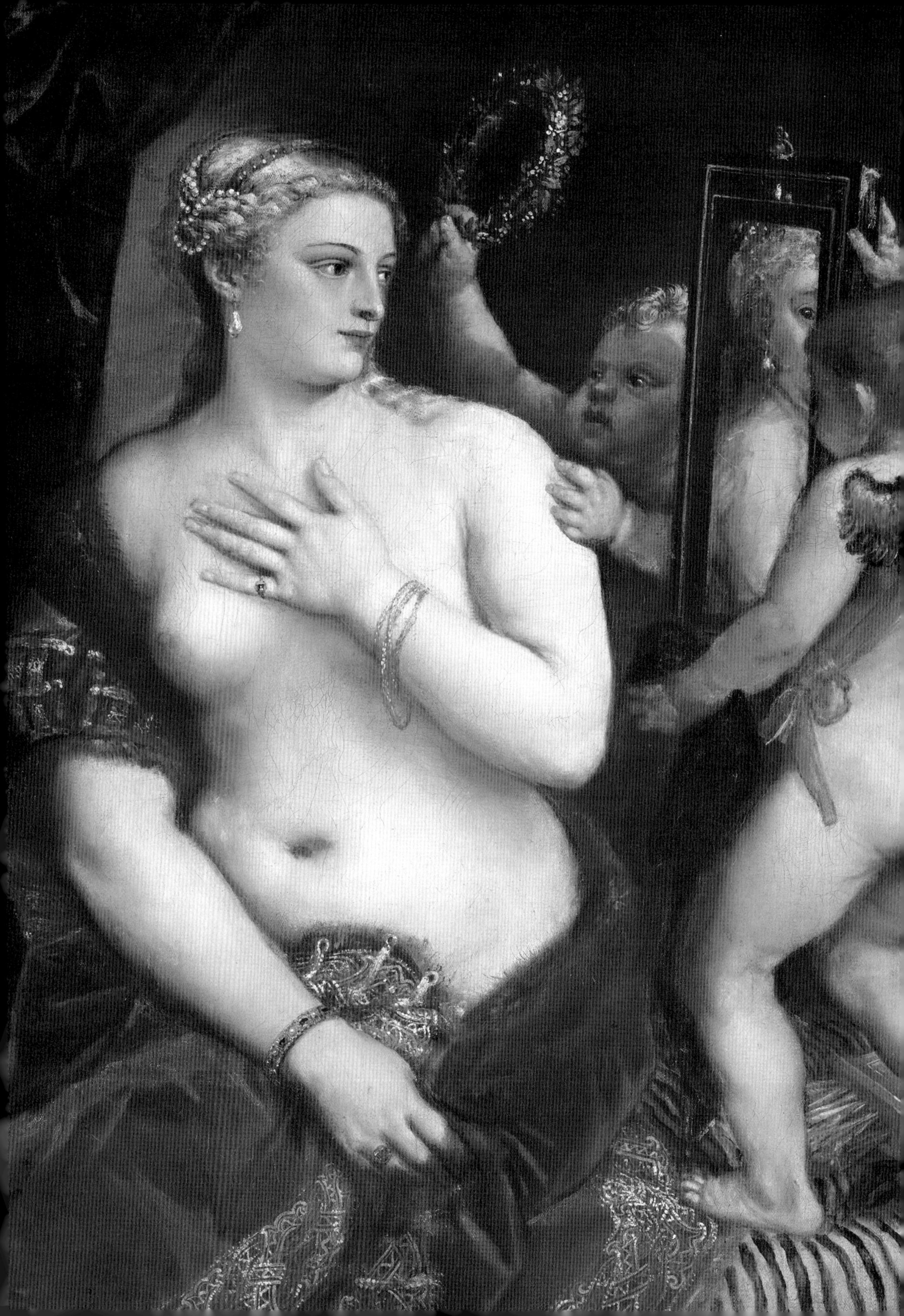

1

"Speculum cum macula"

MATERIALITY AND DESIRE

When Titian painted the so-called *Mellon Venus* (plate 8) in the mid-sixteenth century, he returned to an iconographic subject and compositional type, what is generally referred to in art-historical scholarship as the woman at her toilette, that had interested him and other Venetian painters starting nearly a half century earlier (figs. 9 and 10).[1] Paintings of this type depict a sensuous woman in half-length who gazes at her own reflection in the mirror while either a depicted or an implied male lover looks on.[2] Like all spurned lovers, he is made to wait fruitlessly for his beloved to direct her gaze to him, at the same time that seeing her sensuality and beauty fuels his affection. If these tensions are not apparent from the images themselves, then certainly the many cinquecento poems on the subject would have informed a viewer's experience of the paintings. In one such poem by Serafino dall'Aquila, one of these poet-lovers implores her, "Now let go of the mirror and look at my eyes, for in me you will know who you are."[3]

The subject, first appearing in Italian painting in the early years of the sixteenth century, allowed painters to explore themes central to the theoretical foundations of the art of painting and its subsequent elaborations in cinquecento visual culture. These themes included desire, feminine beauty, and specularity[4]—and all three intersect with an unprecedented mythological specificity in Titian's *Mellon Venus.*[5] The sumptuously bedecked Venus, placed against an abstract background with a curtain suggestive of theatrical presentation, appears to look at herself in the mirror held by a cupid, while a second cupid crowns her with a wreath of flowered greenery.[6] With her compelling nude body positioned to face the viewer, she is the focus of everyone's gaze, a situation that she registers by assuming the simultaneously concealing and revealing pose of the Venus *pudica.*[7] Her beauty also figures the beauty of painting and the way in which painting evokes the structure of desire by depicting so vividly that which can never be

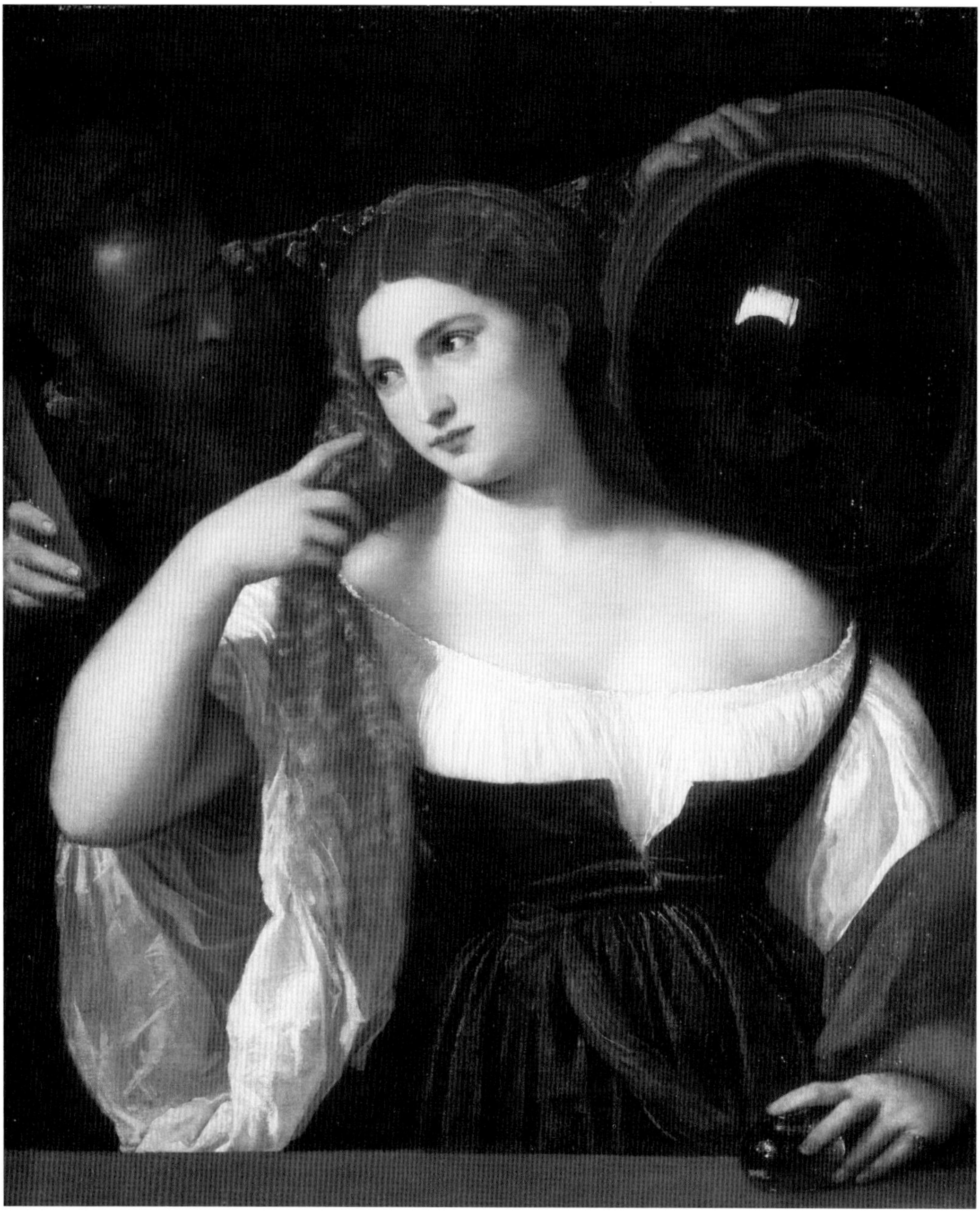

Fig. 9 Titian, *Woman before the Mirror,* Louvre, Paris

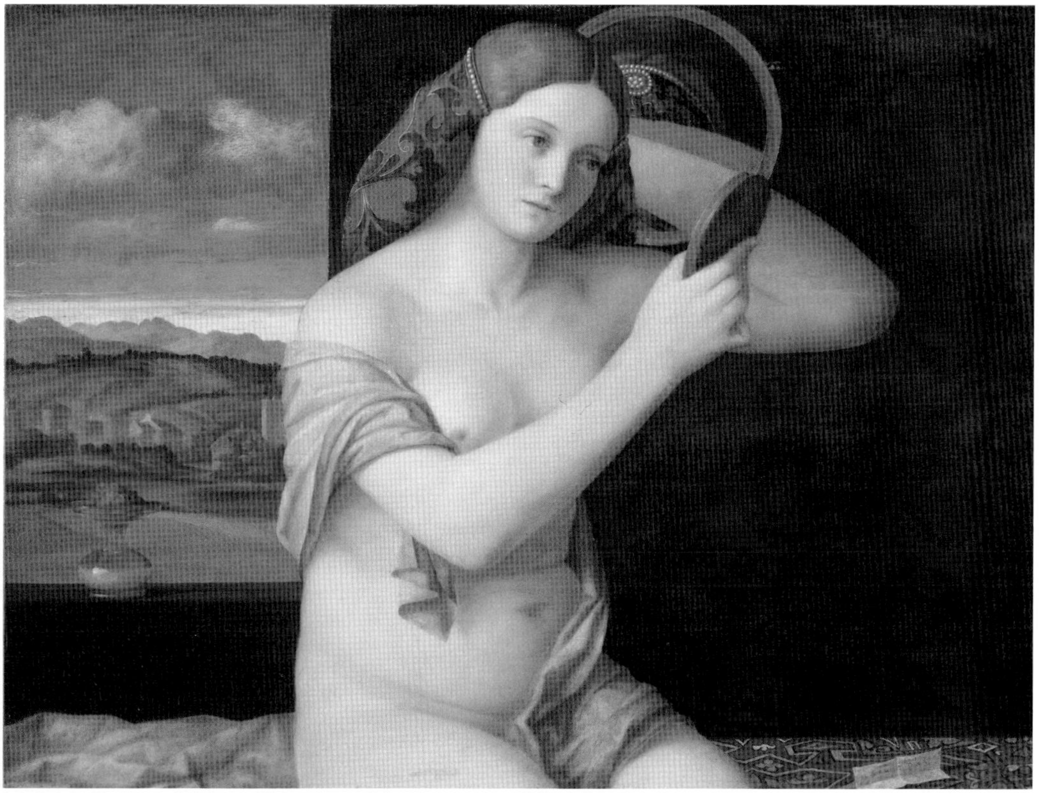

Fig. 10 Giovanni Bellini, *Woman Before the Mirror,* Kunsthistorisches Museum, Vienna

reciprocated and acquired.[8] In looking at this depiction and not possessing that which is depicted, we find ourselves thinking of and experiencing the pleasures and frustrations of another mythical figure before a reflective surface, that of Narcissus, the Albertian inventor of painting.[9]

The *Mellon Venus,* for all of its evocations of the toilette tradition, significantly deviates from the type by presenting a reflection of the goddess that fails to conform to our expectations of how the mirror should appear. The mirror shows a fragment of the goddess seen from behind, whose one visible eye looks directly at the beholder outside of the picture. She appears to be gazing at her own beauty; however, we have a view of the reflected Venus that, according to the operational tradition of mirrors in this compositional structure, we do not expect to have. Rather than seeing her reflected back or being denied any visual access, viewers see the reflected goddess—and without seeing their own reflection. Titian selects one of the more sophisticated positions for the depicted mirror, whereby the mirror becomes a medium for seeing another person without seeing oneself. Our reflected access to Venus comes courtesy of the intervention of Love himself, here in the form of Cupid, who, with his back to us and his love-inducing arrows at his feet, tilts the mirror toward us.[10]

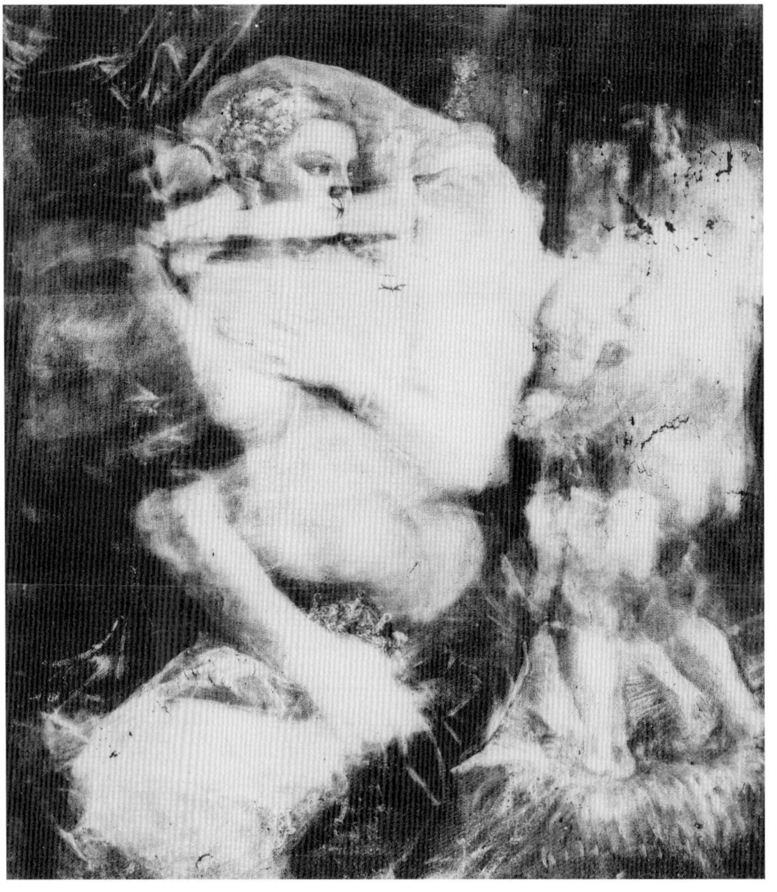

Fig. 11 X-ray of *Venus with a Mirror,* Andrew W. Mellon Collection, National Gallery of Art, Washington, D.C.

An additional and significant aberration in this mirror is that the surface of the reflection appears more loosely and thickly executed than the Venus herself, leading one scholar to refer to the reflection, somewhat proleptically, as having the pictorial sensuality of Rubens.[11] The body of the reflected goddess is splotchy and loosely painted, and the cupid's hand at the far left of the reflection is suggested by stubby peach brushstrokes. This is not the image made without human hands—as is often claimed for mirrors and reflective surfaces—but an image very evidently worked.

Viewers of the painting have considered the materiality of the reflection—if they have noticed it—as part of a broader stylistic consideration of Titian's later work.[12] The open, thick brushwork, the limited palette, and the use of paint to undermine representational form exemplify Titian's approach to the oil medium in the mid-sixteenth century.[13] To some art historians—who see these qualities as a notable shift in, rather than as a continuation of, Titian's pictorial practice—the striking materiality of the mirror suggests that the *Mellon Venus* is unfinished or was brought to completion by necessarily inferior studio hands after Titian significantly changed the orientation and subject of an earlier painting on the same canvas (fig. 11).[14] Contributing further to these *nonfinito* and interventionist claims is the written evidence that the painting remained in Titian's studio at the time of his death, when, in fact, a more likely explanation for Titian's possession is one of professional interest.[15]

If, however, we take seriously this variant mirror, we leave open the possibility that Titian employed a compositional type associated with illusion and desire in order to question the Renaissance paradigm of visuality that the *Mellon Venus* seems to exemplify and uphold. The obvious presence of the physical medium and of the artist's hand throughout the entire painting, not just in the mirror, requires a different approach to viewing, a new paradigm that does not depend on the fiction of looking *through* a painting, but on experiencing the painting *on* the canvas.[16] In this newly evolving paradigm, desire does not depend on illusion exclusively for its figuration or articulation. The physicality of oil paint on canvas elicits desire through the material qualities of the medium and its handling, so that the viewer's experience of the picture is mediated through physical conditions, such as thickness and thinness, and contact and separation.

Inexact Reflections

Early modern culture offers many precedents for a mirror that reflects approximately or that produces an entirely dissociated image. Following the tradition of medieval specula, the Renaissance mirror can show you as you should be, as you are, or, as in *memento mori* images, as you unfortunately will be (fig. 12). The mirror, standing as a metaphor for speculation, also can pierce through self-delusion with clarifying, even horrifying, precision to reveal an unexpected and undesirable self-image.[17] As truth-teller, the mirror reveals the ravages of time on the body and the corresponding changes in the self. Petrarch knew this well: "My faithful mirror, my weary spirit, and my changing skin and diminished agility and strength often say to me: 'Do not pretend anymore, you are old.'"[18] As an instrument of self-reflexivity, the changeable mirror figures the mutability of the self, the impossibility of locating a fixed identity. Consider, for example, Parmigianino's *Self-Portrait in a Convex Mirror* (fig. 13), which presents the distortions of the artist's body as indicative of his technical skill and as suggestive of the sometimes dislocating experience of oneself.[19]

In Renaissance representations of women (figs. 9 and 10), the mirror less often signifies the self-awareness that potentially emerges from the subjective engagement with a reflection, and more often conveys the moral dangers of such self-regard. A woman who gazes at her own reflection involves herself in superficial, ephemeral concerns, such as her own beauty. Recall, for example, the words spoken by the spurned poet-lover cited at the outset of this chapter: "For in me," unlike in the false mirror, "you will know who you are." The vanities of womanly existence are like the transient and impermanent reflection in the mirror, which only registers that which passes before it.[20] The mirror, like beauty and wealth, constantly changes.

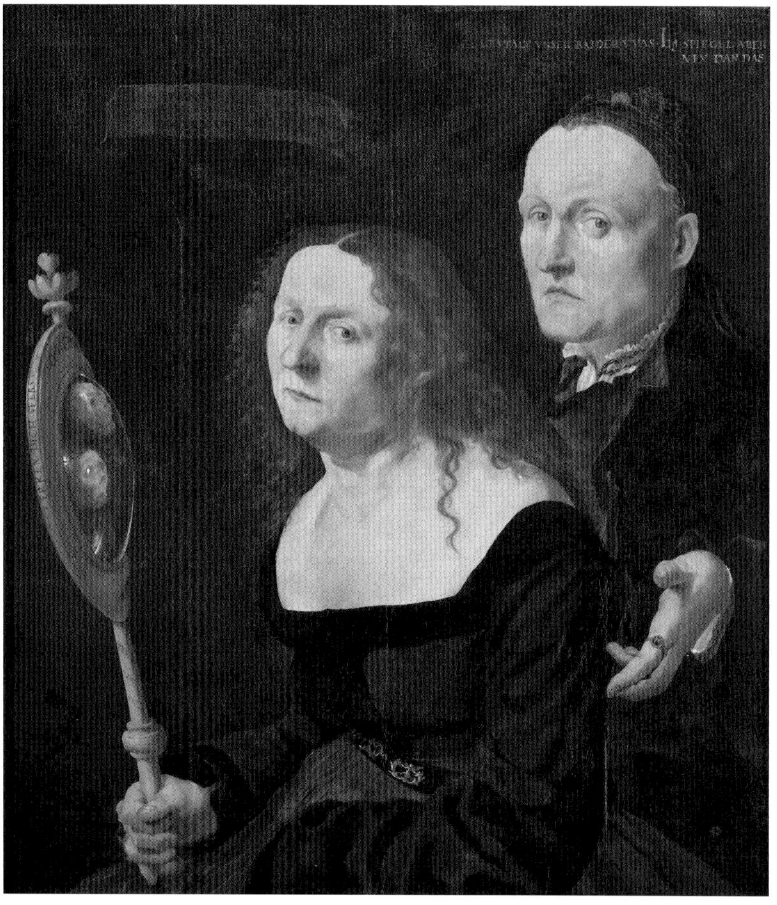

Fig. 12 Lucas Furtenagl, *Portrait of the Artist Hans Burgkmair and His Wife Anna*, Kunsthistorisches Museum, Vienna

The approximate reflection in Titian's *Venus* alludes to these projective, ontological associations with the mirror but does not specifically or precisely enact any of them. Consequently, many readers have offered interpretations that move away from selfhood and related moralizations and involve this picture in the broader thematics of Renaissance aesthetics—and, in particular, the *paragone* between painting and sculpture. The painting easily fits within the tropes of this discourse: Venus, after reclining for a few decades in Titian's oeuvre, sits up and assumes the pose inspired by her ancient sculpted sister; and the painted Venus, like statuary, displays a different side of her body in the mirror.[21] The painting appears to allude to another standard trope of the *paragone* literature: the lost or legendary painting, attributed to Jan van Eyck, which reportedly depicted a beautiful female bather in multiple views that were furnished by reflections in a mirror and an adjacent stream.[22]

The fragmentary, even obscured, reflection in Titian's painting distances the picture from the common Renaissance association between mirrors and the disciplinary self-reflexivity of painting. Typically depicted mirrors give us, quite literally, a fuller picture of the figures inhabiting the painted world or of the imagined space outside the frame. When, for example, Jan van Eyck painted his reflection in the convex mirror of the *Portrait of Giovanni Arnolfini and His Bride* (fig. 14) or Petrus Christus included the reflection of spectators in his *A Goldsmith in His Shop, Possibly Saint Eligius* (Metropolitan Museum, New York) or Giovanni Bellini depicted the vague face in the convex mirror of *Allegory of Prudence* (Galleria degli Uffizi, Florence), he acknowledged the prosthetic and testimonial function of mirrors: these depicted mirrors extend and heighten vision while simultaneously affirming and legitimating presence.[23] These pictures also explicitly acknowledge and defy the limits of the painted surface by including an imagined or an actual beyond on that very painted surface. The *Mellon Venus* draws upon the optical (prosthetic) play of these earlier fictive mirrors, but substitutes for a clear depiction of an "other" the implied representation of the beholder through her gaze—and a gaze that is surprisingly indirect and fractional, considering the recognized potential for displaying pictorial bravura in what is, in effect, a picture within a picture.

Significantly, though, Cupid creates through his positioning of the mirror a reflection that clearly resembles the composition of an image-type popular in the early sixteenth century, the *ritratto di spalla,* a portrait-type in which the sitter is seen from behind (fig. 15).[24] The turning pose, developed from the rhetorically inspired

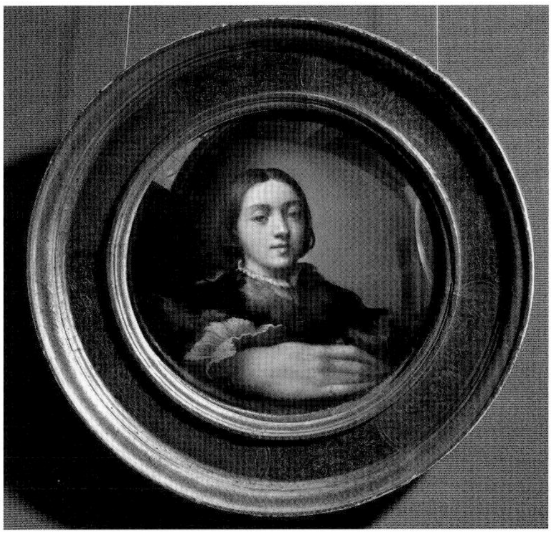

Fig. 13 Parmigianino, *Self-Portrait in a Convex Mirror,* Kunsthistorisches Museum, Vienna

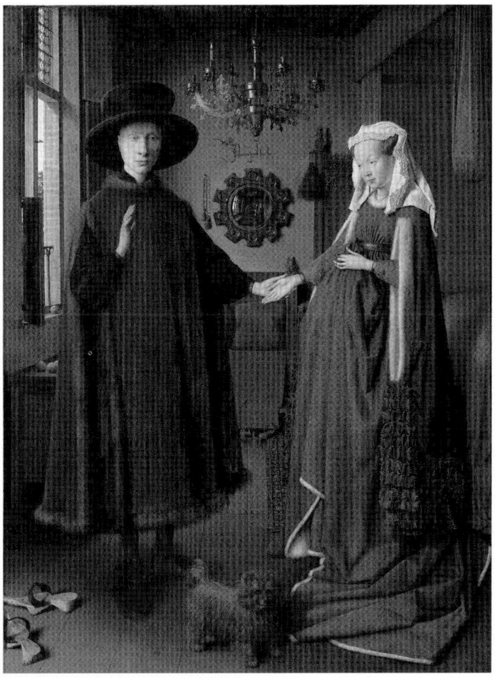

Fig. 14 Jan van Eyck, *Portrait of Giovanni Arnolfini and His Bride,* National Gallery, London

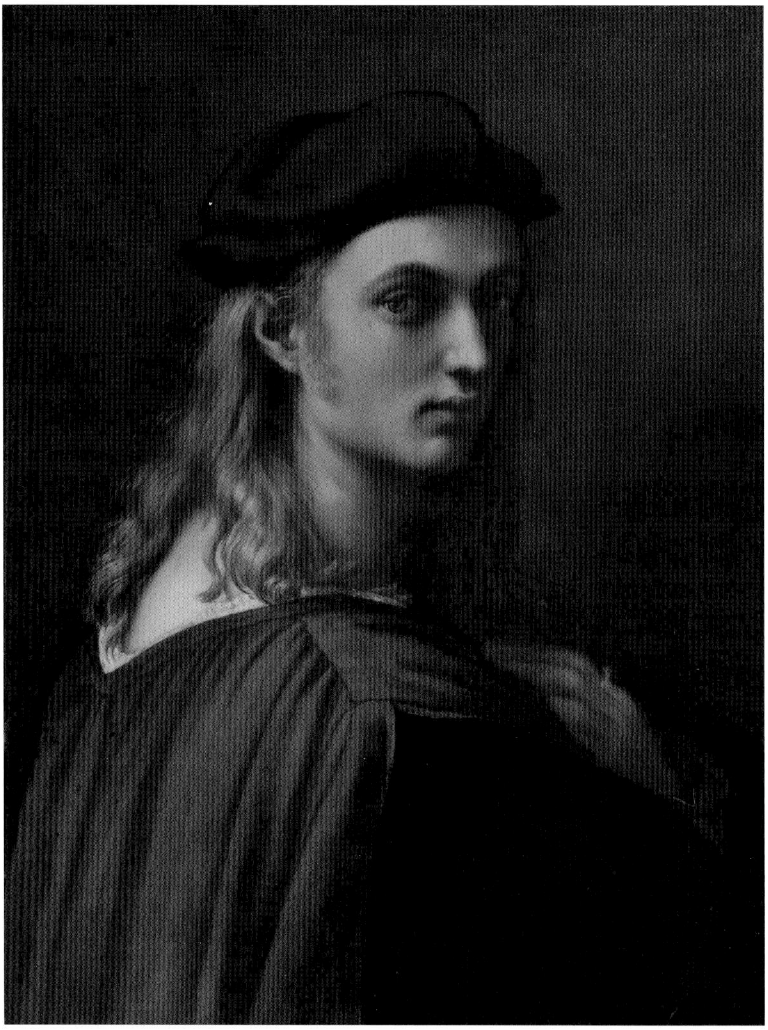

Fig. 15 Raphael, *Bindo Altoviti,* Samuel H. Kress Collection, National Gallery of Art, Washington, D.C.

contrappostal pose and the related *figura serpentinata,* first appeared in the portrait-types of Leonardo and Giorgione as a figuration of revelation, especially in theological situations (fig. 16).[25] Those examples, as well as works by painters more contemporary with Titian, such as Palma Vecchio (*Portrait of a Woman,* Kunsthistorisches Museum, Vienna), quickly acknowledged the potential seductiveness of the turning figure, especially when adopted by a beautiful female figure who, in her turn, registers the presence of the beholder—either the sensuous woman who looks at herself in the mirror or at a different beholder outside of the painting's frame. In adopting this image-type for the reflection of Venus, Titian recognizes and articulates the reflexivity embedded in the turning pose and the resulting ambiguity in reading the painted

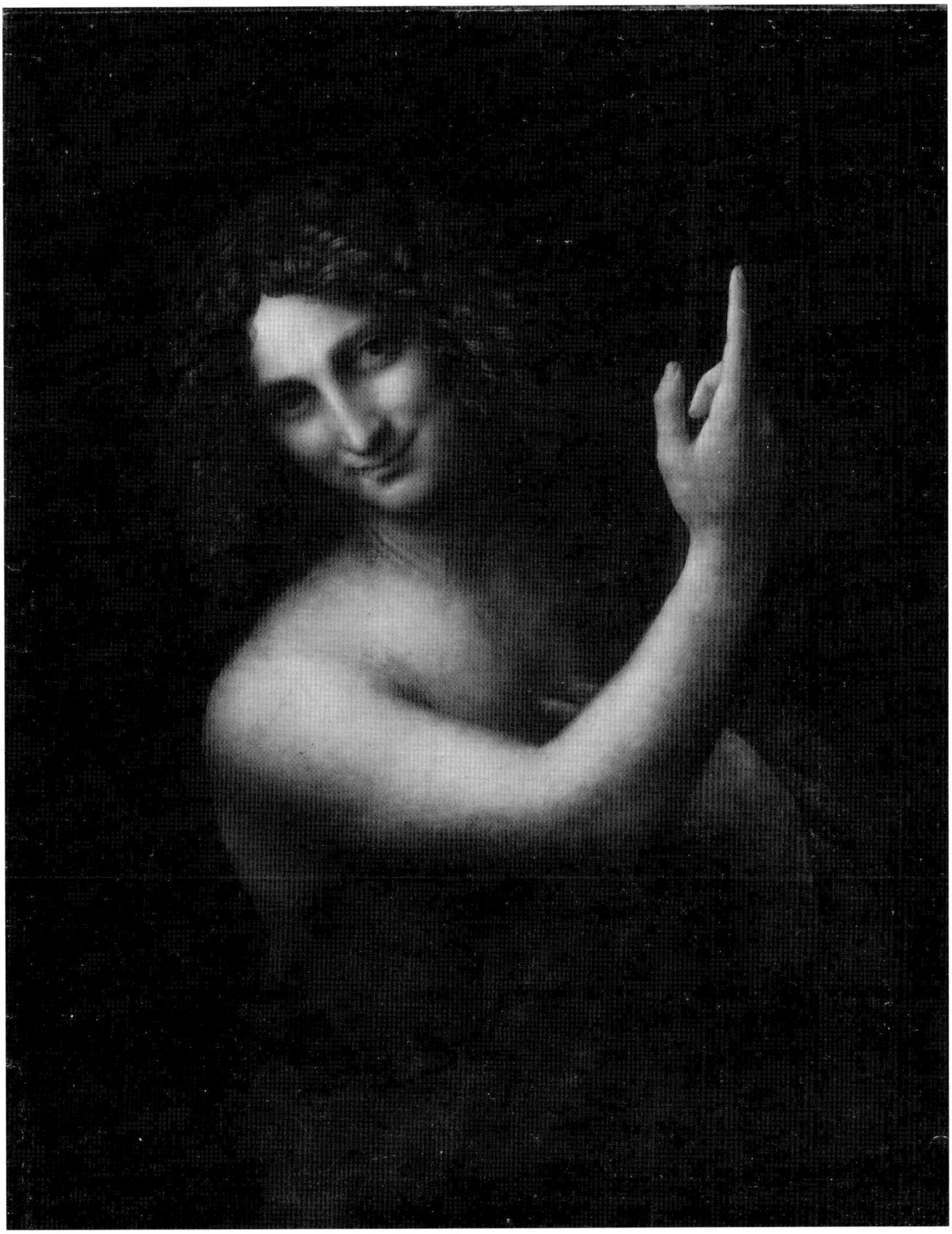

Fig. 16 Leonardo da Vinci, *Saint John the Baptist,* Louvre, Paris

surface as a painting or as a mirror reflection. He also clearly situates this mirror reflection as a sign of desire with a pictorial heritage, which the flat, framed mirror and the careful handling (or presentation) with the dark cloth emphasize.

But like all *ritratti di spalla,* this mirrored one elicits in the viewer both desire and fear, the seemingly unlikely pair suggested by the physical turn of the sitter. The tentative pose, where the turn toward us could easily lead to a turn away, figures a common trope in early modern love poetry, especially in the Petrarchan lyric. There the lover enacts the very antithesis suggested by the turn of the beloved: he feels the pleasure of his beloved's attention—however imagined or momentary—but also fears the intensity of his own affections and laments the future, crippling absence of his beloved.[26] The mirror reflection in the *Mellon Venus* emphasizes this temporariness because of its changeable position and surface. Cupid bears the responsibility of exactly what kind of interaction the beholder establishes with Venus: any movement from his current position will turn the picture from an exchange between Venus and viewer to the more strictly voyeuristic situation found in earlier toilette scenes, where the woman gazes at her own reflection (figs. 9 and 10). Regardless of the movements of the youth, her sensuous body remains available for the delectation of the viewer—heightened by the notably ineffective *pudica* pose—but her visual contact, especially because mediated by the mirror, directly implicates the viewer in the efforts and effects of Love.

As much as the depicted reflection resembles a painting in its compositional structure, it displays a materiality that, at first glance, appears unrivaled by the rest of the painting.[27] Loose brushwork and a thick application of paint create a reflected image of the goddess that fails to correspond to the representation of that part of her face and body.[28] Titian's different, later versions of the "Venus at her toilette" type do not repeat this notable feature of the *Mellon Venus,* suggesting to the few scholars who note this that the inexact reflection reflects technical issues.[29] At an early point in its recorded history, Crowe and Cavalcaselle reported the damaged condition of the painting, an assessment that has confused restorers and viewers who note its fine condition and that might have been motivated by expectations of consistency in this most ostensibly mimetic section of the painting.[30] No later copies of this painting exist, making a comparison impossible.[31]

Perhaps some of the difficulty in recognizing the materiality of this depicted mirror results from its conflict with the expected role of the immaterial mirror in Renaissance painting theory. The mirror, because it replicates the natural world and strips bodies of their matter, served as a fitting metaphor for the art of painting and led Alberti to credit Narcissus as the inventor of the art.[32] Leonardo more decidedly confirmed this immateriality when he discussed the practical assistance provided by the mirror and advised the painter to use one as a guide in evaluating his own work: "You should take your mirror as your guide—that is to say a flat mirror—because on its surface the objects appear in many respects as in a painting. Thus you see, a painting done on a flat surface displays objects which appear in relief, and the mirror—on its flat surface—does the same. The picture has one plane surface and the same with the mirror. The picture is intangible, in so far as that which appears round and prominent cannot be grasped in the hands; and it is the same with the mirror."[33]

The Renaissance expectation that mirrors produce immaterial images without human interference depended not only on their actual operation, but also on much earlier devotional traditions. In these examples the mirror metaphorically conveyed the purity of the subject as well as the collapsing of subject and object in the relationship between God and the devout. The Virgin Mary, for instance, is described as "the flawless mirror of the active power of God and the image of his goodness" (Wisdom 7:26), the "speculum sine macula." The surface of the mirror is valued for its passivity, its clarity, and its light-bearing and receiving properties.[34]

In the portrayal of a very different type of woman, Venus, we find a "speculum *cum* macula"—a mirror painted in the style of Titian's "pittura di macchia."[35] We would hardly expect the representation of the goddess of Love to conform entirely or signify according to devotional iconography. And yet Titian, as well as many of his contemporaries, revealed his sensitivity to the potential openness of secular and devotional pictorial devices, especially the half-length type.[36] The *Mellon Venus* bears its closest resemblance not to his recumbent Venuses, but to his earlier *Mary Magdalene* (fig. 17), which exhibits the *pudica* pose to convey her identity as the reformed sinner.[37] The Magdalene, as prostitute, fittingly assumes the pose of an ancient Venus as she looks heavenward to God.[38] Our Venus takes the pose of her ancient sculpted source—perhaps mediated through Titian's earlier picture—and keeps her eyes downward in this world—both painted and actual. Desire is not completely sublimated or frustrated in the *Mellon Venus,* as it is in earlier toilette images, but encouraged through reciprocity of gaze—even if momentary—and through the fragmentary, inexact reflection that in its apparent difference demands greater involvement from the early modern spectator. Scholars are much more willing to recognize this paradigm or mode of viewing and painting for seicento painting.[39] Consider, for example, two paintings with similarly blurry reflections, Velasquez's *Las Meninas* (fig. 18) and, more thematically relevant to the present discussion, the *Rokeby Venus* (fig. 19).[40] The latter painting, obviously inspired by Titian's paintings of recumbent nudes and without the *nonfinito* baggage that has limited some interpretations of the *Mellon Venus,* has led recent readers to consider the "ghostly" reflection as a metaphor for, among other things, projections and transfigurations of desire.[41] The idea that the figuration of desire in the early modern period might not occur exclusively through illusionism—which, in being seductively real, also incites desire—suggests possibilities for thinking about the splotched mirror and Titian's later style.[42]

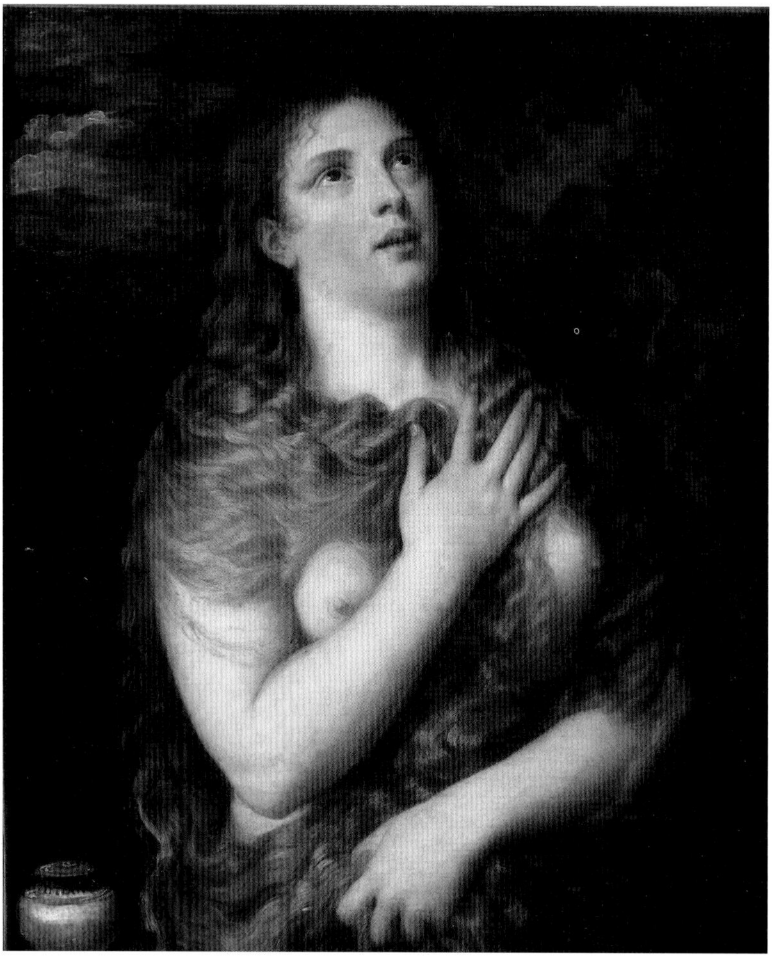

Fig. 17 Titian, *Mary Magdalene,* Galleria Palatina, Palazzo Pitti, Florence

Macchie

Cinquecento writers, who had little investment in upholding a singular standard of illusionism, turned to metaphors of formless clouds and smoke to convey an inexpressible beauty that spurs desire. "O beauty which resembles airy smoke, no sooner eyed than gone and leaving only tears," exclaims Gismondo, one of the discussants in Pietro Bembo's *Gli Asolani.*[43] About a century later Cesare Ripa gave visual form to this ineffability in his *Iconologia* (first published in 1593) by figuring feminine beauty as a nude woman whose head remains partially obscured behind a screen of clouds (fig. 20). The caption reads: "Beauty must be painted with her head lost in the clouds; for there is nothing about which it is more difficult to speak in a mortal language, or that can be less easily understood by human intelligence."[44] This is the "non so che" discussed so frequently in cinquecento painting theory, which articulates a rich network of visual figures for ineffability, such as veils, shadows, and other figures of omission.[45] These motifs articulate the limits of representation in expressing and of human perception in observing certain forms; but these motifs, in obscuring or obstructing the viewer's access to depicted form, also grant the beholder an unprecedented projective capacity that exceeds and surpasses the limits of visual and verbal expression and comprehension; that leaves the beholder without words, over-

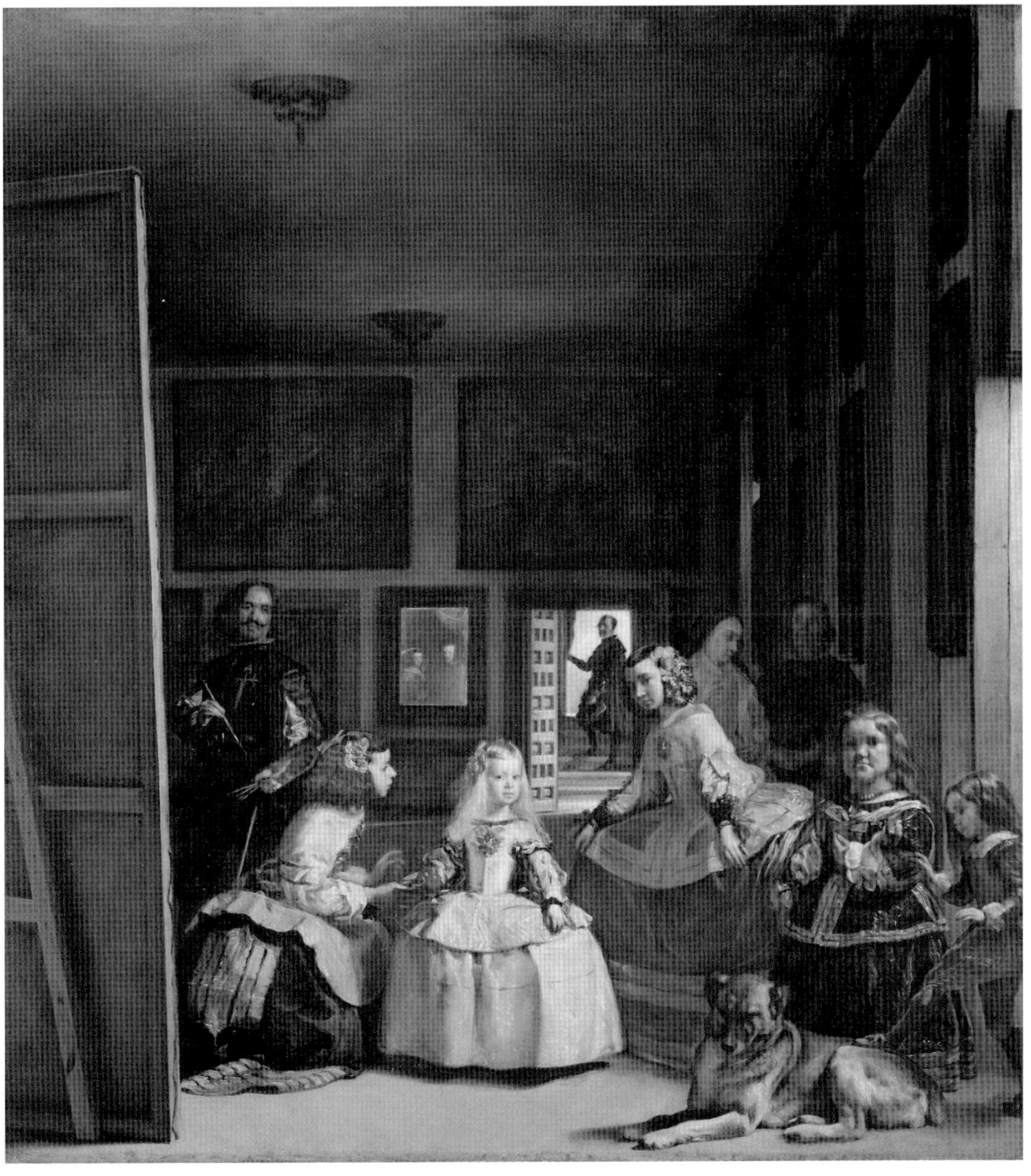

Fig. 18 Velázquez, *Las Meninas,* Museo Nacional del Prado, Madrid

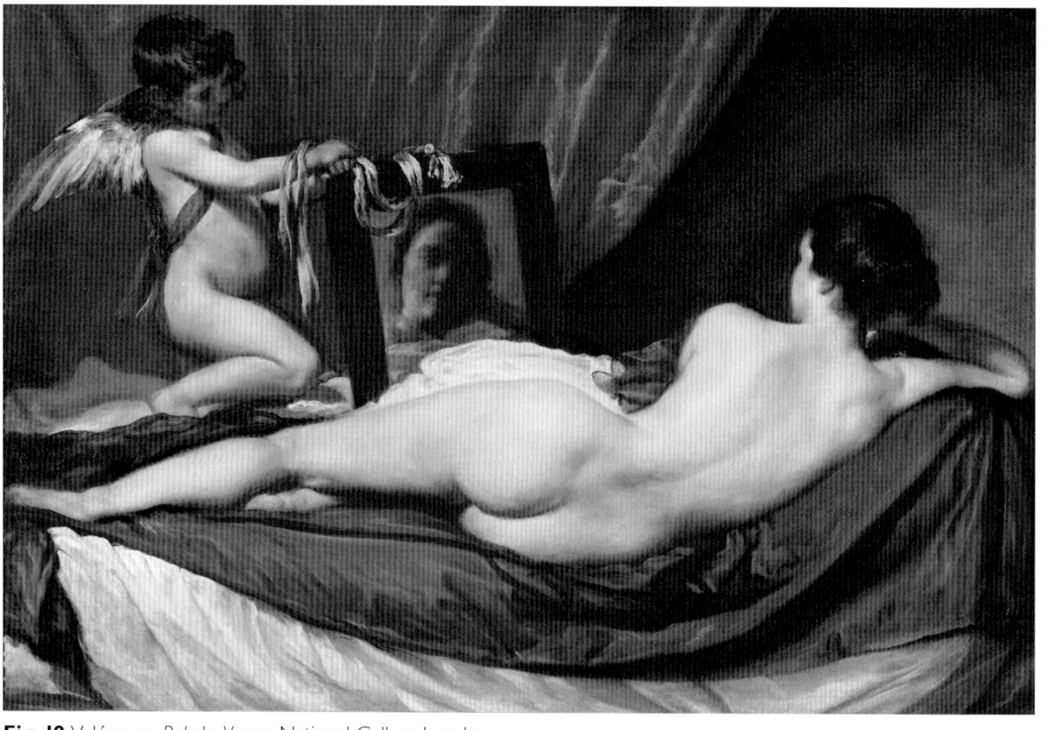

Fig. 19 Velázquez, *Rokeby Venus,* National Gallery, London

whelmed by emotion and desire for the inaccessible.

The metaphors of clouds and smoke are provocative for considering the blurry mirror in the *Mellon Venus,* and indeed the many loosely executed passages of the entire painting, as visualizing the inexpressible and imperceptible beauty of the goddess. But these poetic figures, with their emphasis on formal concealment, also depend on the idea of perfect illusionism as the normative standard, or at least as the horizon, for the interpretation of these mists. Smoke and clouds indicate the limits of signification for the Renaissance imagination in that both are forms found in nature, but forms that are formless or without a fixed form. Renaissance theorists emphasized these pictorial elements that hovered on the boundaries of the nonrepresentational as exceptional, sometimes even deviant, because of and despite the opportunities that they presented for mimetic projection. These early moderns were, to a great extent, inspired by the thoughts of ancient writers, such as Pliny, who embraced paintings left unfinished at the artists' death for their invitation to projective imagination;[46] or those ancients who extolled the ascriptive invitation offered by "images made by chance."[47]

Renaissance art theorists repeated these ancient tropes as evidence of the intellectual basis of the art and the affinity of painting with the naturally occurring artistry of the divine.[48] Leonardo engaged in one of the most extensive inquiries into the various implications of these inherited stories for the production and interpretation of form.

> I shall not fail to include among these precepts a new discovery, an aid to reflection, which, although it seems a small thing and almost laughable, nevertheless is very useful in stimulating the mind to various discoveries. This is: look at walls splashed with a number of stains or stones of various mixed colors. If you have to devise some scene, you may discover a resemblance to various landscapes, beautified with mountains, rivers, rocks, trees, plains, wide valleys and hills in varied arrangement; or again, you may see battles and figures in action; or strange faces and costumes, and an endless variety of objects, which you could reduce to complete and well-drawn forms.[49]

The painter projects form into formless matter, without regard for the material support—Leonardo turns to base, even abject stuff—and this form resembles objects in the natural world.

Underlying Leonardo's discussion of chance images is the larger question of how viewers find significance in specific deviations from illusionism. "Complete forms" and resemblance precede signification in Leonardo's consideration. The passage continues as follows: "And these appear on such walls confusedly, like the sound of bells in whose jangle you may find any name or word you choose to imagine."[50] The formless finds form through resemblance to some prior semiotic system. In another passage concerning the same projective operations, in this case a criticism of Botticelli for including a stain as a landscape in one of his paintings, Leonardo writes: "It is like the sound of bells which can mean whatever you want it to."[51] Although the range of meaning is left open here, Leonardo suggests its possible extension into states of being when he raises the issue of stains in a discussion of how to represent the "motions of the mind" of a figure. "These stains," he writes, "while wholly in themselves deprived of perfection in any part, did

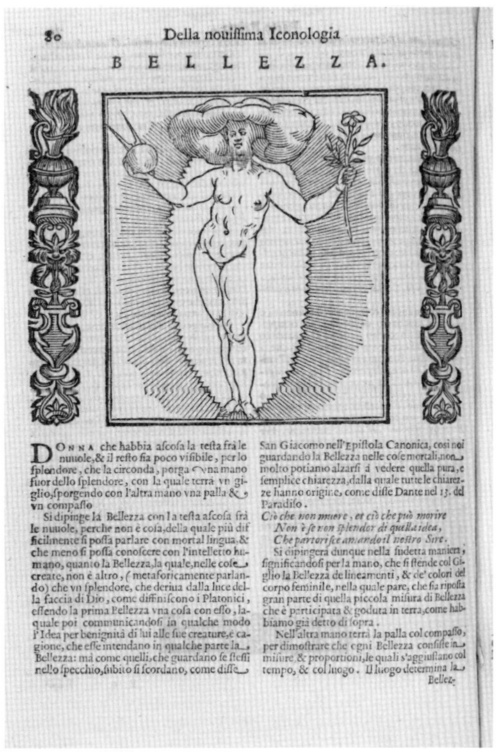

80 Della nouissima Iconologia

BELLEZZA.

DONNA che habbia ascosa la testa frà le nuuole, & il resto sia poco visibile, per lo splendore, che la circonda, porga vna mano fuor dello splendore, con la quale terrà vn giglio, sporgendo con l'altra mano vna palla & vn compasso

Si dipinge là Bellezza con la testa ascosa frà le nuuole, perche non è cosa, della quale più difficilmente si possa parlare con mortal lingua, & che meno si possa conoscere con l'intelletto humano, quanto la Bellezza, la quale, nelle cose create, non è altro, (metaforicamente parlando) che vn splendore, che deriua dalla luce della faccia di Dio, come diffiniscono i Platonici, essendo la prima Bellezza vna cosa con esso, laquale poi communicandosi in qualche modo l'Idea per benignità di lui alle sue creature, è cagione, che esse intendano in qualche parte la Bellezza: mà come quelli, che guardano se stessi nello specchio, subito si scordano, come disse San Giacomo nell'Epistola Canonica, cosi noi guardando la Bellezza nelle cose mortali, non molto potiamo alzarsi à vedere quella pura, e semplice chiarezza, dalla quale tutte le chiarezze hanno origine, come disse Dante nel 13. del Paradiso.

Ciò che non muore, et ciò che può morire
Non è se non splendor di quella idea,
Che partorisce amando il nostro Sire.

Si dipingerà dunque nella sudetta maniera, significandosi per la mano, che si stende col Giglio la Bellezza de lineamenti, & de' colori del corpo feminile, nella quale pare, che sia riposta gran parte di quella piccola misura di Bellezza che è participata & goduta in terra, come habbiamo già detto di sopra.

Nell'altra mano terrà la palla col compasso, per dimostrare che ogni Bellezza consiste in misure, & proportioni, le quali s'aggiustano col tempo, & col luogo. Il luogo determina la Bellez-

Fig. 20 Cesare Ripa, *Bellezza* from *Della più che nouissima Iconologia* (Padua, 1630), Spencer Collection, The New York Public Library, Astor, Lenox, and Tilden Foundations

not lack perfection in regard to their movements or other actions."[52] Stains behave, and therefore signify, like the gestures of a figure: they convey the affect of the figure and contribute to the larger thematic direction of the painting. "Unperfected" splotches may not mean anything in and of themselves, according to Leonardo, but they respond to the projective imagination and to the predominant early modern preoccupation with finding meaning in form.

With his own vapory contribution of *sfumato,* Leonardo's interest in clouds reflects the changing aesthetic in painting around 1500. The dry, hard manner of quattrocento painting, with its emphasis on contour, dissipated with the intervention of new modeling techniques and media—an approach that initiated the "modern manner," according to Vasari.[53] As paintings became cloudier, clouds themselves emerged as protagonists in these paintings, often punctuating the narrative movement occurring on the ground (reflecting Leonardo's formalist reading) while also maintaining their traditional roles of demarcating heaven and giving structural support to heavenly figures. But in nearly all of their appearances, and especially when sensually occupying broad expanses of the picture, depicted clouds actually complicate rather than reinforce the priority of form associated with illusionism by eliding form, subject, and medium. Like represented fabric and flesh, these pillowy nebular passages reveal the challenges of painting precisely because they require the application of a limited range of color, and sometimes over a large area. Painters represented clouds that appeared intangible and immaterial, but that also seemed changeable and unstable, as though allegorizing the tension between form and matter in illusionism; as though reminding us that the formal integrity of the cloud is bound up with the inevitable dissolution of form.

Correggio's *Jupiter and Io* (fig. 21), devoting half of the composition to a soft, engulfing cloud, gives mythical expression to these fundamental premises. Jupiter disguised himself as a cloud in order to conceal his seduction of the young maiden Io from his wife Juno (Ovid, *Metamorphoses* 1.587–688). The sensual interaction between an alluring female body and a notionally insubstantial one, and the depicted textural contrast between flesh and puffy cloud, affirm the interrelationship between illusion and desire, but also detaches desire from illusion. Jupiter is simultaneously form and formless. He appears to be overwhelmingly present, and yet his dissipation as immaterial cloud both evokes the sensual inaccessibility of the painted female figure to the desiring viewer and shifts the sensuality of the event to the imagination—and the body—of the beholder. In another scene of Jupiter's nebular exploits (plate 10), Titian makes explicit the separation of desire from illusionism by drawing attention to the disproportion between the thickness of paint on the canvas and the vast effects it aims to produce by roughly painting the clouds and divine light.[54] The formless clouds of Jupiter, which indicate his seduction of Danaë, remain closely connected to the blotches of paint that comprise them.

The consideration of formless matter as imperfect, even threatening, in the context of

Renaissance painting reflects one of the central metaphysical antinomies governing early modern thought.[55] Repeating ideas expressed by ancient writers, especially Plato, Renaissance theorists on the arts privileged form over matter in their related privileging of two facets of painting, *disegno* over *colore:* "Every material, though it be base," wrote Armenini, "is transformed by design into a thing of great value since when it is shaped into various forms . . . it is esteemed by honorable men."[56] This is one of countless similar expressions found in Renaissance writings on the arts. Recall, for example, the passages just cited by Leonardo. *Disegno,* like form, assumed masculine values, whereas *colore,* like matter, found expression through figures of femininity.[57] Although beautiful, color, like women, could be without rule and dangerous.[58]

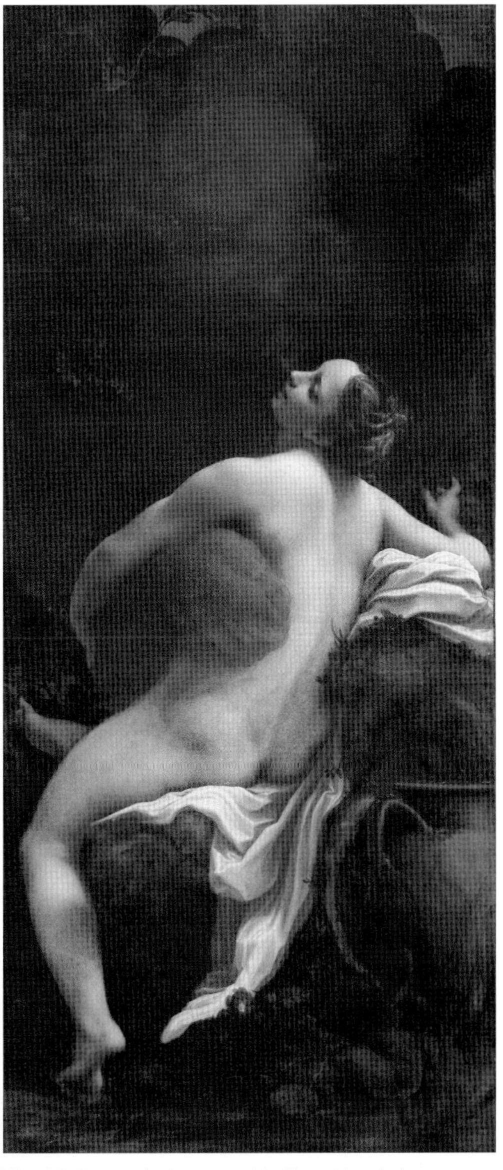

Fig. 21 Correggio, *Jupiter and Io,* Kunsthistorisches Museum, Vienna

Similarly, *macchie,* as unformed splotches of paint, were associated with the pathological conditions central to the different meanings of the word. Well before writers employed the word to describe a sketch, *macchia* suggested an actual stain on a surface, a sore on the flesh of plague victims, and a metaphorical stain, such as a sin or moral failing.[59] Other related meanings gradually accumulated, so that by the early seventeenth century *macchia* also referred to a dark forest and to furtive actions.[60] Naturally occurring *macchie* often elicited and attracted embarrassment, suspicion, or illness. For example, Leonardo dismissed his advice to painters cited above even as he recommended it. Another painter, Piero di Cosimo, followed Leonardo's inventive practice according to Vasari, and in doing so emphasized the abject horizon of and for *macchie.* According to Vasari, "[Piero] would sometimes stop to gaze at a wall against which sick people ['malate'] had been for a long time discharging their spittle, and from this he would picture to himself battles of horsemen and the most fantastic cities and widest landscapes that were ever seen; and he did the same with the clouds in the sky."[61] Bodily fluids of the unwell seem an unlikely basis for intellectual invention in the Renaissance. In fact, Vasari most likely chose this anecdote to support his opinion that Piero di Cosimo possessed a bizarre mind ("la stranezza del suo cervello") that produced *bizarrie.*[62] Later writers, such as Marco Boschini, warn viewers that they, too, could be driven crazy by *macchie.*[63]

Such negative, pathological associations with *macchia* reinforce the idea that we should not consider *macchie* in Renaissance painting as inert, formless matter, but as a deformed form, a disfigured figuration.[64] Vasari implies this distinction when he criticized Titian for not using drawing but also celebrates the artfulness and labor of his later style.[65] But Vasari's strict paradigm of negligible material interference in the production of art limits his articulation, even his appreciation, of how significantly Titian advanced a different approach to figuration. It was not until the seventeenth century that Marco Boschini suggested the possibility that "painters use form without form, even with form deformed."[66] The idea that form could be an unconstructive, even destructive and antagonistic, process surfaces in Palma Giovane's well-known description of Titian's approach to painting at the end of his career, as related by Marco Boschini.[67]

But what is the relevance of these tropes to how we interpret Titian's *Mellon Venus,* which, alluding to the toilette tradition, would presumably represent the assertion of immaterial form so central to that subject?

Materials

If we look more closely at the entire painting, we find that the mirror stands as only one of many loosely and heavily worked passages on the canvas. Not far from the reflection, for example, extends a splotchy arm of Cupid, composed with a few daubs of the loaded brush. His left foot, resting on the striped cushion and the intricately patterned drapery of Venus, draws attention to another area of apparent facture: the black stripes, loose and uneven, and the fur hem of Venus's garment both retain the traces of the painter's instruments used to make them—in this case, the brush and, quite probably, his fingers. The striped lines vary in width and tone, with very little adjustment within the lines themselves to suggest the rotundity of the cushion, and the fur hem results from an uneven smudging of the then still-wet black stripes of paint and red edge of Venus's garment. The lack of precision and consistency in these passages carries into the flesh strokes on the right forearm and shoulder of the goddess and the rough abstraction of pattern on her right sleeve.

Titian explores in the *Mellon Venus* these extremes between the substance of painting and the transubstantive capacity of representational painting to make that pictorial stuff into a flawless, shimmering surface. This range suggests itself most clearly through the varied representation of different fabrics unified under the foot of Cupid. Precise interlocking patterns on luminous red velvet give way to a hem created by undoing or by deforming the upper section of the unevenly striped pattern and edges of the red gown. We do not see the smudged line as either represented fur or as paint, with each mode of reading excluding the other. We cannot separate in our viewing the materials and action necessary to create the smudged line from what it represents.

Rather than approach the subject *or* the surface of the *Mellon Venus,* we can think of the ways in which the subject and the medium transform, even deform, one another. Consider again, for example, the passage of the painting that extends along the right hem of Venus's cloak. Rather than read this line either as representing fur or as a smudging of the striped cushion, I suggest that we recognize the interplay of these readings. The depicted subject of Venus transforms and directs the fuzziness of the line into our notional texture of fur; and the smudged line, made by wiping out earlier strokes, stands as a sign of the artist's intervention, which here simultaneously creates and unmakes. This physical, bodily presence in the painting transforms this ostensible scene of looking and pure reflection even as it recalls the tradition. In comparison, for example, we find the very different registration of the painter's continued making in Giovanni Bellini's *Woman Before the Mirror* (fig. 10) in which he inserts a *cartellino* signed with the word "faciebat." His use of the imperfect tense refers to an ongoing action in the past.[68] Titian's presence in this painting, although similarly without temporal restriction, is not at all as rhetorical, directed, and succinct.

The *Mellon Venus* serves as a unique demonstration of this alternative paradigm advanced by Boschini because, as a scene of looking, the painting enacts the limits and failures of considering the representational subject without regard for the medium and the means of making. As we have discussed, the mirror reflection, as the paragon of illusion, draws attention to the unexpected materiality of the image. However, Titian conceives this reflection more as a painting, and as a painting that signifies desire, structurally emphasized by the *ritratto di spalla* type. The thickness and looseness of the paint only further our desire by appealing to us as embodied viewers; and, in appealing to us as embodied viewers, the materiality transforms the visual focus and thematization of the "Venus at her toilette" tradition. Our experience of such heavily worked brushstrokes is not exclusively visual, as a scene of looking would suggest, since we read their appearance according to how the strokes were made. The striped cushion and smudged fur signify *because* of the action of the brush; they have a motion unexpected for an inanimate pattern or fabric but also a thickness that evokes the texture of these represented materials. Facture signifies in this painting by evoking ontological conditions involving surface and contact, and we experience desire through a different kind of visuality, one that involves not just the eyes but the entire body.[69]

The significance of the physical stuff of painting and this mode of experiencing this kind of painting was available in Renaissance art theory and written responses to Titian's later work. However, the negative view of matter—and our inheritance of this view in art-historical method[70]—has directed most approaches away from a consideration of how Titian's later paintings draw upon precisely these negative views and sublimated meanings of matter.[71] Matter had no place in a paradigm of intellectual invention, and so art theorists emphasized the control of materials through form. If we pierce through this rhetoric of denial, we find that defenders of an intellectual ideal actually tell us what matter can mean: corporeality, abjection, chance, and desire, among many others.

Some Renaissance theorists advanced a less distinct relationship between form and matter by turning to Aristotelian thoughts on the subject. Defenders of both painting and sculpture marshaled for their own ends the argument of composite form, which conceives of form and matter as inextricably linked. Paolo Pino incorporates this idea of form and represented matter as *tutto composto* in his argument for the universality of painting:

> The sculptor cannot endow a figure with anything beyond its form, which is its essential being; whereas we painters, in addition to form and being, adorn it with specifications [that make] for integral being. And this consists in our feigning the whole composite carnal form, in which one may discern the diversity of complexions, the distinction of the eyes from the hair and other members, not merely in their form, but also in their colors, just as they are distinguished in the live model.[72]

A near-contemporary of Pino, Benedetto Varchi, developed in his defense of sculpture the idea of *tutto composto* to include form and actual matter.

> That which is generated by nature, or made by art, is not only in form, nor only in material; but the whole is composed together ["tutto composto"]; such that, if one asks what is that which a sculptor has done when from a mass of bronze he has cast, for example, a Perseus, we ought to reply that as he has not made the material, that is the bronze, so similarly he has not made the form of Perseus, but the whole *composto,* that is, the material and the form together. . . . A man is not in form only, that is, the soul, nor matter only, that is the body; but the soul and body together.[73]

The intertwining of form and matter allows Varchi to affirm, and to ennoble, the importance of the senses of vision and of touch in experiencing sculpture.[74]

Although these philosophical arguments developed in the mid-sixteenth century, the concept of an embodied viewer already had structured viewer responses and prescriptions for viewer responses through synaesthetic metaphors. Lorenzo Ghiberti, for example, described his experience of viewing an ancient sculpture of a hermaphrodite and eloquently involved the amorous connection between touch and sight. "In this statue," he observed, "there were a great many delicacies ['dolcezze'], the sight discerned nothing [of them] if the hand by touching did not find them."[75] Responding to the physical presence of the sculpture, Ghiberti expresses the connection, if not dependence, between touch and sight in experiencing the sensuous body of the reclining figure. In doing so, he alludes, of course, to the myth of Pygmalion.

But he also appears to rely on a rhetorical framework for the expression of his erotic and amorous response. The *dolcezze* that touch apprehends in the sculpture refer to an intimate aspect of the animating potential of words in rhetoric, that is, the sensual endowment of inanimate objects or the "narration of pleasures which are represented to the use of our . . . senses."[76] The sculpted hermaphrodite, with its smooth surfaces and spatial presence, appeals to an embodied viewer who feels as he sees and sees as he feels.

The combination of vividness and sensual pleasure found in the concept of *dolcezza* elicits similar synaesthetic responses to other media. Ghiberti, this time criticizing his own sculpted work, once again returns to mixed modalities of senses while abandoning the eroticism of his earlier response to the statue. Here he employs the combination of taste and sight to distinguish between ornament and significance in his "historie" for the east doors of the Baptistery in Florence. "I want to have two things in the representation of the Old Testament: one is *illustri* and the other is *significanti.* We refer to as *illustri* that which feeds the eye ['pascere l'occhio'] with variety of design, and *significanti* as that which is important to remember."[77] Feeding the eye has less to do with fully satisfying the viewer on some profound intellectual level and more to do with occupying the eye with a pleasing variety, a sensuousness of ornament. Similarly, cinquecento writers such as Castiglione and Dolce came to use the phrase *pascere l'occhio* to suggest a distraction that requires little intellectual engagement.[78] The phrase has amorous origins, beginning in the work of Propertius and Lucretius, and appearing in the first stanza of Poliziano's *Stanze per la giostra.*[79] The latter poet's Cupid, for example, "finds [Venus] seated on the edge of the couch, / just then released from the embrace of Mars, / who lay on his back in her lap, still feeding his / eyes on her face."[80] Lovers "feast" their eyes on the faces of the beloved, just as they "caress" them with their eyes, as a figuration of their mutual and all-consuming affection.[81]

Such mixed modalities of different senses began to surface more frequently in cinquecento *dialoghi dell'amore.*[82] Love literature, much like most writing on the arts, followed Platonic thought and emphasized vision as the sole operative sense.[83] If any of the "lower" senses entered into the discussion, they exemplified the experience of a mistaken or flawed love, a bestial rather than a divine love.[84] A few writers moved away from the Platonic rhetoric and theorized a more sustainable human love that involved the entire body.[85] Sperone Speroni warns in his *Dialogo d'amore,* "foolish is he who neglects his essential appetites and tries to be bodiless like an angel." He repeats this idea later in his dialogue: "The senses are a stairway and road to reason: therefore, whoever is foolish in love that he does not care for appetites, but acts only as an intellect without any body and searches to satisfy only the mind, is similar to the person who in gulping food without touching it or chewing it becomes ill rather than nourished."[86]

Other love treatises advanced the possibility of an embodied experience of love, even if it remained a minority view in the contentious dialogue form. Pietro Bembo devotes the second book of his *Gli Asolani* to such a view, even though the main advocate, Gismondo, discusses, albeit with some hesitance, the senses including those other than sight and hearing.

> As a painter can delineate the whiteness, but not the coldness of snow, for something which can be appreciated only by the touch is not revealed to the eye, whose proper field is painting: so I have to some extent been able to describe love's benefits to you, but love's delight, which captures all the senses and overflows them all as if it were a fountain much more plentiful than this beside us, can never be concerned by ear alone, however long we speak of it. (2.42–49)[87]

Dolce will later allow for a projective operation in viewing that causes the viewer to imagine a multisensory engagement when beholding depictions of "those things which stand subject to touch (like, for example, the coldness of snow), or to taste (like the sweetness of honey)."[88] The painter, Dolce continues, "depicts . . . the thoughts and feelings of the spirit ['gli pensieri e gli affetti dell'animo']."[89]

Once imagination and thought could cohabitate alongside the five senses in generating the experience of love, whether inspired by an actual or a depicted beauty, there remained the possibility of an absorptive experience, where the boundaries between the two bodies threaten deliciously to dissolve. We remember Leonardo's often-cited embodied experience in viewing a depicted beauty:

> It will inspire you with love and not only of the eye but all of your senses with a longing for possession; and all the senses will seem to compete with the eye, as if the mouth would like to swallow it bodily, as if the ear took pleasure in listening to the descriptions of its beauty, as if the sense of touch liked to draw it in through all its pores and as if the nose would like to inhale the air which continually breathes from it.[90]

The Lyric Touch

All of these writers, in seeking the bodily dimensions of love, return us to analogous tropes in Petrarch's *Rime sparse* and their relevance to the *Mellon Venus.* Lyric poetry served as an important inspiration for the painting and viewing of sensuous female half-length images of the Renaissance.[91] The *Mellon Venus,* although far more specific in her mythological identity than these indeterminate sitters, stands as no exception. The picture, through its subject matter, engages many of the same Petrarchan tropes of beauty, desire, and longing; however, the materiality of the picture recalls the repeated physical metaphors—that is, metaphors of touch and the physicality of sensation—in Petrarch's *Rime.* In several of the poems, he included metaphors of touch in order to convey his frustrated efforts to imagine and feel Laura's presence inwardly and bodily and to draw attention to the materiality of his poetic language.

Written and spoken words assert a sensual, even physical, presence that may never be the beloved herself, but come deceptively close, especially when the beloved is not near at hand. In *Rima* 37, Petrarch skeptically, and then jealously, looks upon his poem as precisely this kind of complex sensuous mediator. He raises his concerns of the unsupervised public life of his poem in the envoi to his song.

Canzon, s' al dolce loco
la donna nostra vedi,
credo ben che tu credi
ch'ella ti porgerà la bella mano
ond' io son sì lontano;
non la toccar, ma reverente ai piedi
le di' ch'io sarò là tosto ch'io possa,
o spirito ignudo od uom di carne et d'ossa.

[Song, if in her sweet place you see our lady, I believe that you believe that she will reach out to you her hand, from which I am so distant; do not touch it, but reverently at her feet tell her that I shall be there as soon as I can, either as a disembodied spirit or a man of flesh and bone.][92]
(lines 113–20)

The poet-lover's relationship to his song sharply contrasts with that in his source text, Ovid's letter from Leander to Hero: "Go to my love . . . in her fair hand she'll take you, happy note; perhaps she'll kiss you, nibbling, I hope, with lips and snow-white teeth the envelope."[93] Far less harmoniously complicit, Petrarch indulges his song in its vain hope that it will have physical contact with Laura in the act of reading and more intimacy than the poet himself has had in the act of writing. But, just as quickly as he disavows the thought, he succumbs to the possibility of contact and commands the poem not to touch. "Non la toccar": his words of intervention resonate with the urgency of the resurrected Christ's imperative to the Magdalene at the tomb. However, Petrarch quickly takes the role of the Magdalene by positioning himself (and his poem) at the feet of Laura, and thereby suggests the transcendent spirituality of touch as a form of cognition or figurative intimacy (as the disembodied spirit) and suggests the sensuality of enacted touch (as the man of flesh and bone).

Petrarch extends the concept of touch as a physical expression of his sensual love by exploring the connection between the tactile and thought in the discovery, and recovery, of love in the mind of the lover. In the dozen or so sonnets beginning with *Rima* 190, he turns to the metaphor of the breeze, *l'aura,* a tactile pun on Laura, as a sensual figuration of his beloved. The calm, gentle breeze at times causes him to remember his love, but more generally it softly suggests, and connects, his own physical presence, his poetic ambitions, and the presence of the idea of his beloved.

L'aura gentil che rasserena i poggi,
destando i fior per questo ombroso bosco,
al soave suo spirto riconosco
per cui conven che 'n pena e 'n fama poggi.

[The gentle breeze that makes the hills clear again, awakening the flowers through this shady wood, I recognize by its soft breath on whose account I must rise in labor and in fame.][94]

(194.1–4)

L'aura serena che fra verdi fronde
mormorando a ferir nel volto viemme
fammi risovenir quand' Amor diemme
le prime piaghe sì dolci profonde.

[The calm breeze that comes murmuring through the green leaves to strike my brow makes me remember when Love gave me the first deep sweet wounds.][95]

(196.1–4)

L'aura celeste che 'n quel verde lauro.

[The heavenly breeze that breathes in that great laurel.][96]

(197.1)

The breeze sometimes acts like the heavenly "spiritus" or the breath that inspires the poet-lover to write and sometimes acts upon the body as a spur to—or even a medium for—imagination. Unsubstantial and unseen except for its effects, the breeze figures desire and love as felt, and passes just as quickly as it comes.

The potential sublimation of desire connoted by Petrarch's *l'aura* led Renaissance writers on the arts to use the related term *aria* when describing a mode of painting unlike that found in the *Mellon Venus. Aria* was a pictorial quality that surfaced almost entirely in paintings that conformed to an ideal of illusionism and to a figurative tradition of gestures first espoused by the quattrocento Florentine tradition.[97] Alberti, as an initiator of that tradition, connected *aria* to the visual expression of the soul of a figure when he recommended that painters include fluttering hair, leaves, branches, and clothing as a way to visualize emotions.[98] Followers of his advice, most famously Botticelli, who in his *Primavera* (Galleria degli Uffizi, Florence) also allegorically included the wind source itself among the agitated draperies, recognized the potential grace of *aria,* whether as a responsive indicator or as a pictorial quality of softening the figures by making them both palpable and distant.[99] The wind-stirred drapery clings to and gives virtual relief to the depicted bodies, making contact visible and visual but not actual. In the cinquecento, Vasari, among others, described how successive painters employed *aria* to convey not merely "sublimated physicality" but also "sublimated sexuality."[100] Although the aesthetic term derived from Petrarchan writings, the aesthetic qualities it connoted conformed to the aesthetic ideals of ancient statuary, particularly of sensuous youths. The corresponding formal values—such as a smooth, seductive nude figure—find their best expression in the inviting, because unthreatening, androgynous body.[101]

Petrarchan tropes also gave rise to image types closer to that of the *Mellon Venus,* such as the sensuous female half-length image—even if they failed to share the materiality of Titian's painting. Renaissance viewers guided their responses to actual and imaginary depictions according to lyric structures and metaphors of frustrated desire; and the paintings, with their contrasting depicted textures of fabric and flesh, sustained the discourse. Modern viewers, in their own responses to these paintings and, more specifically, Titian's recumbent nudes, have acknowledged amorous structures of distance and proximity and the interdependence of the senses, of sight and hearing and of sight and touch in particular.[102] Titian's *Mellon Venus* expands the medium of the metaphors to the physical medium of painting itself. The perspectival inset in the *Venus of Urbino* or the contrast between depicted actual flowers and decorative patterned flowers figures the tensions of desire through devices of illusionism.[103] In the *Mellon Venus* these tensions are worked out on the surface of the canvas and paint, where brushstrokes and passages of the canvas figure proximity and distance, entanglement and resolution, the fullness of presence and absence in the traces of the brush. It is a desire figured and disfigured in the physical stuff itself.

Love, accordingly, requires labor and creates unease as much as it leads to unequaled pleasure. Similarly, our Cupid possesses physical weight, measured by the depression in the cushion, and appears to labor under the weight of the mirror. His wreath-bearing accomplice also demonstrates a lack of ease as he steadies himself against the shoulder of the goddess. Instinct as well as effort appear to be instrumental in effecting love since Cupid is shown to be working blindly. Rather than employ the more conventional motif of a blindfold,[104] Titian instead effaces his Cupid's eyes through the view of the figure's head in profile *perdu.* With his eyes turned away from his victim outside of the frame, he guides the mirror in our direction without seeing where we are. In not looking directly at us, our Cupid also suggests that love and desire depend on more than a mutual gaze for their beginnings and sustenance over time. Love and desire also require physical effort, result in physical benefits, and inflict physical costs, as the red-splotched arrows testify.

In linking the labor of painting to the labor of love, and in failing to conform to earlier allegories of sight, the *Mellon Venus* articulates, if not initiates, what could be considered an epistemological shift or moment in early modern painting and thought. Titian is reported to have talked about pursuing a "new path" when he returned from Rome in the mid-1540s, and, whether or not this is a legendary account or an episode of rhetorical posturing, his contemporaries certainly noted the stylistic differences in his later work.[105] But the *Mellon Venus* offers strong pictorial evidence of the self-consciousness of this later mode and of the extent to which Titian's later paintings articulated their critical formal and signifying differences from their apparent earlier sources. In this light, Titian's often-noted tendency after the mid-cinquecento to replicate earlier compositions might indicate that there is more substance in the matter, or, as the case might be, more substance in matter.

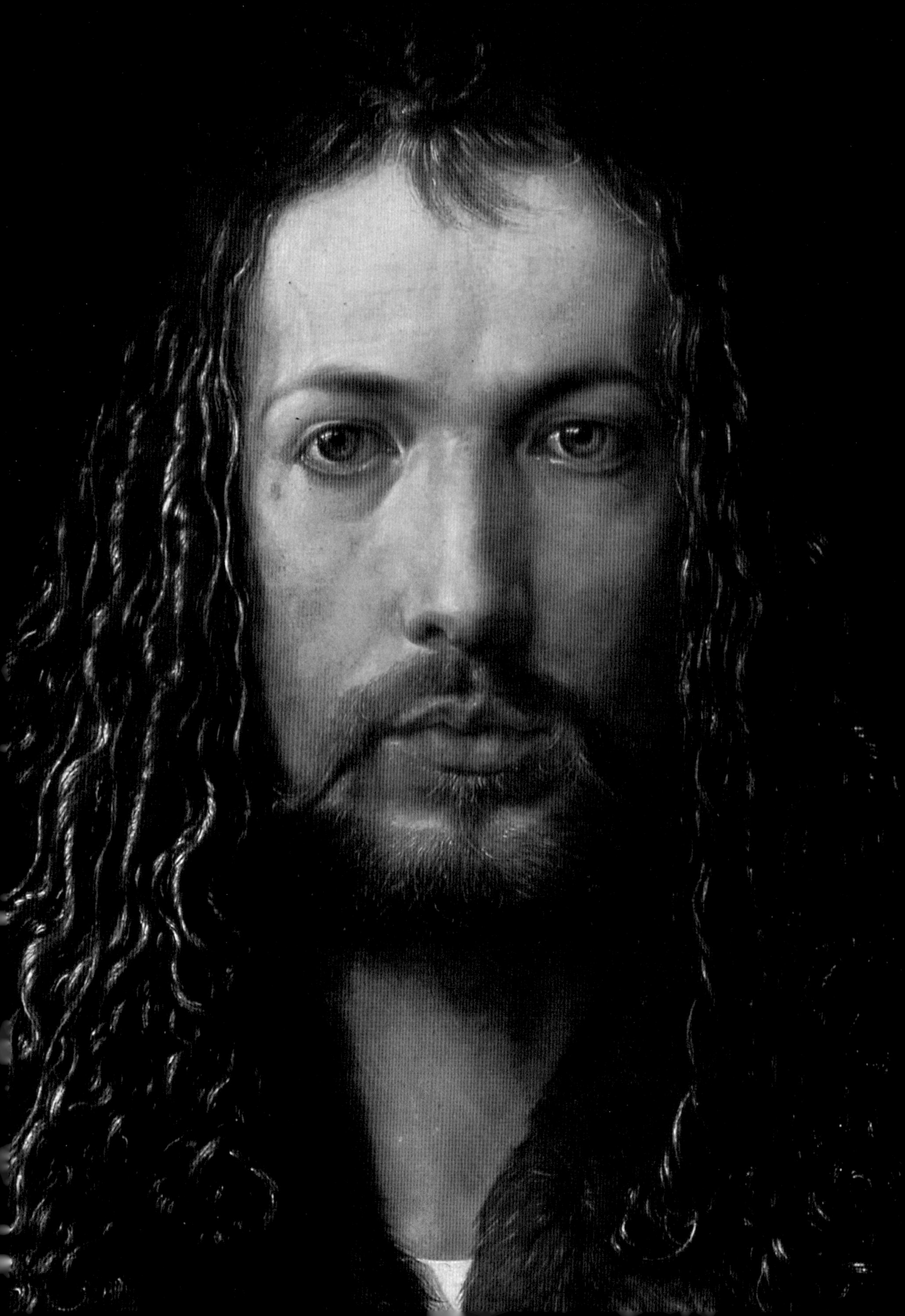

2

Myths of (Un)Making

The idea that the beholder's experience of Titian's later paintings displaces the purely reflective paradigm advanced by Renaissance visual culture effectively muddies the waters of Narcissus. This mythical inventor and beholder, so pervasive in the theoretical approach to and execution of Renaissance painting, fails to support the visual reality—the approximation, the disfiguration of mimesis, the effort—of these later works by Titian.[1] Other myths of making, such as tracing a shadow or replicating the creative operations of the Divine, continue to circulate in the later cinquecento imagination, but they, like all such myths, remain tied to a reflective sensibility that idealizes and suppresses variations in artistic production.

Well before the literature on the visual arts acknowledged and even articulated any deviations from illusionism, Titian offered what could be interpreted as a pictorial and mythological formulation of this mode of making when he depicted the *Flaying of Marsyas* (ca. 1570–75; plate 3).[2] As a subject, the myth of artistic competition between the god Apollo and the satyr Marsyas bears an obvious professional relevance—in terms of both inspiration and technique—to potentially any artistic project, visual or otherwise.[3] Titian's depiction of the myth specifically invites the comparison between the mythological subject and the act of making: the kneeling flayer, with his knife held against the body of the victim, evokes the activity and equipment of the painter outside of the frame, and the seated figure of Midas takes a pensive pose often associated with the melancholic pose of creative genius.[4] Such analogic relationships have opened the *Flaying* to interpretations that allegorize the painter and painting according to widely held assumptions about the rationality and divine inspiration of the artist and the art.[5] These figurative allusions have contributed further to a perceived presence of the painter through the materiality of the painting, which, with its visible brushstrokes, signifies as an index of the artist. But the signifying

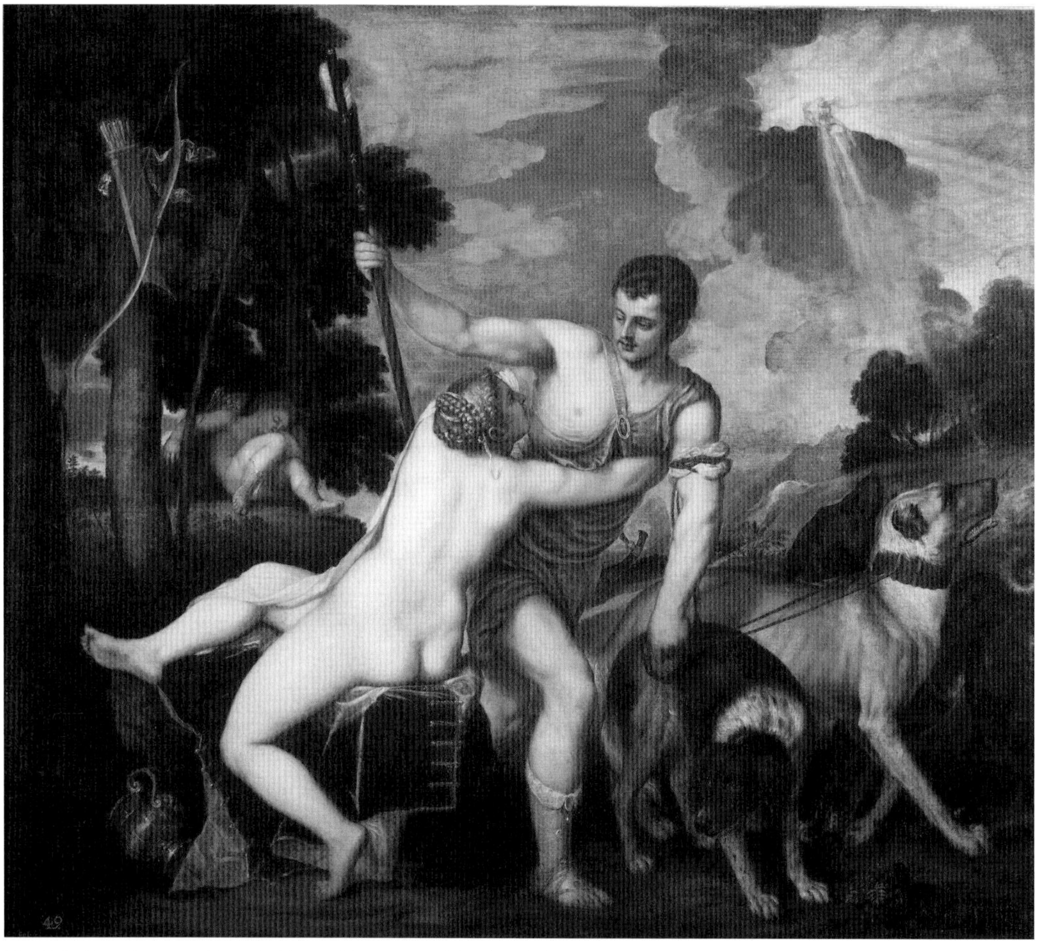

Fig. 22 Titian, *Venus and Adonis,* Museo Nacional del Prado, Madrid

connection between painter and brushstroke is never consistently simple, direct, and self-explanatory.[6] Additionally, such a scene of destruction and unmaking affects the nature of the maker's presence and subjectivity. I see the allusive connection between the depicted figures, the technique, and the painter as overturning the very assumptions that it has been seen as upholding. The allusion questions the nature of an artist's presence and self-reflexivity by suggesting a complex relationship between violence and (un)making that challenges our conceptions of early modern creativity as intentional and productive.[7] These challenges, not limited to Titian's *Flaying,* carry broad implications for reconsidering the central myths of making circulating around cinquecento art and for thinking about Titian's work within this larger historical and epistemological shift rather than as indicative of melancholic introspection oftentimes associated with old-age style.[8]

Although painted roughly twenty years after the *Mellon Venus* (plate 8), the *Flaying* stands as a conceptual pendant to the earlier

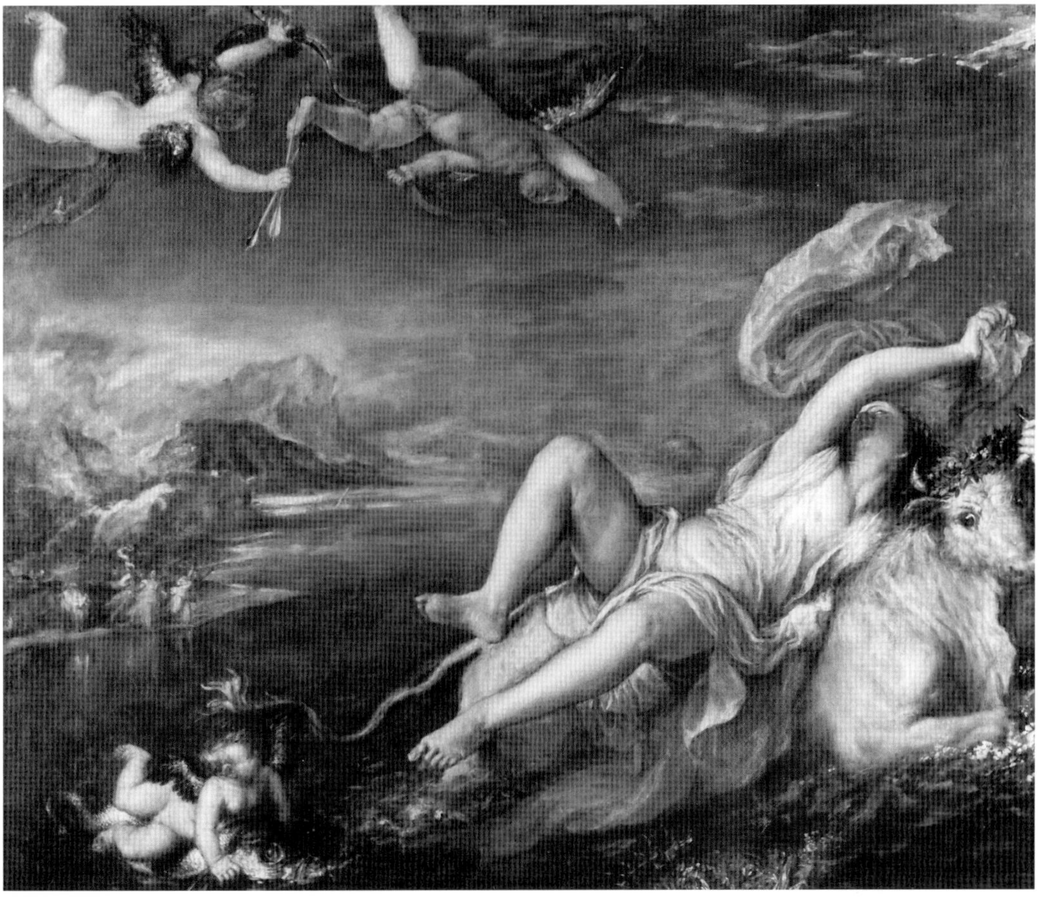

Fig. 23 Titian, *Europa,* Isabella Stewart Gardner Museum, Boston

picture. Both mythological, both harking back to earlier compositional types, both in the artist's studio upon his death,[9] the two pictures address the varied relationship between material substance, corporeality, and subjectivity. The *Mellon Venus* explores the engulfment in the object through desire in a pictorial tradition associated with viewing—with sight—and with selfhood. The *Flaying* considers the other side of (abject) matter—the horror of violence and its destabilizing of the self—from the perspective of making.[10] If the horrific scene, emphasized by, among other details, the dog lapping up blood,[11] threatens to dissolve the presumed self-coherency of the Renaissance viewer, then the enactment of violence through depicted surrogates of the painter and through the painter's brush undermines the early modern and our modern conception of the singular, self-sufficient Renaissance artist.[12]

Sacra Mythologia

Titian's *Flaying* enacts the dramatic competition and horrible punishment of Marsyas as told by numerous ancient writers, but perhaps best known through Ovid's *Metamorphoses* (6.384–400).[13] Having found the pipes invented, and then abandoned, by Minerva, the satyr challenges the god Apollo to a musical contest, and both agree that the victor will choose the punishment of the defeated. Not surprisingly, Marsyas, who competes with the lesser instrument, the pipes, loses to Apollo, who plays the lyre, or some variation of the stringed instrument. The triumphant Apollo decides that the defeated Marsyas should be flayed alive. A series of antinomies structures the story, including divine and mortal, rational and bestial, mind and body, Apollonian and Dionysian, living and dead, all of which emphasize the tragedy of the event. The *Flaying* responds to the dialectical structure inherent in the myth with its iconic composition, in which the upside-down satyr hangs in the center of the canvas, his hooves defining the upper edge of the painting, his suspended, bent arms nearly reaching the bottom, and his torso unnaturally stretched to fulfill this structural role. To his (and our) right appear three figures: another satyr, the seated figure of King Midas, and a young satyr who restrains (caresses?) a dog.[14] These figures are more closely aligned with the bestial ways of Marsyas, whereas the figures on his left represent the rational divinity in his administration of justice.

Although there are numerous sixteenth-century Venetian representations of the myth of Apollo and Marsyas, possibly because of the themes of justice and music, Titian's composition departs from the established tradition of representing the story with the activity and motion expected of narrative.[15] Titian's representation emphasizes the isolation and the suspension, if not the dislocation, of the continuous time expected of a narrative. The seemingly pensive, somewhat unresponsive Midas in Titian's painting, for example, heightens the stasis created by the iconic composition through his failure to react in the moment, extending the event in timeless rumination. The musician, who here engages directly with the instrument, creates a permanent suspension of time as the just-played notes still linger over the scene; he does not set the time of the story and resists being read as representing an earlier, separate moment in the myth, the "before" that is presumed to culminate in the actions of the other figures.

Titian clearly conceived of the *Flaying* in nonnarrative terms, and, in this regard, the painting differs fundamentally from his depictions of other myths from Ovid's *Metamorphoses.* Beginning with his work for Philip II of Spain, Titian turned to these stories of change and dramatized the temporal, emotional, and physical conditions of such transformations, in part, through compositions and poses that reinforce the lateral movement and progression of narrative—for example, his *Venus and Adonis* (ca. 1554; fig. 22) and *Europa* (1559–62; fig. 23).[16] An Ovidian story represented in a later work, *The Death of Actaeon* (ca. 1559–75; fig. 24), establishes a dominant horizontal movement from the gracefully and heroically striding Diana, her arms still directed in their deployment of the arrows to the already-struck victim.[17] Such a movement is completely absent in the *Flaying.*[18]

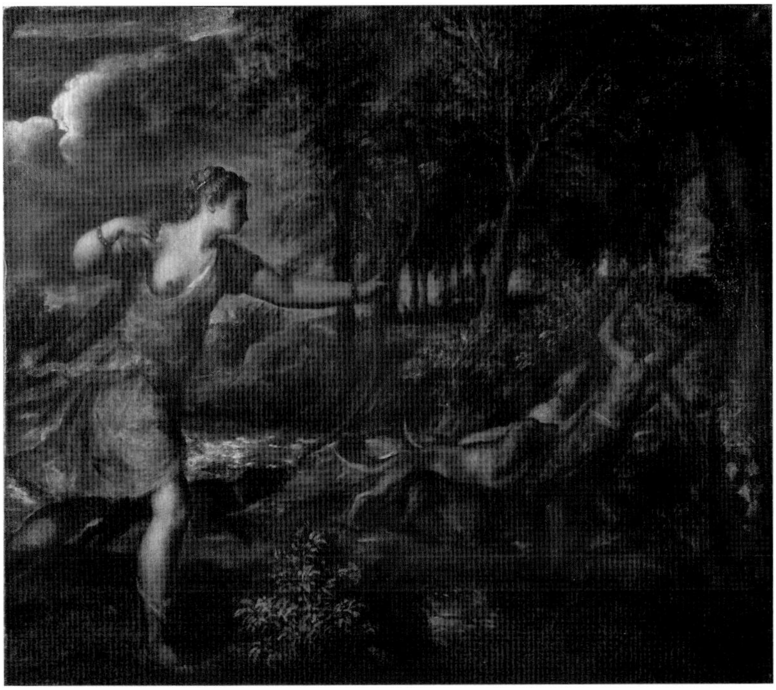

Fig. 24 Titian, *Death of Actaeon,* National Gallery, London

The formal structure of the *Flaying* composition, with the central figure of suffering and sacrifice flanked by persecutors and mourners, evokes most clearly that employed for, or more importantly expected for, the representation of martyrdoms of saints and of the Crucifixion, Deposition, and Pietà, and alludes generally to the formal organization found in fifteenth-century *sacre conversazioni* and depictions of the Adoration of the Magi.[19] These earlier types of devotional images (figs. 25 and 26) structured their compositions around the presentation of the central figure, whose position declared the unchanging presence, the eternal "thereness," of the divine to the devout viewer standing before the image.[20] The hypostasizing of an inherently narrative event encourages viewers to meditate on the scene, to see the eternal presence of the divine unaffected by history, and to develop its potential temporal extension in their own minds.[21]

By the mid-sixteenth century, the frontal, centralized devotional composition appeared less frequently as artists in the early decades of the cinquecento, including Raphael, Michelangelo, and Titian, explored the expressive potential of the altarpiece.[22] With Titian's early altarpieces, the painter embarked on what would become a lifelong effort to dramatize the activity of the miraculous, the holy, and the spiritual through his constant revisions to the traditionally balanced spatial structure of the altarpiece and his use of color to suggest tragedy, transcendence, and redemption.[23]

As his career progressed, Titian generally moved away from static compositions for

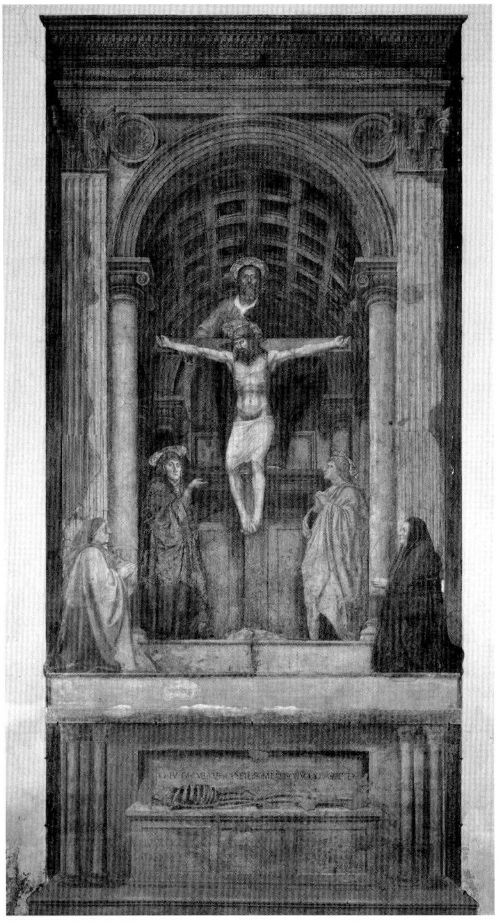

Fig. 25 Masaccio, *Trinity,* Santa Maria Novella, Florence

altarpieces and clearly inscribed a narrative direction in his mythologies. What is the significance, then, of his turning, or returning, to such an archaic compositional structure for his *Flaying,* and to one that has clear origins in earlier devotional images?

In representing a mythological scene according to a devotional type, Titian's *Flaying* returns us to the very origins of independent, full-scale mythological painting in the Renaissance. Although mythological scenes appeared in print and other media throughout the fifteenth century, it was not until the last two decades of the quattrocento that depictions of pagan divinities appeared in monumental panel painting; among the earliest images are Botticelli's *Primavera* (ca. 1482?) and *Birth of Venus* (ca. 1484–86; both Galleria degli Uffizi, Florence). Scholars have remarked often on the similarity between these compositions, in which various divinities assemble in a unified space, and that of a *sacra conversazione.*[24] The turn to more contemporary devotional art as a source for representing classical subject matter reverses the earlier habit among Renaissance artists of turning *to* classical models for sources of pathos *for* devotional art, the *Pathosformel* first discussed by Aby Warburg.[25] Perhaps in response to the intense meditation and the visionary experiences of classical deities described and advocated by neo-Platonism and the lyric tradition, Botticelli created an image that, following the *sacre conversazioni,* facilitated and shaped such contemplation of and conversation with mythological figures that were not connected by a single, coherent narrative.

In abandoning the motion of narrative, the *Flaying,* like the *Primavera,* inscribes the mythological story within the iconic tradition of devotional images, but to very different ends. Botticelli's sinuous, graceful lines and brilliant colors transport the viewer to a lyric paradise of eternal celebration and praise, of joyous meditation. Not so lithe and welcoming, Titian's *Flaying,* with its somber, earthy colors and the central physical presence of the tortured body, evokes the tragic dimensions of its devotional sources, especially representations of the crucifixions of Christ and of Saint Peter.

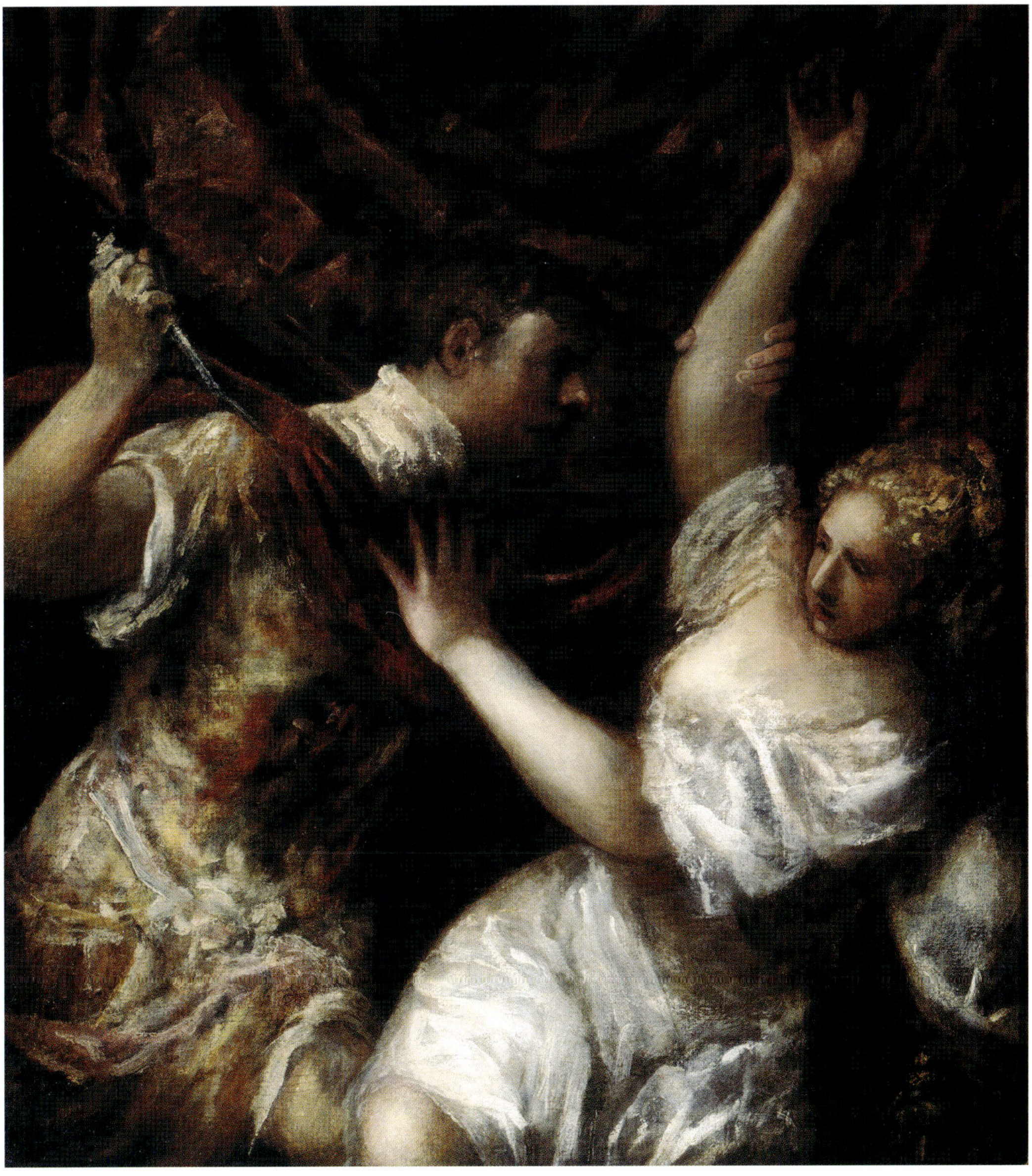

Plate 1 Titian, *Tarquin and Lucretia,* Gemäldegalerie der Akademie der bildenden Künste, Vienna

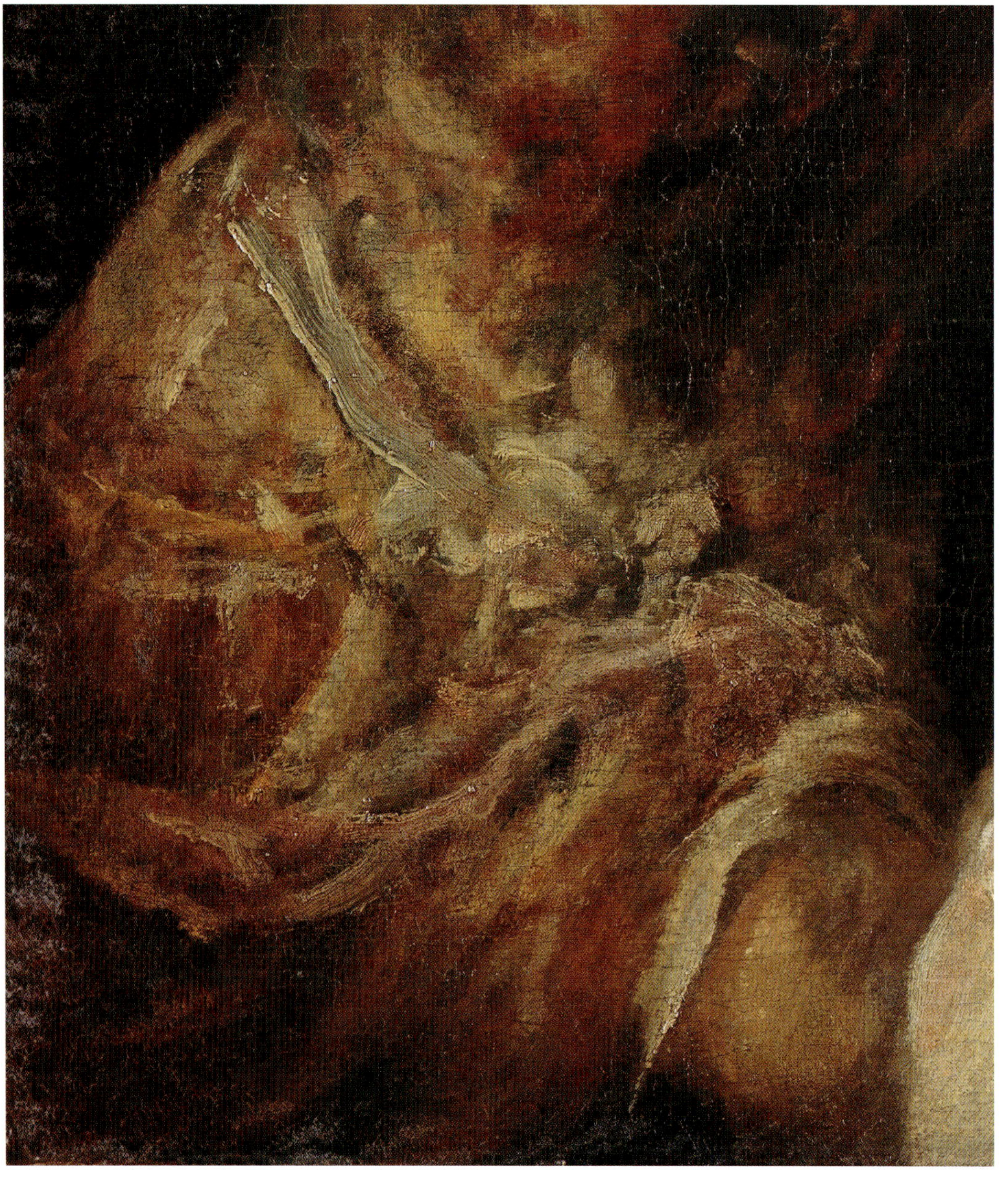

Plate 2 Titian, detail of *Tarquin and Lucretia,* Gemäldegalerie der Akademie der bildenden Künste, Vienna

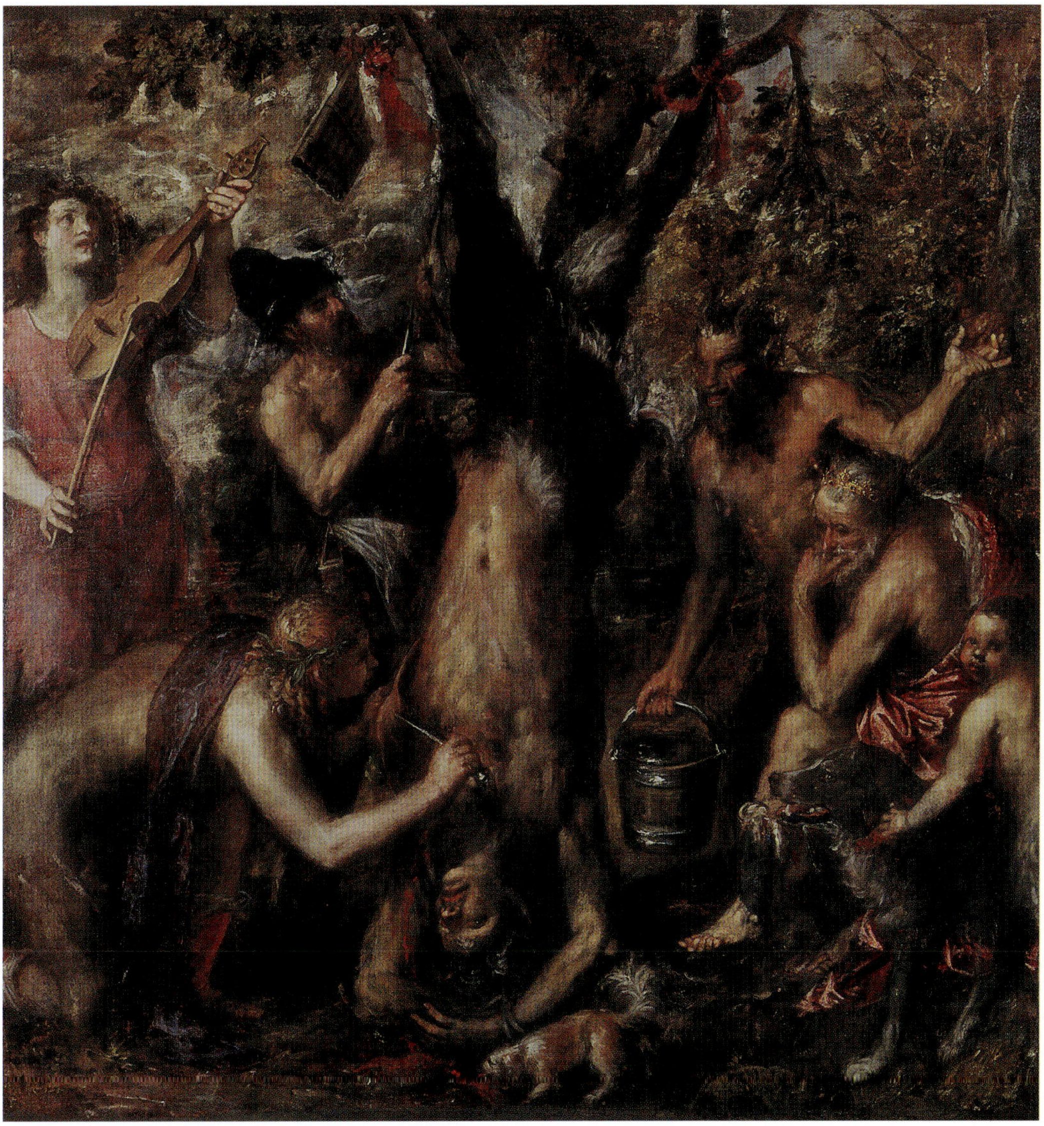

Plate 3 Titian, *Flaying of Marsyas,* Archbishop's Palace, Kromeríz, Czech Republic

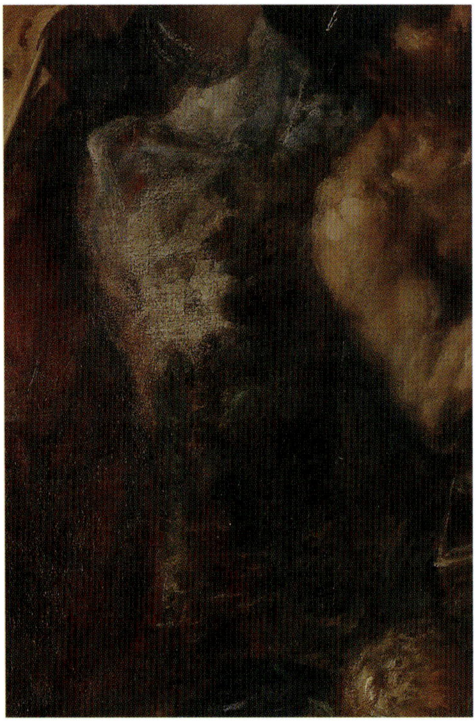

Plate 4 Titian, detail of *Flaying of Marsyas,* Archbishop's Palace, Kromeríz, Czech Republic

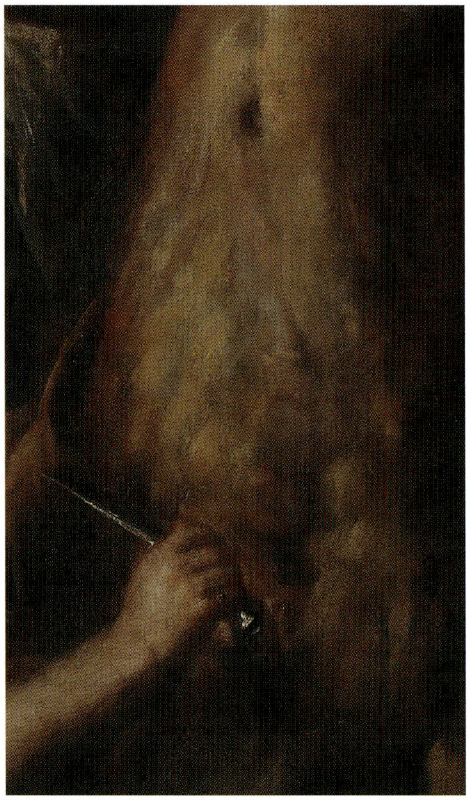

Plate 5 Titian, detail of *Flaying of Marsyas,* Archbishop's Palace, Kromeríz, Czech Republic

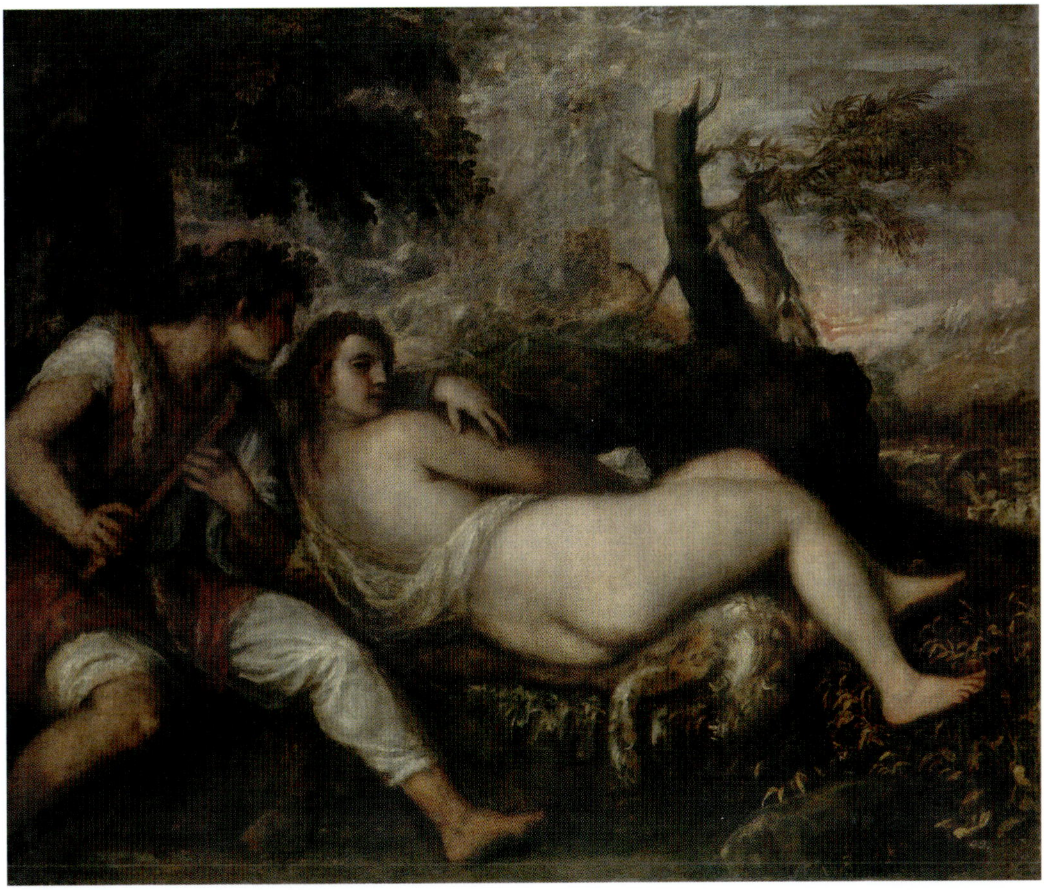

Plate 6 Titian, *Nymph and Shepherd,* Kunsthistorisches Museum, Vienna

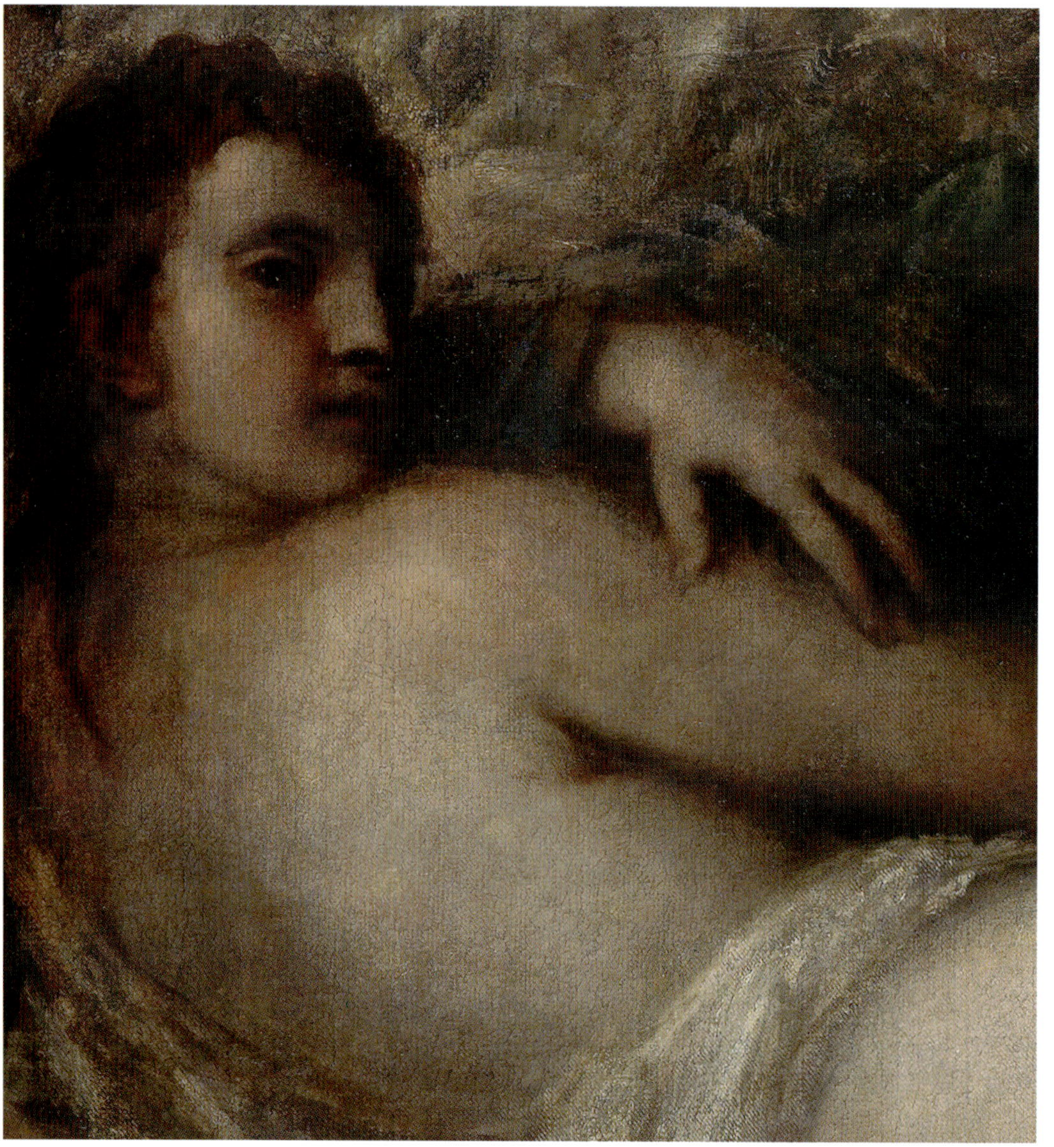

Plate 7 Titian, detail of *Nymph and Shepherd,* Kunsthistorisches Museum, Vienna

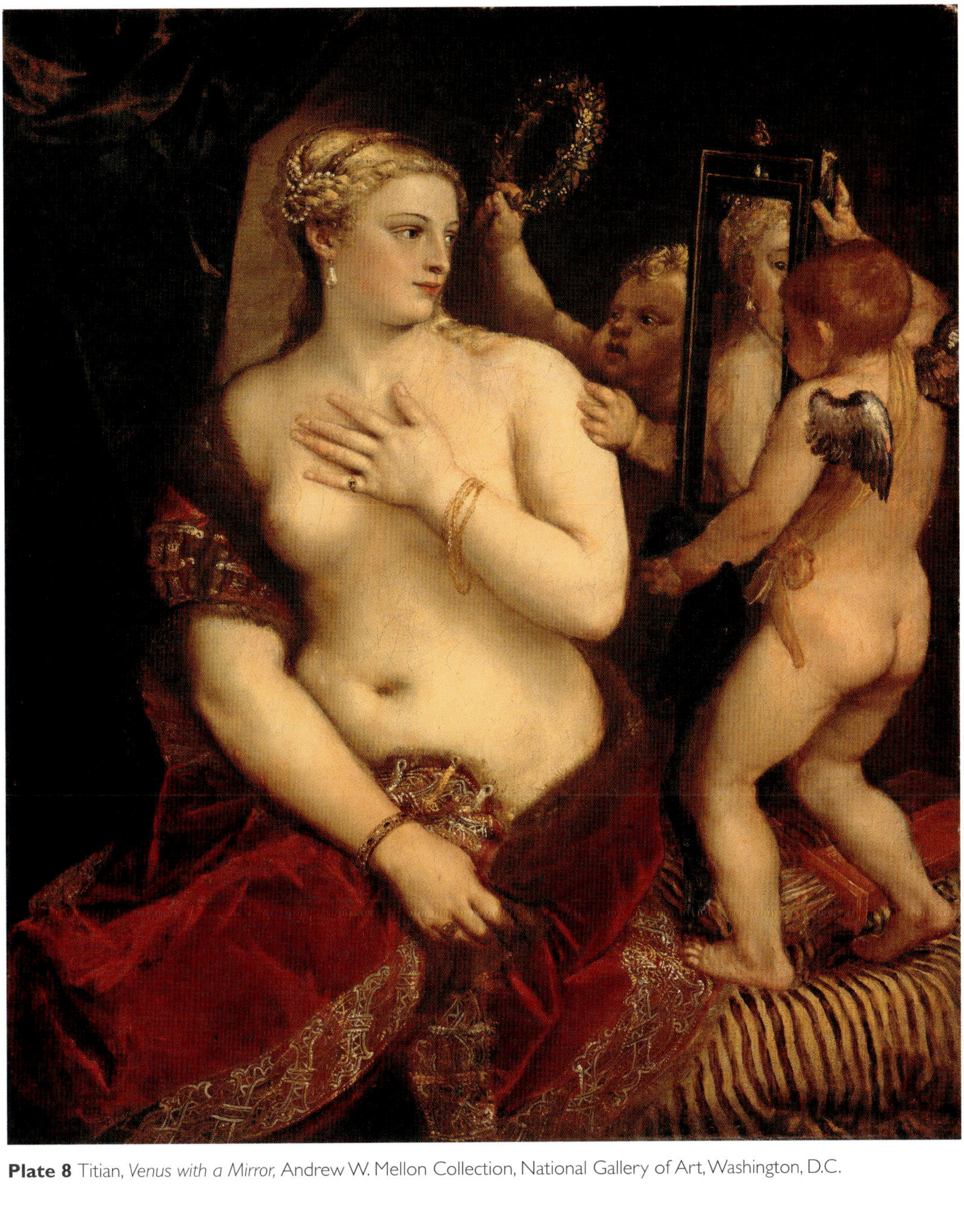

Plate 8 Titian, *Venus with a Mirror,* Andrew W. Mellon Collection, National Gallery of Art, Washington, D.C.

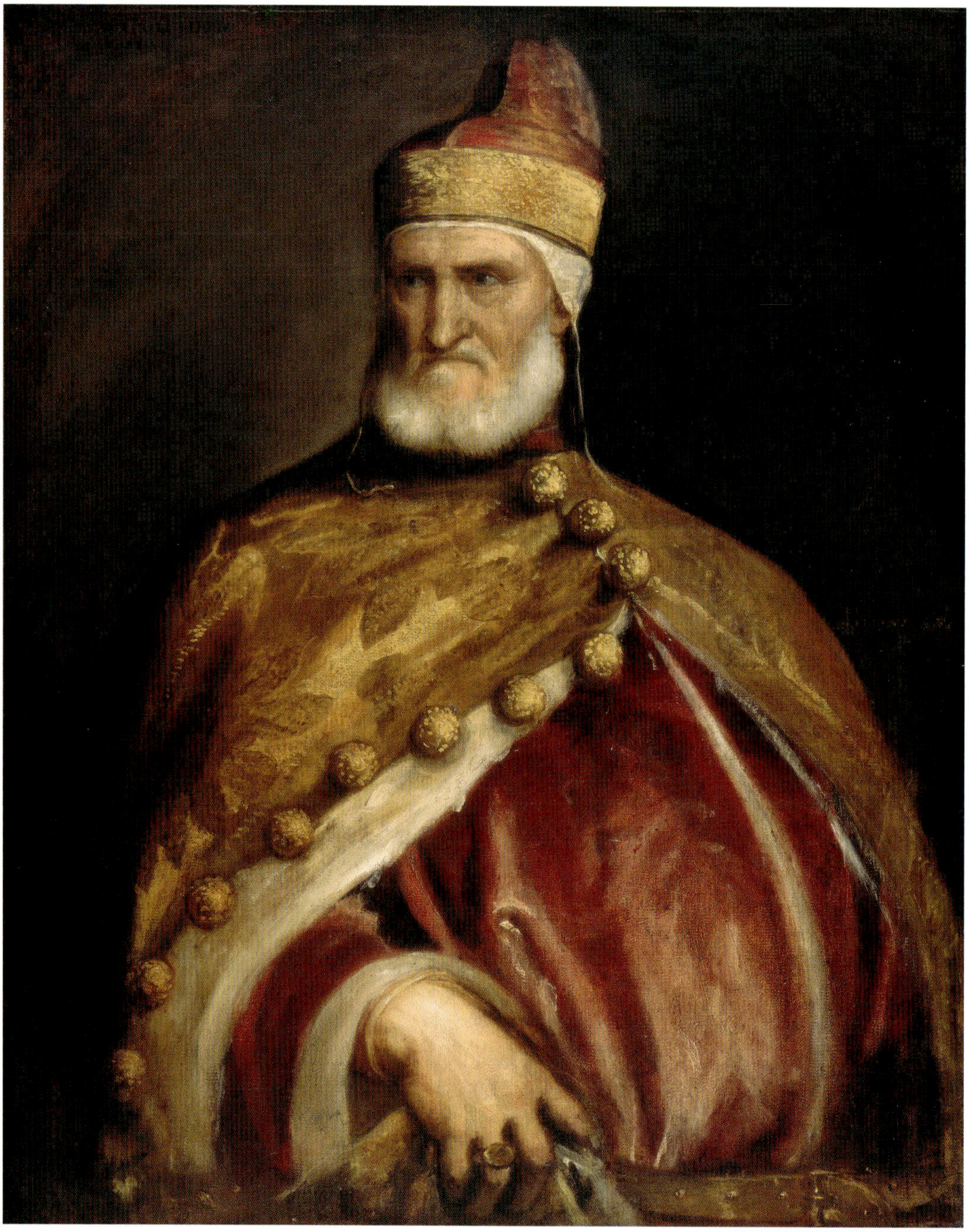

Plate 9 Titian, *Doge Andrea Gritti,* Samuel H. Kress Collection, National Gallery of Art, Washington, D.C.

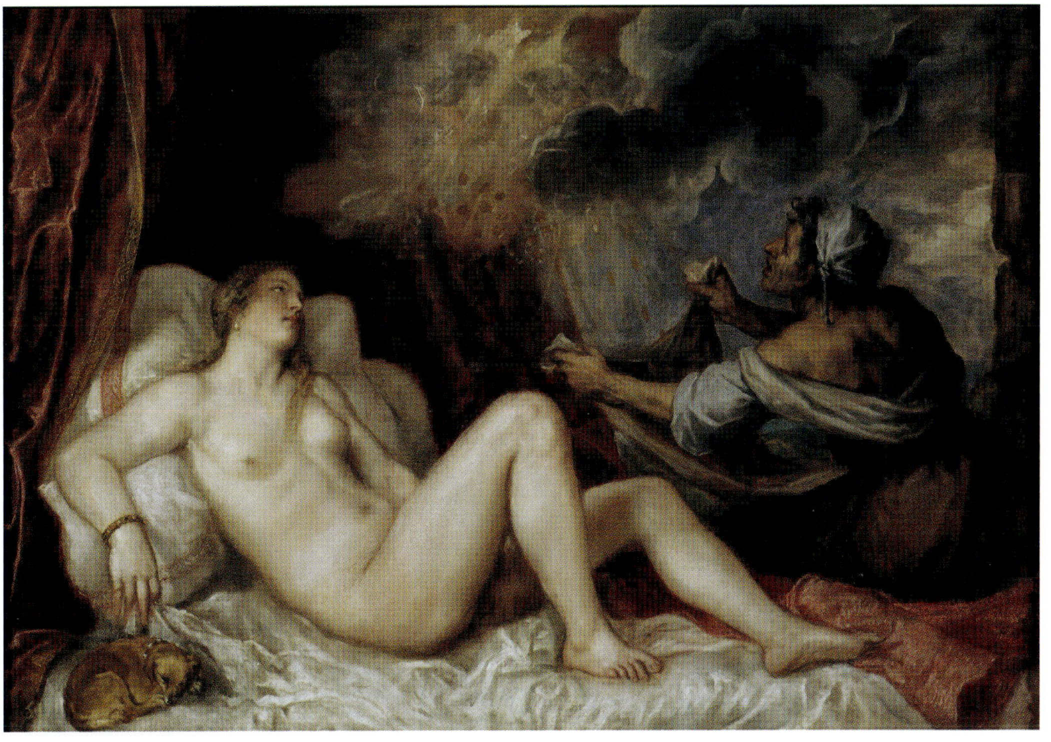

Plate 10 Titian, *Danaë,* Museo Nacional del Prado, Madrid

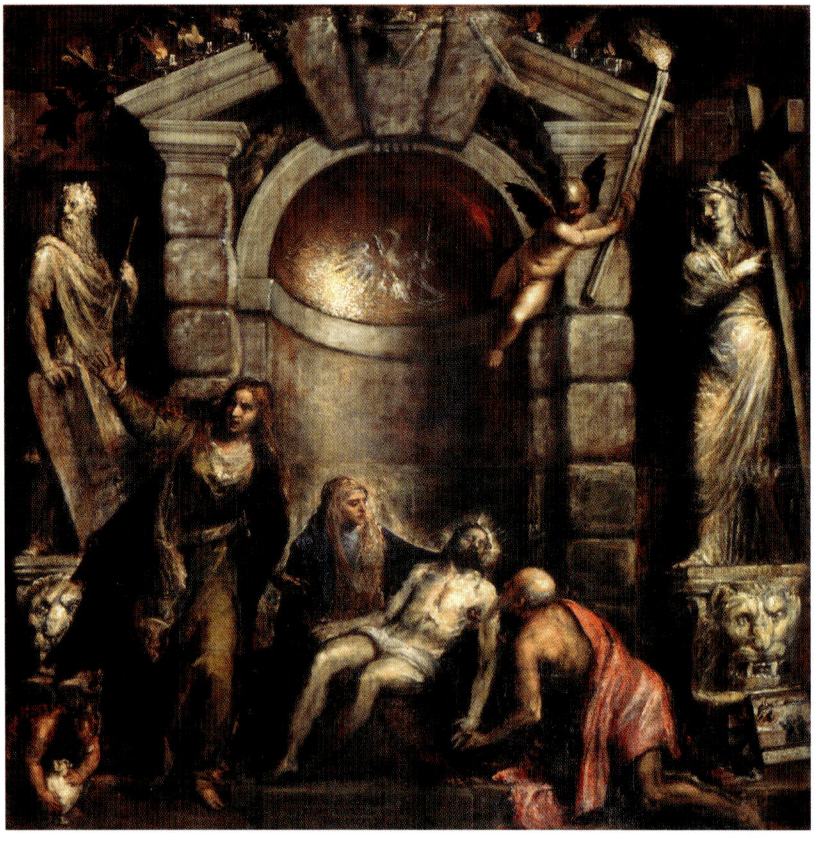

Plate 11 Titian, *Pietà,* Accademia, Venice

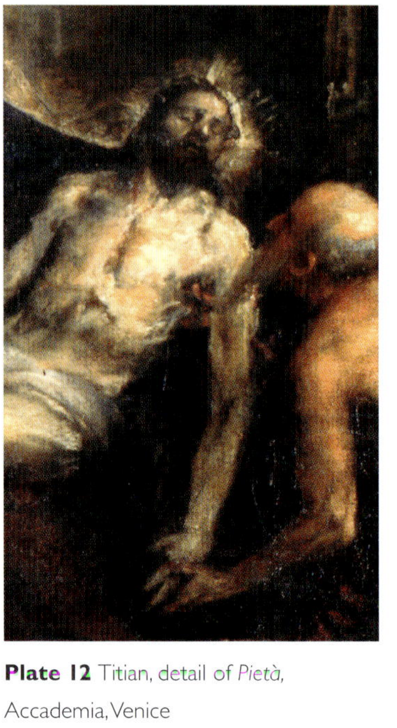

Plate 12 Titian, detail of *Pietà,* Accademia, Venice

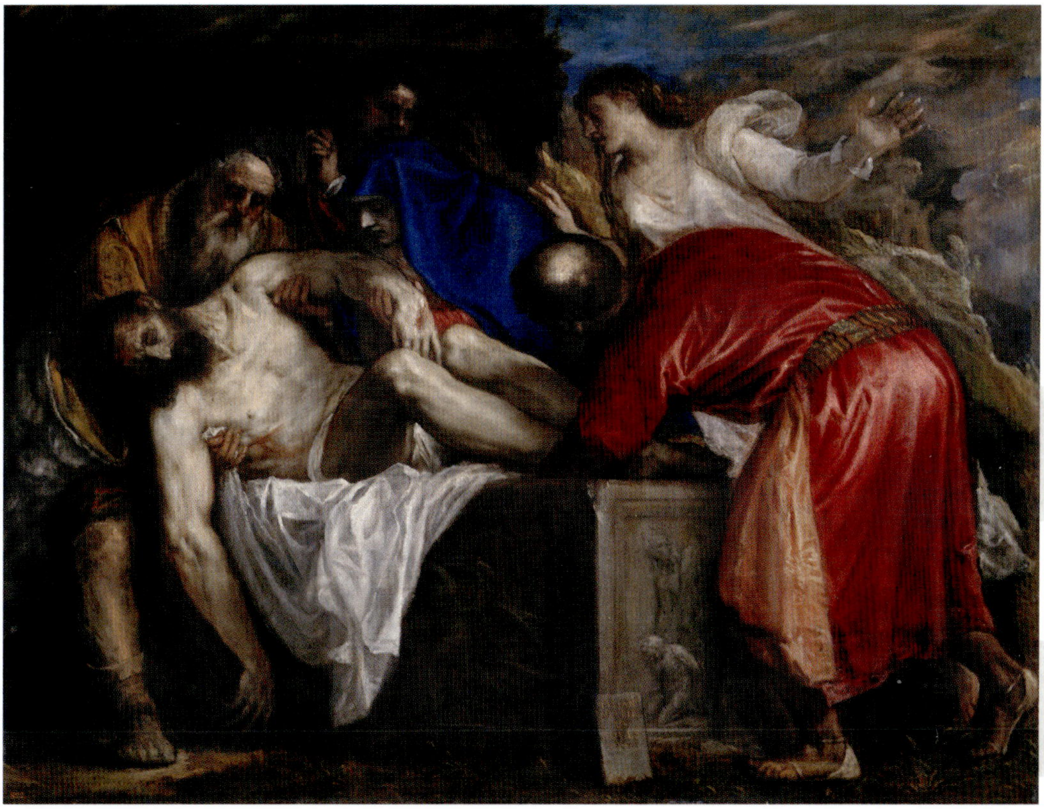

Plate 13 Titian, *The Entombment,* Museo Nacional del Prado, Madrid

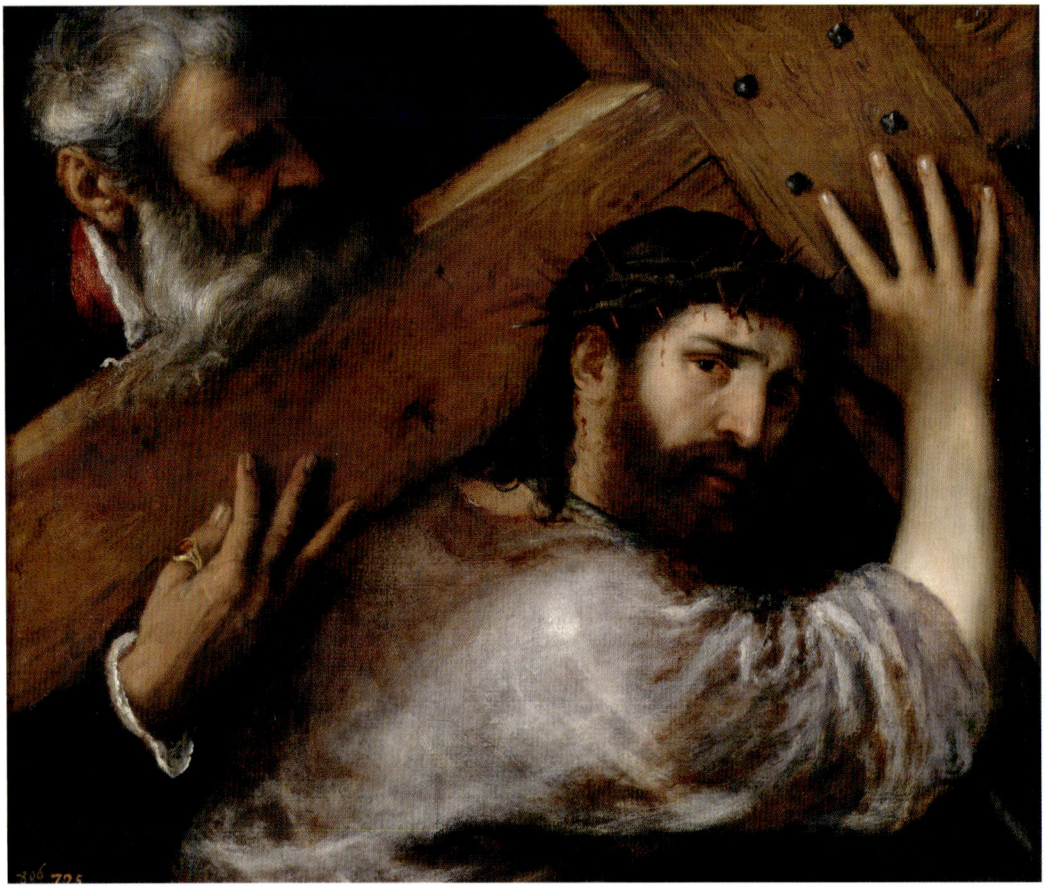

Plate 14 Titian, *Christ Carrying the Cross*, Museo Nacional del Prado, Madrid

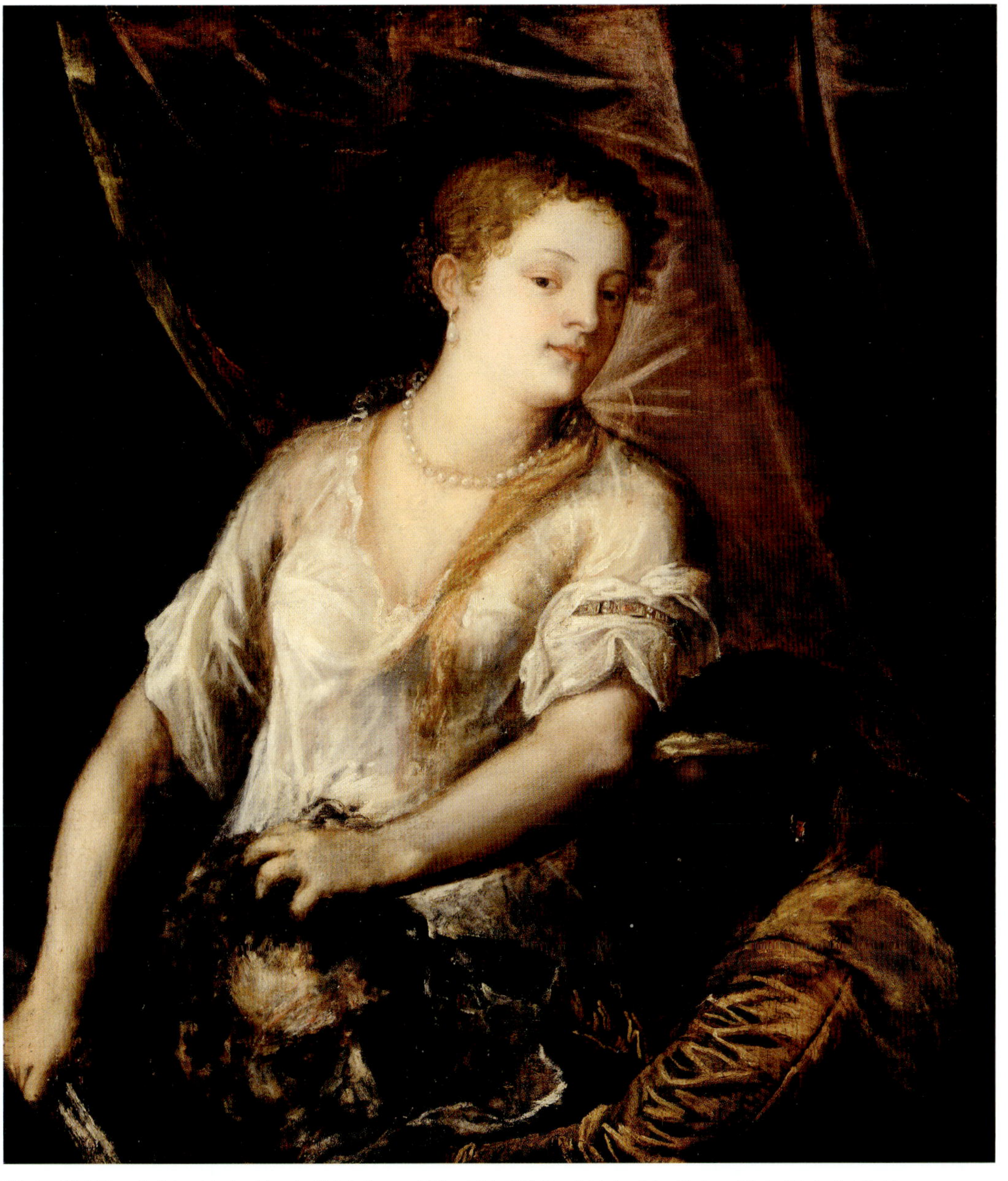

Plate 15 Titian, *Judith with the Head of Holofernes,* Gift of Edsel B. Ford, Detroit Institute of Arts, Detroit, Michigan (© 1989 The Detroit Institute of Arts)

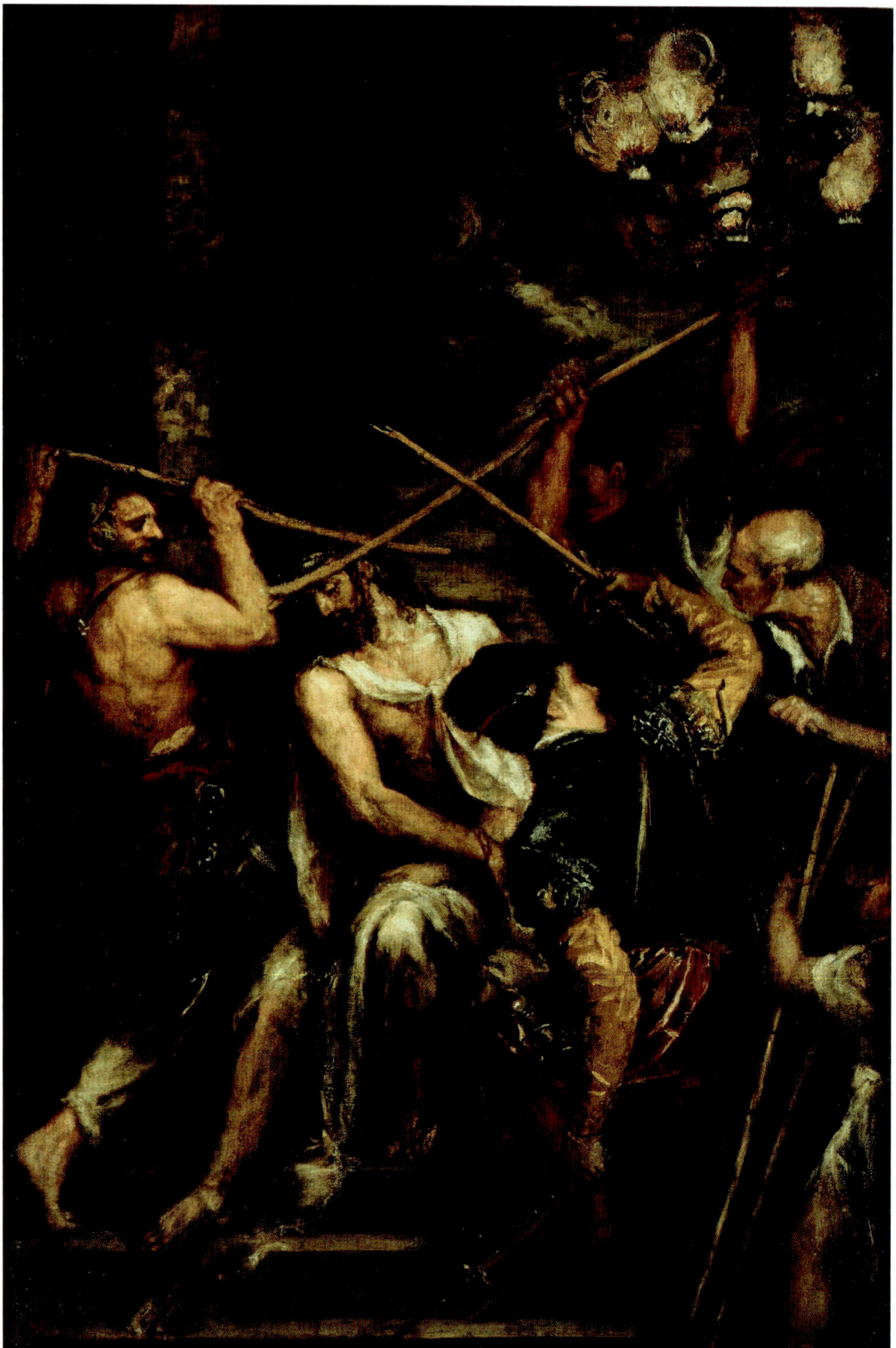

Plate 16 Titian, *Christ Crowned with Thorns*, Alte Pinakothek, Munich

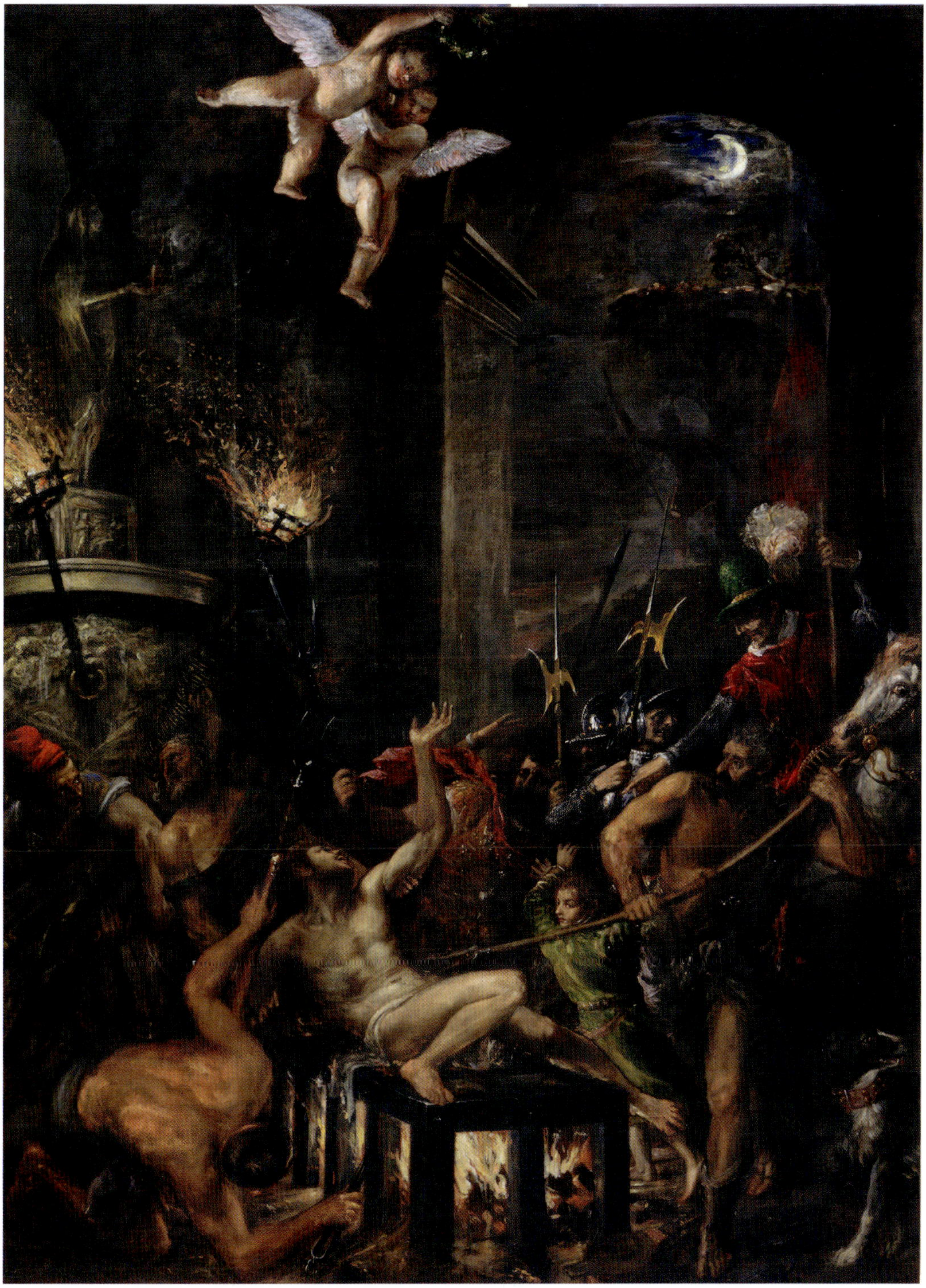

Plate 17 Titian, *Martyrdom of Saint Lawrence,* Escorial, Madrid

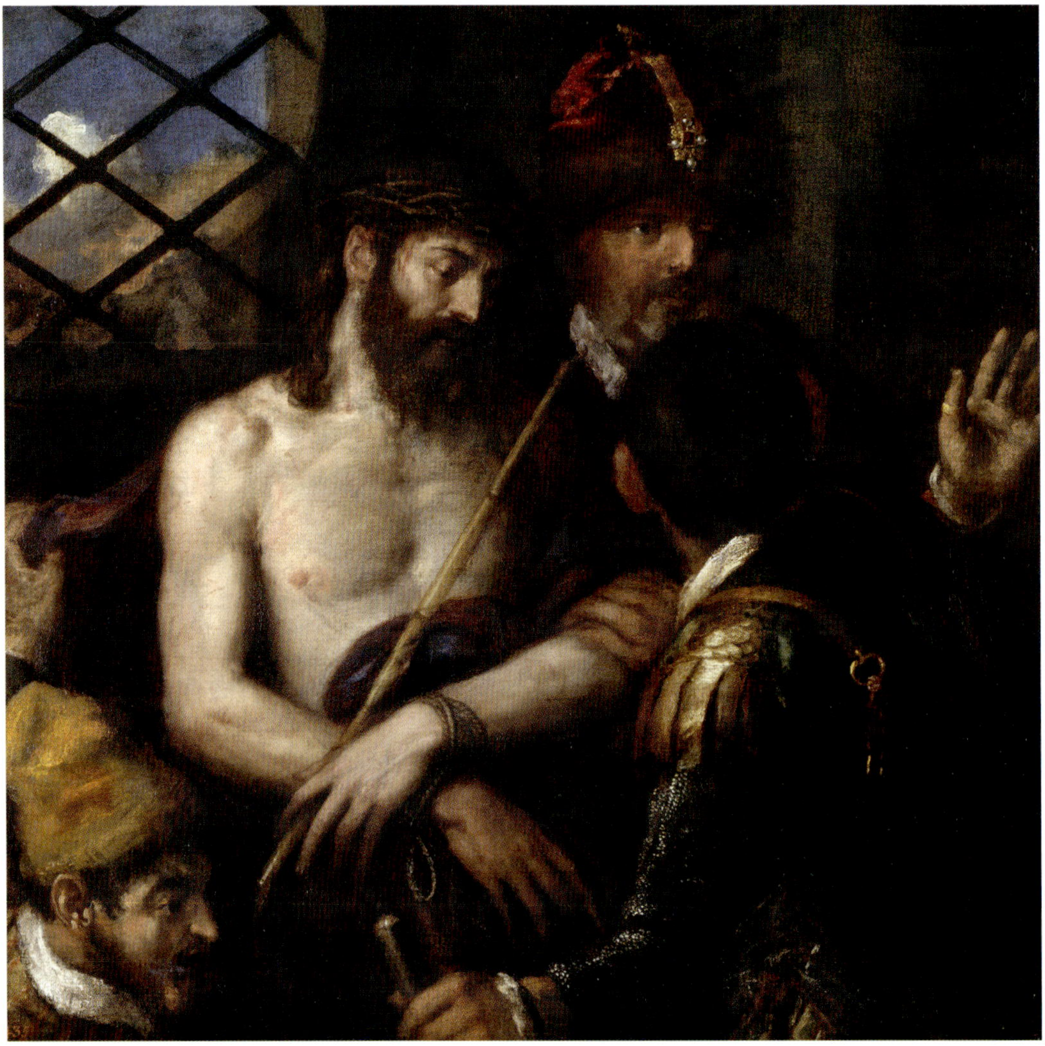

Plate 18 Titian, *Ecce Homo,* Museo Nacional del Prado, Madrid

Like centralized scenes of Christ's death, the *Flaying* makes static a narrative event in order to fragment it, to create the arrested time of decomposition and decay often found in tragedy.[26] With minimal outward expression of suffering, grief, and horror, the figures laconically engage in suspended activities that emphasize the protracted nature of Marsyas's death. The power and impact of tragedy in general are that it dissolves directed structures of narrative time. Terrible events are not immediately resolved, but gain their affective power from the slow failures, missteps, and recognition of their participants and agents. Compared to Giulio Romano's Louvre drawing of the subject for the damaged fresco in the Palazzo del Te (fig. 27),[27] the *Flaying* appears a strikingly quiet and internalized depiction, which, like most tragedies—whether devotional or profane—

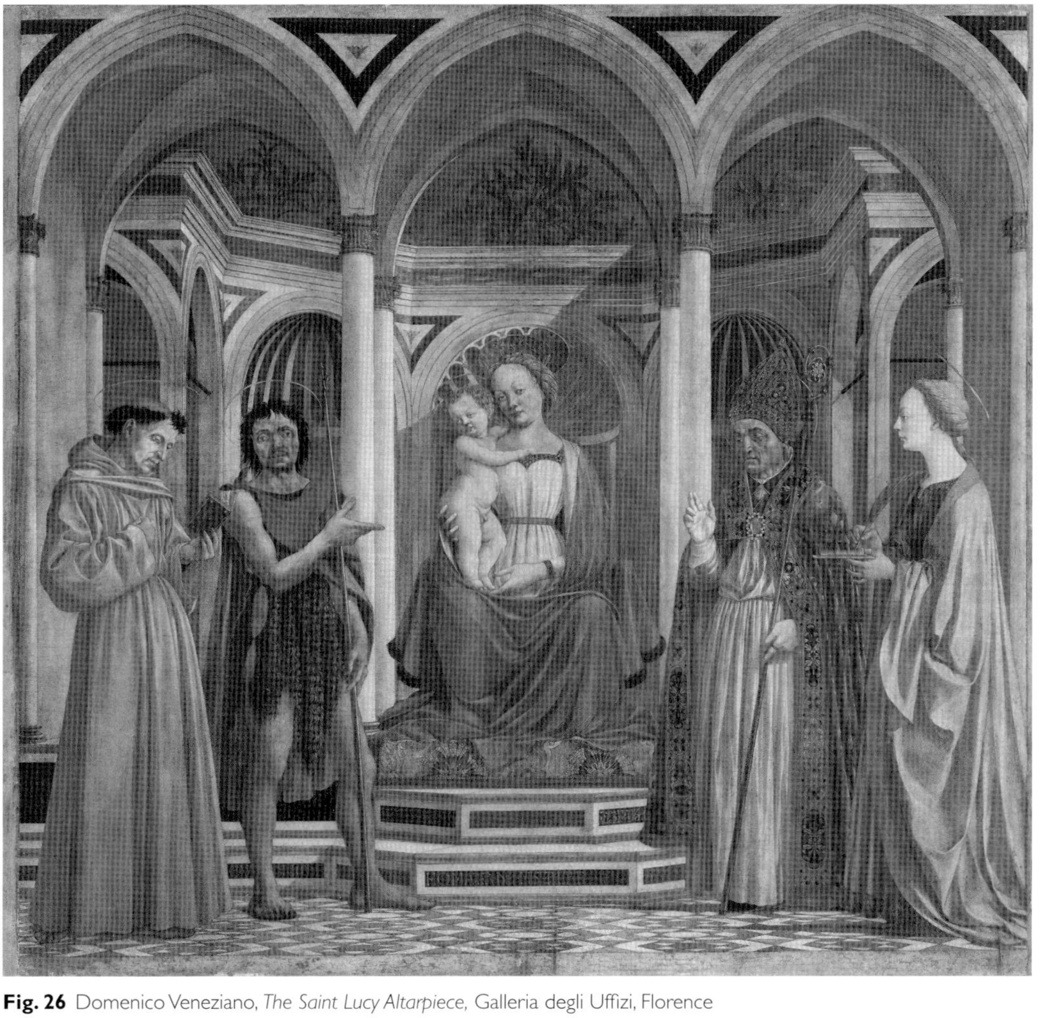

Fig. 26 Domenico Veneziano, *The Saint Lucy Altarpiece,* Galleria degli Uffizi, Florence

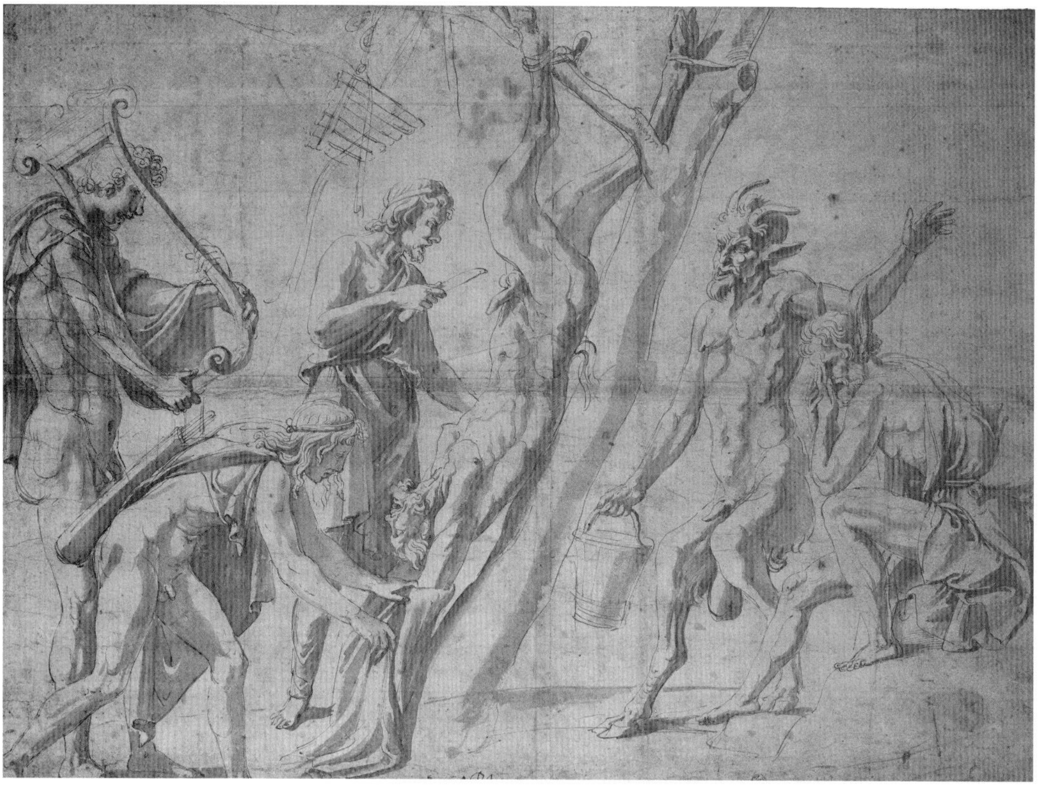

Fig. 27 Giulio Romano, *Apollo Flaying Marsyas*, Louvre, Paris

leaves room for observers to project and feel the range and intensity of their own emotional experiences.

In leaving our experience unguided, the picture challenges one of the central assumptions of Renaissance art, beginning with Alberti, that narrative painting must imitate human affections and thereby direct the sympathies of the beholder.[28] In addition to gestures and facial expressions, perspective helped to prioritize the figures and their reactions. But even painters less committed to such structural formulations abided by a general calibration of emotions for the sake of narrative legibility and sympathetic projections.[29] Giulio's drawing, with the writhing, screaming figure of Marsyas and the horrified Midas who covers his own eyes, attests to this enduring priority in narrative depictions. We easily identify the action and its different effects on the depicted participants and observers—and all of this unfolds on a human level. The a-responsiveness of Titian's figures and the notable presence of the background as an area of significant form—actively encircling, even encroaching into, the depicted figures—suggest the equal physicality and presence of the represented world.[30] This emphasis on the physicality and presence of both human and nonhuman is essentially an antinarrative enterprise that, although it deviates from Renaissance narrative traditions, bears a relationship to the devotional images that appear to inspire the *Flaying*.[31]

A Renaissance viewer might experience Marsyas's death as meaningless, especially compared to the death of Christ, but the *Flaying* nonetheless draws upon the theological significance of embodied subjectivity in devotional images to convey the insistent corporeality of the myth. Images of the Passion, although not often subjects for Venetian altarpieces, symbolize the sacramental significance of Christ's body in their depiction of the deceased.[32] Involved in the celebration of the Eucharist, which takes place on the altar beneath the images, these paintings affirm the presence of the mystical body through the human body of Christ. They allude visually to the (meta)physical events of the Mass, in which participants physically and bodily enact the materiality of Christ's body and the presence of his spirit.[33] Titian explores precisely this embodied experience and response in his *Pietà* (plate 11), in which the figure generally identified as Jerome but sometimes as Nicodemus or Joseph of Arimathea, and often identified as a self-portrait of the artist, enters into the iconic core and sees and feels the body of the dead Christ.[34] In contrast to the imagined world of the visionary, suggested here by the *ex voto* image at the base of the sibyl, Jerome takes in the body and engages in the complexity of bodily involvement with devotional images; he enacts what viewers of iconic, and oftentimes tragic, images are asked to imagine. As a similarly composed iconic image, the *Flaying* offers the possibility of an embodied experience and response, which, by framing corporeality through image types associated with corporeality, deepens the telling of a myth of painful metamorphosis.

Corporeality in the context of Marsyas's story offers little promise of the redemption implied in devotional images and emphasizes the fundamental, oppressive materiality of bodily presence. Compare, for example, the striking similarities between Jerome (plate 12) and the flayer (plate 4) in relation to the bodies of the deceased: both figures appear in a state of absorption, seeing *in* the visible, as they look too closely and touch these horribly disfigured bodies.[35] And yet their contact with corporeality reveals very different experiences of embodiment. Jerome interacts with a tortured, bruised body that hovers as a spectral presence threatening to disappear into a heavenly, disembodied spirit. The white paint creates a desiccated, calcified body, apparently burdened by its physicality and yet, paradoxically, almost insubstantial, as though the body struggles as a flickering suggestion of presence similar to the penumbral signs of divinity around Christ's head and the Virgin's extended arm. Materiality and immateriality intertwine in the *Pietà* to convey salvation through the body. The flayer establishes a related interconnection between materiality and dematerialization by looking into the body of Marsyas as he destroys it; however, the disfiguration does not threaten the existence of Marsyas's body or suggest a condition beyond the body (transfiguration), but emphasizes its very materiality, the body as body.

The inverted body draws our gaze directly, and unexpectedly, to the lower material sphere of the male body, not usually the central focus in Renaissance painting.[36] When Alberti laid out his principles of perspective and of the *historia,* he implied the importance of the figure for determining the centric point of the picture and for conveying the story through gaze and gesture.[37] Even if painters deviated from strict Albertian practice, they still generally respected general principles of decorum by not often making the sexual area of the body, here emphasized by the satyr's literal bestiality from the waist down, the physical center of the canvas. Giulio Romano, and possibly ancient reliefs, served as the most immediate source for inverting the satyr's body.[38] But with its frontal, iconic alignment, Titian's satyr might have as an equally important source the inverted body of the crucified Saint Peter, who, not wanting to emulate the death of Christ, asked to be hung from the cross by his feet.[39] When depicted, the scene potentially situates the viewer in the unexpected position of looking down and, in the example of Masaccio's *Pisa Polyptych* (fig. 28), invests direction with devotional and moral weight.[40] We, like the soldiers, look down at the crucified Peter; when we look up at Christ's crucifixion at the summit, he looks down on us. Michelangelo's *Crucifixion of Saint Peter* (1546–50; Cappella Paolina, Vatican), a more contemporary source for Titian, lifts his head to cast a confrontational gaze to the beholder, eliciting a response of humility through his admonishment and not through a dialectic of high and low, upright and rotated.[41] The inversion of Marsyas, rather than being a respectful deviation from the divine, functions as a pictorial equivalent of the "world turned upside down" sensibility found in the carnivalesque mode.[42]

One does not have to look far in Renaissance commentaries on the Ovidian story to find recognition of Marsyas as a perversion of the divine precisely because, unlike Peter, the satyr fails to recognize importance of humility toward the gods. Lodovico Dolce offers this allegorical interpretation of three unfortunate Ovidian characters, Niobe, Marsyas, and Procne, at the close of the thirteenth canto in the 1568 edition of *Le trasformationi:* "These three *favole* denote the temerity of those who, self-absorbed, presume to recognize that which they do, and possessed by the gods, do the opposite, scorning divine power and making idols of themselves."[43] Marsyas becomes a false god, an impostor.

Similarly, the painting destabilizes the empathy of the viewer by asserting itself not as a seductive illusion but as an object. Red paint, suggestive of blood, issues from the area of contact between the flayer's knife and the satyr's body, travels straight down the canvas, and fails to follow the suggested shape of the body. (Compare, for example, the contour-defining blood flow along Christ's arm in Giovanni Bellini's *Pietà,* fig. 32.) The sign of sacrifice remains at the level of signifier, and the painting asserts itself as an object most clearly in an area of the canvas that is potentially one of the most horrifying.[44] The brushstrokes of the dog lapping up the blood, in which we can imagine the quick flourishes of the paintbrush, only heighten this effect. We expect to be repulsed because of what we see, and, yet, despite the concentration of the abject, we find ourselves strangely unmoved and without stable cues for our response.

Anatomizing the Body of Marsyas

As the flayer in Titian's depiction exposes the body's layers and enacts the gradual undoing of the body, he transforms the complete and autonomous body into "one raw wound," as Ovid wrote (*Metamorphoses* 6.382–400).[45] Apollo seems transfixed by the results of his punishment of the satyr, as he looks closely, inspecting and studying, that which his work effects and reveals; he is singularly focused on the recesses of Marsyas's body. Rather than actively trying to torment his victim, he seems to be performing the careful and painstaking work of a dissection for an anatomy lesson, in which the knife is no longer a weapon but a tool.[46]

The practice of performing anatomies in Italy began in the sixteenth century and offered both medical knowledge and, because of the invasiveness and desecration of the dead, a means for further punishing criminals after their death.[47] With the publication of Andreas Vesalius's *De humani corporis fabrica* in 1543, readers could peruse the written results of his scientific investigations

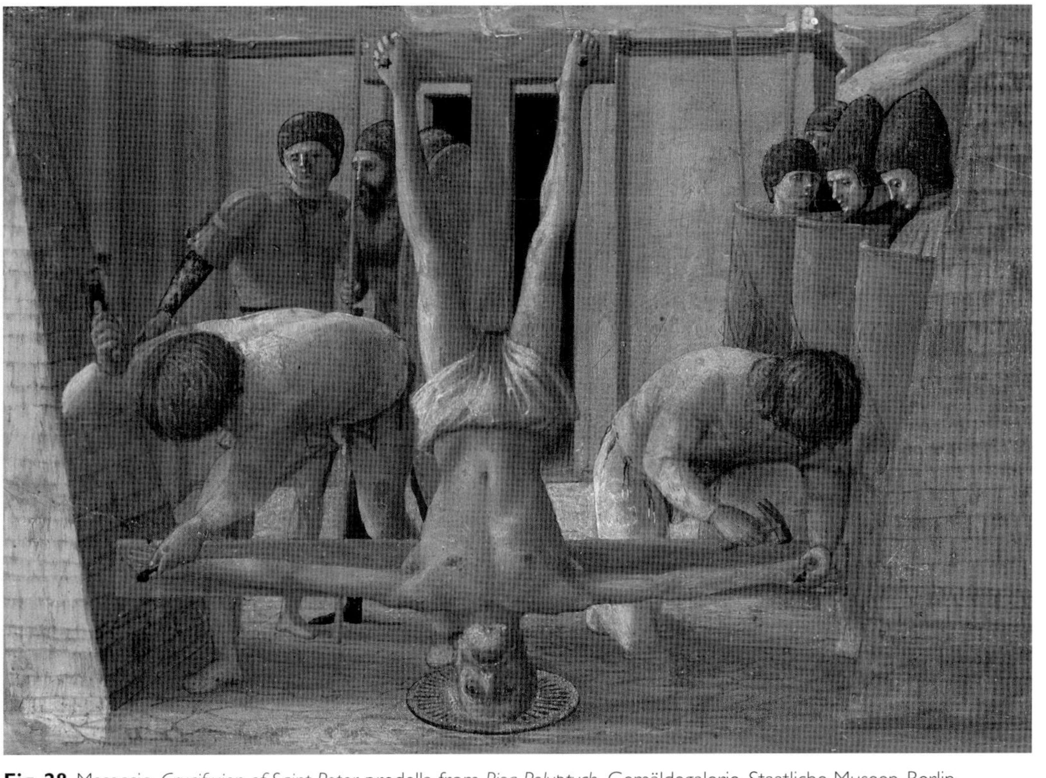

Fig. 28 Masaccio, *Crucifixion of Saint Peter,* predella from *Pisa Polyptych,* Gemäldegalerie, Staatliche Museen, Berlin

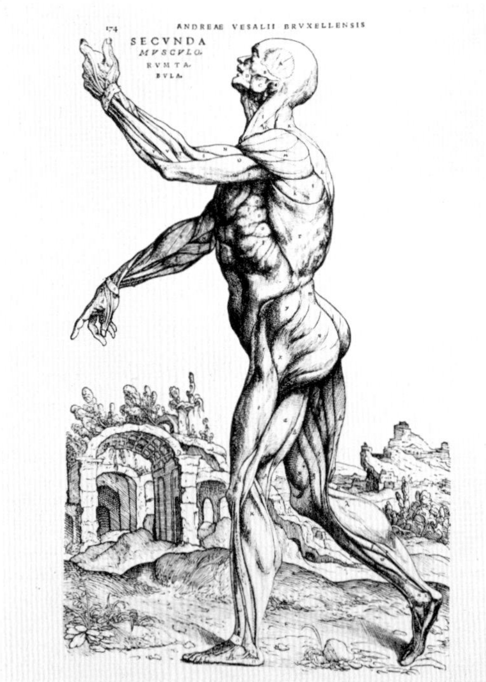

Fig. 29 Andreas Vesalius, *Musculature Structure of a Man* from *De humani corporis fabrica* (1543)

and view in the accompanying illustrations the gradual decomposition of the heroic, idealized male body into the suffering, destroyed, dehumanized form (fig. 29).[48] Anatomies yielded knowledge, but, as these figures clearly show, they did so by compromising, if not unmaking, the assumed perfection of the intact body. Either shown in pain or without the recognizable structure of a face, these figures express the complexity, the materiality, but above all the burden of the body, much in the same way that dancing and speaking skeletons warn beholders of their mortality in *memento mori* images.[49] Such anatomical illustrations also quite naturally seem to call to mind the story of Apollo and Marsyas, and vice versa.[50]

Anatomical investigations, whether mythologized or represented as scientific inquiries, not only approach the body as an object to be explored but justify their violation by choosing subjects with no hope of redemption. In making the inside the outside, the process of anatomical dissection makes everything into surface, into matter, without any acknowledgment or recognition of the transcendent spirit or soul.[51] Clearly, Renaissance anatomists would have considered Marsyas to be a notorious subject: the humanity of Marsyas, as a satyr, is compromised from the beginning, and is certainly in question when he transgresses the divine. Evoking these anatomical traditions, Titian further conveys the unredeemed condition of Marsyas by situating the dissection in a devotional image-type that typically conveys the promise of redemption. There is no spiritual salvation for the satyr, only the overwhelming physicality of the body in the present and his imminent transformation into a stream.

This materiality is not figured as an unambiguous result and sign of violence and destruction, but also appears to be intimately connected through the hands of the flayer to production and creation. What exactly is this Apollo doing when he takes the knife to the flesh of Marsyas? Absorbed and careful, he seems to act more like a painter with a palette knife, who creates rather than destroys the body with each move of his arm. The productive creator and punitive destroyer inhabit the other, with the direction of the reference shifting between the two: the action of the flayer suggests that of the painter, and vice versa, so that making and unmaking are inextricably linked, if not a form of each other. The simultaneity of such seemingly opposed processes characterizes many of the transformations in Ovid's *Metamorphoses,* where the desecrated and dismembered body is the changed and newly formed body, where chaos attends and marks creation.[52]

Not only the central dynamic in Ovidian stories, violence and making also interconnect in contemporary discussions of Titian's technique and approach to painting in the final years of his career.[53] We return again to the description given by Marco Boschini, cited earlier in this book.[54] The passage is striking for the metaphors of violence, which convey the act of creation as antagonistic (considering his paintings as "mortal enemies") or as painful surgery. As it happens, much of Boschini's vocabulary for describing the brushwork in late sixteenth-century Venetian painting includes terms of combat and of fencing, metaphors that not only capture the rapid, striking movements of the artist's hand but also articulate the way in which color no longer creates a sense of union and harmony in constructing a coherent, mimetic form.[55] Pigment, as used by Titian, undermines, conceals, and reveals form; it gives form to the immaterial and makes immaterial the most solid of forms.

Titian's handling of the paint in his representation of the body of Marsyas, and on the entire canvas, draws attention to the physicality of paint, its status as matter, as substance; the agitated brushwork affirms the opacity of the pigment and undermines bodily structure at the same time that it gives the flat surface of the canvas the appearance of palpability, relief, and motion. At times the canvas weave itself appears to shape the paint, to have an active role in creating texture. Immaterial qualities and conditions of light, shade, and atmosphere here take on a depth of substance through the application of thick strokes of white and flesh-colored impasto, sometimes worked with thick brushes and in other paintings with the hands. Passages delineating flesh and musculature are a network of patches of color, rather than integrated into a consistent whole. This is not the transparent window but a compressed plane, which conveys the slow action of metamorphosis through the motion of brushstrokes and through the accumulated layers of paint and its active shaping by the hands of the artist and the canvas ground.[56]

The Portrayal of the Painter

The subjectivity of the painter, whether technically implied or analogically suggested through the depiction of the flayer, fails to conform to the presumed self-sufficiency and constructiveness of Renaissance artists. However, modern viewers of the *Flaying* respond to these mimetic figurations and nonmimetic indications of presence as evidence of the uncomplicated iteration of the heroic, inspired, and intellectual artist that so often circulated around and defined Renaissance notions of the creative genius. The implied self, not surprisingly, suggested to some readers the actual, depicted self, which, in the *Flaying,* takes the form of a self-portrait of Titian in the guise of Midas.[57] Seated in a contemplative pose that recalls the long-standing visual tradition of the inspired genius, the aged figure, especially

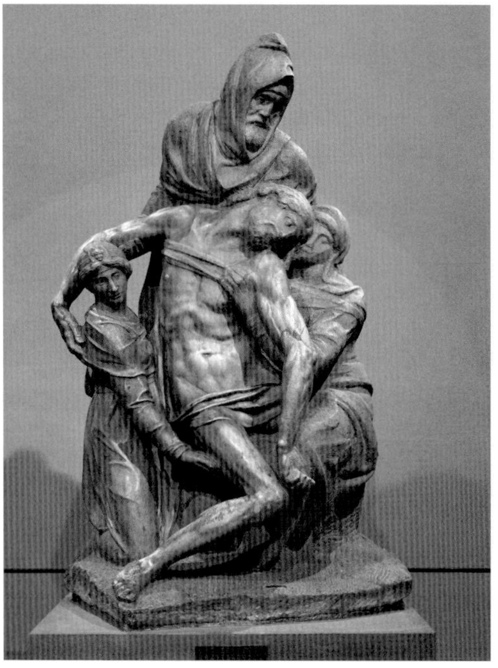

Fig. 30 Michelangelo, *Pietà,* Museo dell'Opera del Duomo, Florence

compared to Giulio Romano's recoiling Midas, appears to engage intellectually with the scene before him, meditating without any emotional reaction.[58] The physiognomy of Midas, with his gray hair and beard and aquiline nose, also appears to share features with those found in Titian's nearly contemporary self-portraits.[59] But how does the identity of Midas, considered to be the embodiment of foolishness and impaired judgment, relate to the projected and implied identity of Titian? What is the significance of a painter representing himself as Midas? Why would a pose traditionally associated with inspiration seem appropriate for Midas? Is this identification of a "disguised" self-portrait as much an indication of the decentering of the self as it is an assertion of the self? And is this decentering indicative of a personal situation associated with old-age style or of a broader historical phenomenon? In asking these questions, I am as much interested in the historical tradition of disguised self-portraiture and its manifestation of a changing subjectivity of the artist as I am in the recent art-historical practice of asserting these depictions as self-portraits.

The identification of Midas as a self-portrait of Titian remains one of many suspected, but not confirmed, self-portraits of the artist in narrative scenes. Modern identifications of possible disguised self-portraits proliferate in Titian's later works—as Nicodemus in his several Entombments (plate 13) and as the hermetic saint in his variations of Saint Jerome (Monastery of San Lorenzo, Escorial; Museo Thyssen-Bornemisza, Madrid) and the *Pietà* (plate

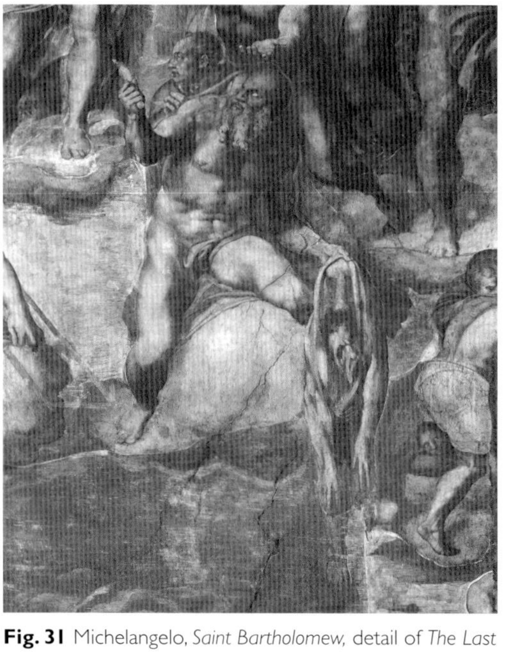

Fig. 31 Michelangelo, *Saint Bartholomew,* detail of *The Last Judgment,* Sistine Chapel, Vatican

11)—primarily because of physiognomic resemblance to the visage in his independent self-portraits.[60] Working backward in time from the Prado and Berlin pictures (figs. 3 and 4), scholars also have found self-portraits in Titian's earlier works, such as the decapitated John the Baptist in his *Salome* (fig. 37) and again as Nicodemus in his Louvre *Entombment.*[61] Without any historical confirmation, these modern identifications—motivated by perceived resemblance—most certainly find support from the repeated identifications by Vasari of artists appearing in their own work[62] and, more specific to the subject of the Entombment, from the legendary association between a figure like Nicodemus and artists—including the documented identification of a disguised self-portrait by one of Titian's rivals, Michelangelo's self-portrait for Nicodemus in his *Pietà* (fig. 30).[63] Additionally, Titian's reputation as a worldly painter with an active studio and a widely dispersed group of patrons offers a commercial and authorial explanation for these identifications. His presence through presumed physical likeness could function as an assertion of control over his work, despite his no longer working on the painting, but also emerges from and confirms a specific notion of authorship as a controlled and controlling process.[64]

This notion of authorship fails to consider the varied identities possibly assumed by the painter. Some of these disguises seem unworthy of a self-assured creator: the decollated head of John the Baptist, the mythological King Midas, or, turning to an example from Michelangelo's oeuvre, a flayed skin in the *Last Judgment* (fig. 31).[65]

The impulse to give a name to a face, to engage in an autobiographical mode of reading, actively surfaces in modern considerations of Renaissance art but has its origins squarely in the work of one of the most influential Renaissance art historians. Vasari, following the lead of ancient histories and conduct books, approached works of art as reflections of the personality of the artist and, more often, created artists in the image of their works.[66] Mild-mannered Raphael, for example, produced works of equal refinement and sweetness.[67] The troubled Rosso executed paintings with jarring color contrasts and other *bizarrie.*[68] Specific events in an artist's life, such as love or illness, could affect his manner of painting and sometimes even the choice of subject matter. As a history of art constructed on the anecdote, Vasari's *Lives* asserts an eyewitness quality of truthfulness that undermines the fictional dimensions of these stories and their reinforcement of tropes involving all aspects of art.[69] The circularity of self-referencing between work and artist in this mode of reading reflects the interrelationship of the life of an artist and the idea of the artist as a cultural hero.[70]

Renaissance art reinforces and sustains this textual and critical approach by including pictorial structures and/or iconographic features that foreground a self-consciousness associated with authorship. Artists frequently depicted themselves as participants or as donors in larger narrative scenes, such as in so-called *in assistenza* self-portraits, which first developed in quattrocento Florence.[71] Among the more frequent formal inventions signaling the artist's presence was a direct gaze by the figure to the beholder, often accompanied by a signature or identifying *cartellino* (fig. 32). This acknowledgment of the viewer creates a spatial and temporal connection with the present moment, a visual equivalent of "I am here," that recalls the direct view that the artist has of himself before the mirror used for self-portraiture and that often contrasts with the absorption of the other figures in the central narrative. As figures within the narrative and yet simultaneously outside of it, they occupy a liminal role in which they oftentimes seem to know too much about both sides of the picture frame. Consider, for example, the self-portrait of Raphael in his *School of Athens* (fig. 33).[72] Inhabiting a pictorial field populated by contemporary artists in the guise of ancient philosophers, the painter looks directly out at the beholder, distinguishing himself from the various groups of engaged philosophers at the same time that he appears among them.[73] Existing both there and here, the figure encourages the viewer to think of his identity in terms of a

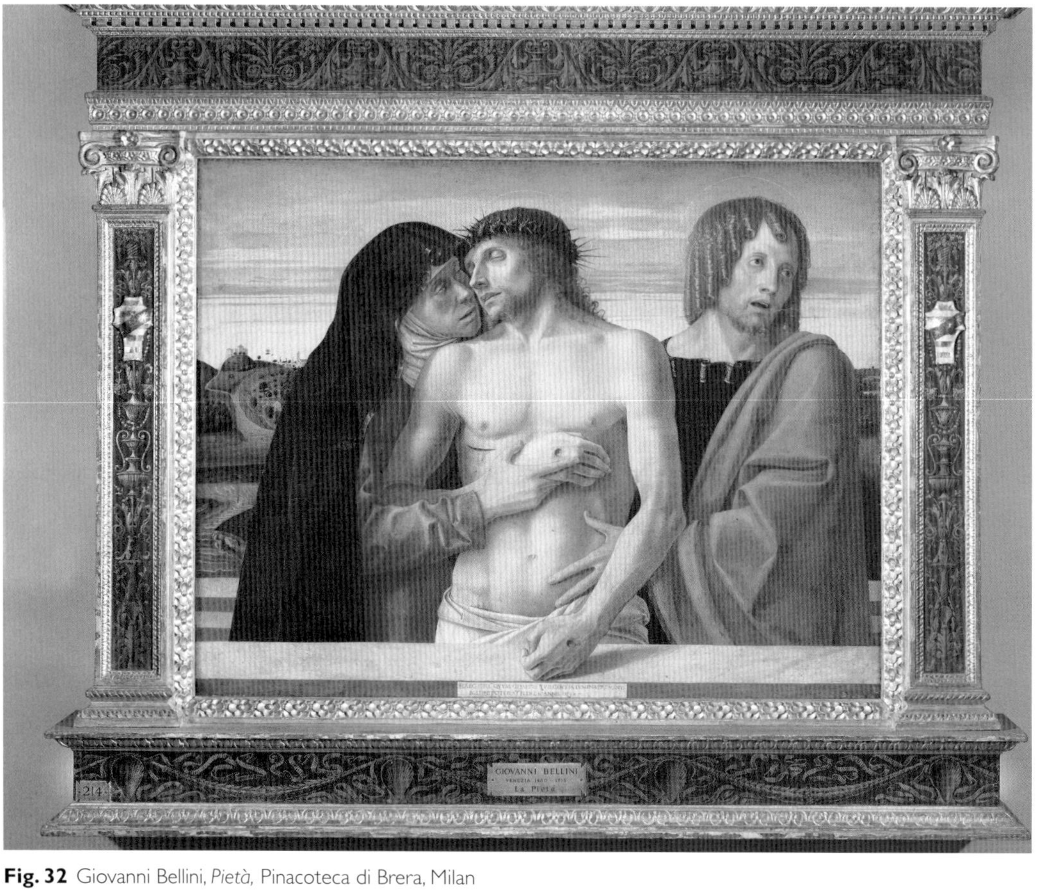

Fig. 32 Giovanni Bellini, *Pietà,* Pinacoteca di Brera, Milan

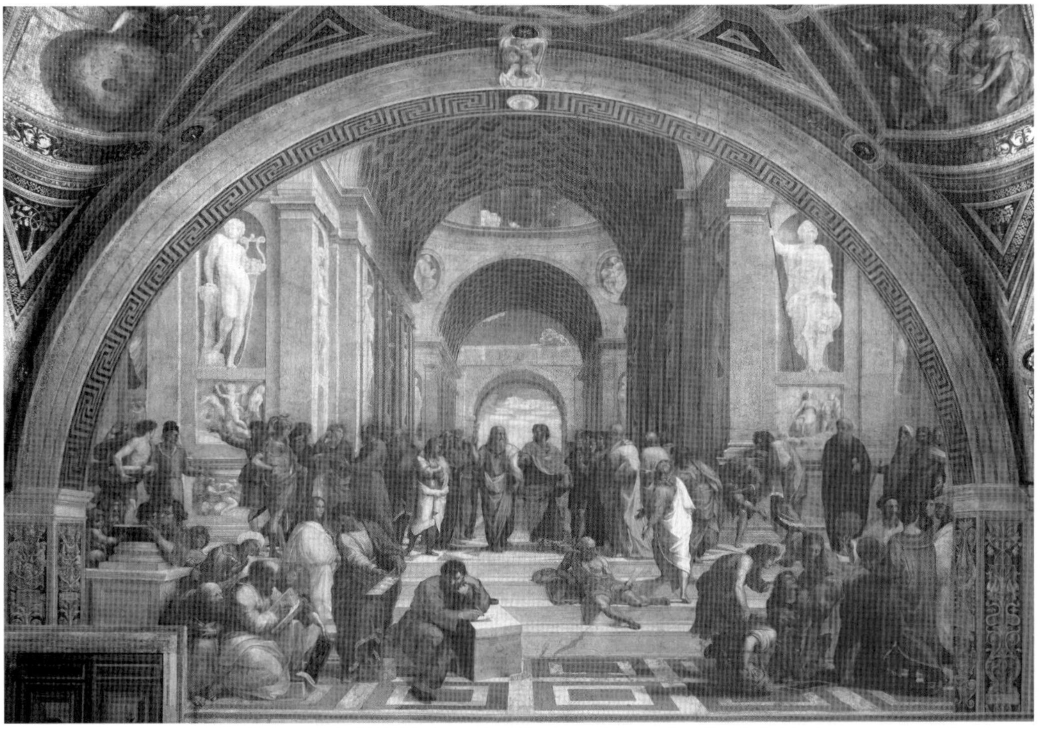

Fig. 33 Raphael, *School of Athens,* Stanza della Segnatura, Vatican

person installed in the past and worthy of recognition in the present. The self-aware, mimetic figuration seduces viewers into thinking that identification of the figure forecloses interpretation. The face has a name and we think that we know, courtesy of Vasari et al., who he is and how this depiction supports an anecdotal history (and vice versa).

Raphael's depiction of himself in the *School of Athens* marks an important moment in the tradition of the included self-portrait: after this fresco, very few Italian painters rely on the direct gaze to indicate their presence in a multifigure or narrative composition[74] (although painters, especially in Venice, continued to include portraits of contemporaries in narrative paintings[75]). In fact, Raphael himself might have been emphasizing the retrospective connotations of the device as a way to articulate one of the dialectics advanced in the fresco, the contrast between quattrocento and cinquecento approaches to the visual arts as one of geometry on the right side of the composition versus inspiration on the left.[76] Cinquecento artists gradually turned to other formal structures for their self-representation, foremost among them being the independent self-portrait, which figured selfhood not only through the direct gaze but also through signs of specularity, such as self-referential gestures and the motif of the mirror. Painters extended their representations of themselves beyond a transcription of their specific features in the mirror's surface and began to explore more generalized aspects of selfhood and inwardness. Titian's self-portraits (figs. 3 and 4) exemplify this shift by appearing to be portraits by another hand, as though we are given an image that is a memory of oneself rather than a physiognomic record or transcription.[77]

As the independent self-portrait developed as a potentially flexible and poetic genre in the cinquecento, artists creatively expanded their participatory possibilities in multifigure compositions and the formal structures and inventions used to designate either themselves or a self-consciousness that seemed to refer to the artist. This is most clearly demonstrated in depictions with so-called disguised self-portraits, in which artists assume the guise of a different identity and, rather than announce themselves through structural devices of presence, assume a persona with professional or inferred biographical relevance or a more general iconography of inwardness and self-reference.[78] Nicodemus and Saint Luke served as exemplary personae.[79] Not obviously differentiated from the other depicted figures, these figures do not necessarily suggest themselves as specific biographical figures; they more easily remain on the interpretative level of generalized iconographic types. To understand the difference, one only needs to compare the self-awareness of Raphael's self-portrait in the *School of Athens* to the interaction and absorption of Michelangelo's self-portrait as Nicodemus in his *Pietà*.[80]

In assuming the identity of another and standing as one figure among many, these "disguised" self-portraits suggest the mutability of the artist's self and advance a self-consciousness that paradoxically depends upon being overlooked. A similar phenomenon of disguise occurred in cinquecento portraiture when sitters impersonated legendary or historical figures as a way to figure or to inhabit some aspect of themselves, whether actualized, imagined, or desired.[81] Usually these portraits indicate through inscriptions or reveal through some other motif the disguising mechanism at work. The formal similarity between half-length images of legendary and devotional figures and portraits of ordinary people, the very similarity that facilitated impersonation, requires such indication to make these images understandable as such. Disguised self-portraits, because they appear in narrative compositions that generally signify without requiring the specific identity of a bystander, alert the viewer more subtly, if at all, as the continuous stream in art-historical scholarship of identifications and rejections of possible self-portraits suggests.[82] The submersion in a narrative scene oftentimes develops the very subject of the narrative in which the depicted artist (dis)appears. Self-portraits as Nicodemus in more expanded scenes of the Passion draw, for example, on the devotional significance of being overlooked as a sign of humility in the face of human sacrifice and divine recognition. A similar interpretation could apply to the figure most often identified as Jerome in Titian's *Pietà,* if we accept the identification of a self-portrait. Most of the interpretations of Midas as a self-portrait, for all of their problems, as we will discuss later in this chapter, acknowledge and find significance in the alienation or absenting of the contemplative figure from the punishment of Marsyas.[83]

The subtlety of these "disguised" figures suggests that, in fact, the phenomenon of disguised self-portraiture could be an illusion of an autobiographical mode of reading.[84] Not coincidentally, many of the identifications of the so-called great masters, especially of self-portraits of Titian and Michelangelo, proliferated in the last century, when biography dominated much of the developing discipline of art history, whether in the approach of connoisseurship, the appeal of psychoanalysis, or even methodologies, such as iconography, that seemingly had no basis in the life of the artist.[85] Poststructuralist thought, well known for its elimination of the author/artist, resulted in readings of paintings that, in thematizing the process of their own making, unexpectedly reinstated not just the idea of the author, but the specific details of the author's/artist's life.[86] Not surprisingly, the pivotal moment for the stream of disguised self-portrait identifications occurred in the early twentieth century, beginning with an Italian physician's identification of Michelangelo's self-portrait in the flayed skin held by Saint Bartholomew in the *Last Judgment* (fig. 31).[87] Most art historians have accepted the identification since the disemboweled flesh reflects our inherited idea of Michelangelo—the negative self-image reported through anecdotes in his biographies and in his own correspondence; his antagonistic relationship with Pietro Aretino, whose features, it was proposed, might resemble those of Saint Bartholomew; his neo-Platonic poetic imagery, which repeatedly conveys himself as a soulless husk; and his affinity for Dante, who in his *Divine Comedy* links inspiration with the flayed skin of Marsyas.[88] Other than the curious physiognomic disparity between the skin and the saint and the proximity of Michelangelo's name to the skin in a later print by Nicolas Beatrizet, there is no evidence to support the identification.[89] But the ease with which this figure resonates with the poetics of selfhood circulating around the historical figure Michelangelo is itself productive, especially if we avoid a literal, biographical explanation of his presence.[90] The skin, whether or not a disguised self-portrait of Michelangelo, reminds us of the personal relevance of the Last Judgment and of the inwardness, soul-searching, and fearful alienation attending even the idea of the event in early modern culture.

Titian's "disguised" self-portraits began to be identified at approximately the same time as those of Michelangelo's, but because of the relative obscurity of the picture, the designation of Midas as a self-portrait occurred several decades later.[91] Those scholars issuing and accepting the identification moved away from strictly biographical interpretations of the artist's appearance and offered readings that found more abstracted significance in his self-reference. The first art historian to identify Titian in the guise of Midas interpreted the "disguised" self-portrait as Titian-Midas meditating on the victory of divine art, on the artist's self-confidence and man's humility.[92] Successive scholars also have emphasized the self-punishing gesture of casting oneself as Midas, as though through this identification the artist were criticizing himself for his hubris and impotence in the field of painting.[93] Titian could be contemplating his own Olympian presumption, "but the resemblance," as Sidney Freedberg writes, "is more generic than secure."[94] These predominantly allegorical readings, rather than narrowly personal ones, are possibly suggested by the devotional structure of the composition, which encourages the viewer to think of the myth in exegetical terms.[95] But these formal similarities might also have influenced interpretations along strictly moralizing parameters, so that Titian's identification with an unexpected and negative figure becomes in these accounts a punitive gesture for personal ambition, for striving toward the divine in his creative talents, rather than an identification that reflects a general conception of making as destructive or unproductive.

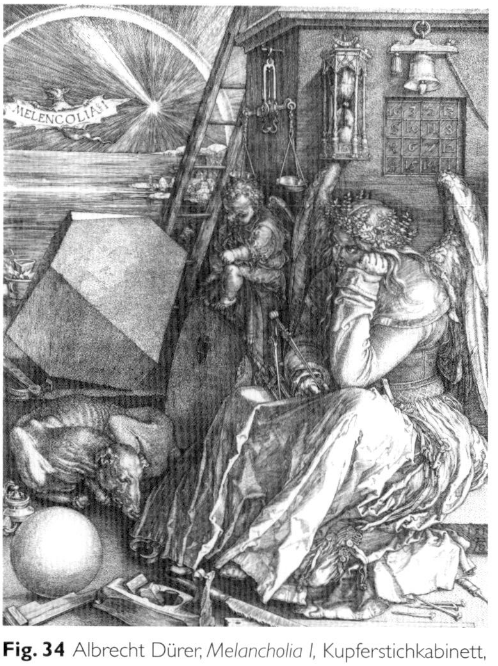

Fig. 34 Albrecht Dürer, *Melancholia I*, Kupferstichkabinett, Staatliche Museen, Berlin

Midas and Melancholy

The figure of Midas challenges a straightforward iconographic interpretation: the melancholic pose seems entirely inappropriate for the flawed and foolish judge who acts without thinking, but understandable when interpreted as indicative of the painter's self-referentiality, even though Midas and Titian seem unlikely partners. Is there a way in which these conditions and identities converge without one direction of identification determining or overwhelming the significance of the figure?

One of the main challenges in recognizing the complexity of Midas is that he assumes a pose that, by the later sixteenth century, had developed into a well-established iconographic type. Seated with his hand on his chin, he appears contemplative and despondent, engaged and curiously unmoved by the scene unfolding before him, especially when we recall his horrified seated predecessor in Giulio Romano's drawing. The pensive, seated figure, paralyzed by thought and inertia, had long symbolized the melancholic humor that dominated the temperament of inspired figures, such as prophets and evangelists.[96] Michelangelo employed the pose for the prophet Jeremiah on the Sistine Ceiling (1512);[97] and, perhaps most famously, Albrecht Dürer adopted the pose for the figure of Melancholy in his engraving *Melancholia I* (1514; fig. 34).[98] Sometime close to the execution of both of these examples, Raphael implicitly extended the inward, self-enclosed pose to a new branch of intellectuals, the visual artist, when he added the Michelangelesque figure, often identified as Michelangelo in the guise of Heraclitus, to his *School of Athens* (fig. 33).[99]

The spiritual and physical isolation of the melancholic figure easily lends a specifically personal autobiographical or biographical connotation to the representations. In addition to Raphael's obvious formal allusions to Michelangelo's pictorial mode (and Raphael's noteworthy deviation from his own), the figure of Heraclitus behaves according to our inherited expectations of Michelangelo's reported character.[100] Viewers have thought similarly of Dürer's *Melancholia,* suggesting that the image could be thought of as a spiritual self-portrait of the artist, as reflective of Dürer's entire personality, rather than any single life experience, and of his creative self.[101]

Infrequently do we find the antisocial, withdrawn melancholic represented as an engaged participant in a larger group, as is Midas in the *Flaying.* When he inhabits a multifigure composition, as does for example Heraclitus in the *School of Athens,* his physical isolation and separation from the collectivity of the group emphasize his self-absorptive and alienating state. Most early modern representations of melancholy focus on the single seated figure, isolated by the actual boundaries of the frame or by fictive dividers included in the depiction.[102] Midas, by contrast, appears fully integrated within the composition, providing the figural transition between the physical postures of the standing satyr and the diminutive *satirino* and dog. He functions as a pivot between the emotional reaction of the satyr and the seemingly emotional appeal to the viewer by the lower grouping, which in turn emphasizes his own spiritual withdrawal. Perhaps the pose registers a disconsolate, grief-stricken observer, someone so overwhelmed with emotion that he falls into a state of inertia. Or perhaps the pose negatively emphasizes the split of physical presence and spiritual absence demonstrated by melancholics. Two decades before his *Melancholia* and the larger occupation with the connection between creative genius and melancholy, Dürer had thought of the pose in approximately these terms when, in a drawing of the Holy Family, he depicted the sleeping Joseph, detached from the nearby Virgin and Child not because of the distractions of creativity but because of his complex role as the pious outsider.[103] Midas, as a far less positive figure, exemplifies the dangers of physical involvement without intellectual judgment, of having thoughts without divine inspiration (hastily judging Pan to be the victor in a different musical competition), and of physically manifesting his lack of thought (with his touch of gold and ass's ears).

In drawing upon the structure, and not the creative content, of melancholy, the mythological figure of Midas disfigures the iconographic tradition in which it appears to participate.[104] Except for a similar miserliness, Midas has very little in common with the early modern notion of melancholy and, as figured in the *Flaying,* assumes the pose almost as though a parody of the introspective tradition.[105] In Lodovico Dolce's commentary on the flawed judge, he emphasizes Midas's absence of inborn talent, judgment,

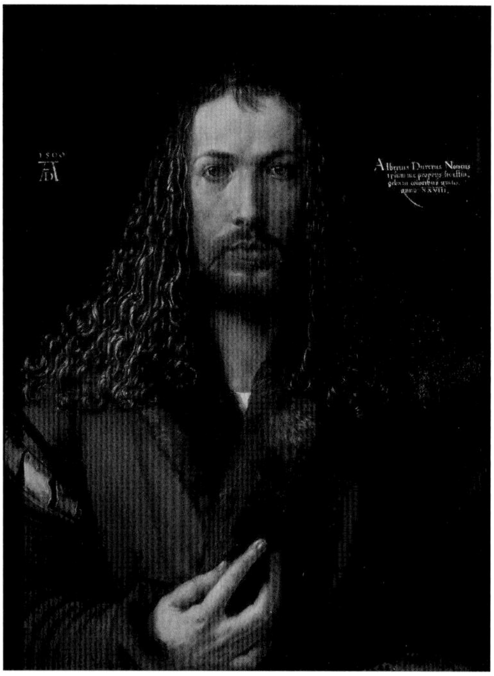

Fig. 35 Albrecht Dürer, *Self-Portrait,* 1500, Alte Pinakothek, Munich

and skill, even after repenting his errors: "But his *ingegno* remained rough and low and his eyes of judgment infirm and short-sighted, even though every day he received favors from the woodland Pan, god of shepherds."[106] According to Dolce's description, with terms more commonly found in contemporary accounts of visual artists, Midas would fail to measure up to the standards expected for the creative genius. Indeed, his brief experience of turning everything to gold, of changing the material of a given object but having no effect on the form, was considered by some cinquecento critics of sculpture, without specific mention of Midas, as anathema to art and, in some cases, artless.[107]

His placement among those woodland satyrs only reinforces his separation from the intellectual inspiration of the muses and might, in fact, indicate an interpretation for this melancholic pose that emerges from the pastoral tradition. Alongside the notion of melancholy as a fixed temperament there existed the poetic meaning of the concept as a temporary mood.[108] Melancholy as an emotional mood was not interchangeable with the condition as an intellectual state, although the two could be complementary. Shepherds in pastoral poetry roam the sylvan landscape with melancholy brow and speech, occupied as they are with thoughts of lost love, longing, sentimentality, and death.[109] Pastoral painting reflects this forlorn world with shadowed faces and the stillness and evocativeness of nature. Titian's *Flaying,* clearly related in subject to and yet technically distanced from the Giorgionesque vision of this lost golden age, figures the actuality and encroachment of sadness and

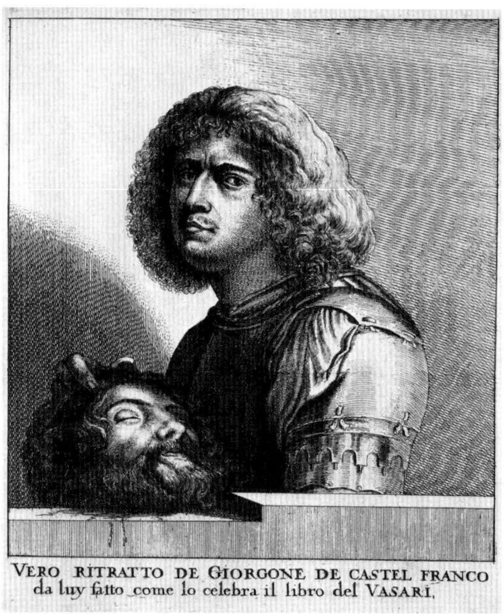

Fig. 36 Wenceslaus Hollar, *Self-Portrait as David, after Giorgione,* 1650, British Museum, London

death into the heretofore protected and isolated pastoral realm—not unlike the equally threatening mood of his roughly contemporary painting, the so-called *Nymph and Shepherd* (plate 6).[110] Midas's isolating pose only heightens this mood, which is created so palpably by the way in which Titian suggests the physical features of this pastoral world, this swirling and compressed sunset landscape. Perhaps the pose evolves out of a more distinctly Venetian milieu in which artists reconnected the mythological father of melancholics, Saturn, to his agrarian and pastoral origins.[111]

As an index for various states of inwardness, the pose remains open and undetermined, suggesting and encompassing all of these different traditions without necessarily limiting them. The richness of the meditative figure—regardless of the composition in which it appears—lies in how it directs viewers to reflect on the production of meaning and its oftentimes ambiguous relationship to contemplation, to inspiration, and to the production of art. This inquiry deepens when the figure appears in a picture with a potentially metapictorial subject and with a strikingly physically engaged counterpart as the flayer. The two figures share a spatial link through their apparent focus on the same area of Marsyas's body, but exhibit contrasting postures and degrees of engagement. Apollo, representative of inspired creativity, enacts an embodied relationship with the body of the satyr; whereas Midas, aligned with the bestial satyrs, assumes a reflective, meditative pose. The contrast brings to mind a similar dichotomy in Titian's *Pietà* (plates 11 and 12), in which the embodied experience of Jerome (another putative self-portrait) with the body of Christ contrasts with the transcendent visionary experience of the artist depicted in the diminutive and archaic *ex voto* image. These sets of figures both establish a comparison between a present way of being (bodily absorption in the moment) and past way of being (whether in an archaic image-type or through a familiar, although somewhat dated pose) that easily extend to describing ways of making—or destroying, as the case might be.

Although such negative self-images of the flayer and Midas might seem out of place in our inherited idea of Titian's or any Renaissance artist's—other than Michelangelo's—subjectivity, they bear a close relationship to the sentiments conveyed by the self-portrait *in malo* tradition.[112] First specifically mentioned in accounts of early seventeenth-century artists such as Caravaggio and Cristofano Allori, these reportedly disguised self-representations as villain and as victim introduced an unexpectedly sinister and antiheroic dimension to early modern subjectivity.[113] Renaissance artists rarely aligned themselves so openly with such legendary enemies. Such negative sympathies seem distant from the idea of the artist as the divine creator, as in Dürer's identification with Christ in his *Self-Portrait* of 1500 (fig. 35). However, in light of these Baroque identifications, some art historians have suggested related pictorial situations in Venetian Renaissance scenes of decapitation. Giorgione's *Self-Portrait as David* (Herzog Anton-Ulrich Museum, Braunschweig; reproduced here in a print by Wenceslaus Hollar, fig. 36), recognized as such by Vasari

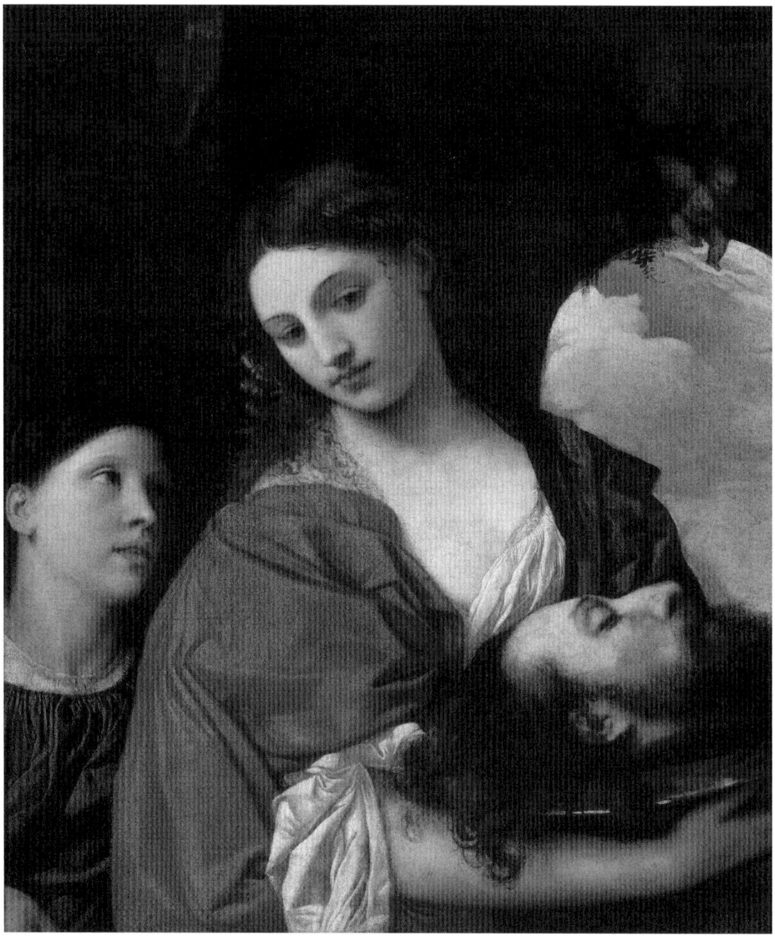

Fig. 37 Titian, *Salome,* Galleria Doria Pamphili, Rome

after an earlier, albeit vague, inventory entry, generated an identification of the painter as the decapitated Holofernes in his *Judith* through physiognomic resemblance to the depicted hero and the unexpectedly intimate relationship between the two figures.[114] This suggestion has reflected back on Giorgione's *Self-Portrait,* causing some viewers to wonder if the artist depicted himself as David or as the decapitated Goliath—who was quite literally cut from the original picture—and to intimate similar disguised self-portraits for other decapitation scenes ranging from Donatello's *David* to Veronese's *Judith* and Palma Vecchio's painting of the same subject (Galleria degli Uffizi, Florence).[115]

Physical resemblance might generate or support these depictions as disguised self-portraits, but the interrelated concepts circulating around decapitation—including sensuality, sexuality, and the head as the locus of thought and identity—suggest a more generalized idea of presence. Such interconnections first found articulation in psychoanalytic theory, specifically in the seminal work of Freud on castration.[116] Not surprisingly, some of the earliest modern designations of the self-portrait *en decapitè*—first among them Titian's self-portrait as the head of John the Baptist in his *Salome* (fig. 37)—occurred in the chronological wake of these psychoanalytic writings. The intimacy and sensuality and focused sense of identity evoked between the perpetrator and her/his victim, accomplished in these Venetian examples through the close proximity of contrasting textures, through provocative glances, through half-length or single-figure compositions, emphasizes an artistic self-consciousness that easily inflects an autobiographical reading onto the disembodied head.

Amorously framed, the association between subjectivity and decapitation also has pre-Freudian roots in Petrarchan poetry and madrigals in which the spurned lover compares himself to decapitated enemies and remains astonished at the absence of pity demonstrated by the beloved.[117] Even David felt pity for his victim, Petrarch writes, "But you, whom pity never makes pale and who have your defenses always ready against Love's bow . . . you see me torn asunder by a thousand deaths, but nevertheless no tear has ever fallen from your eyes, but only disdain and anger" (*Rima* 44).[118] Not only has the poet's love become self-destructive in the absence of reciprocation, but the poetic enterprise itself threatens its own origins by cutting off the generation of love in the eyes and of thought in the head. Love, with all that it generates and inspires, is simultaneously heroic and aggressive, divine and monstrous.

These "disguised" self-portraits, whether verifiable or forming a legendary strand in art-historical discourse, nonetheless resonate for thinking about ambivalent associations with the idea of making in the Renaissance—and, more specifically, Titian's representations of the flayer as maker/destroyer and Midas as the unthinking thinker. Michelangelo, when working through the design for his bronze David and the right arm of his marble David, draws a comparison between his gestures and tools of sculpture and the defenses and actions of the biblical hero when he writes on a drawing sheet: "David with his sling, and I with my bow. Michelangelo."[119] The comparison seems straightforward: David defeated Goliath with targeted physical force, intellectual superiority, and divine favor.[120] Articulating the central tropes in cinquecento art theory, contemporaries argued that sculpture, and specifically Michelangelo's sculpture, required and demonstrated precisely these intellectual and supernatural conditions. But considered in the context of the repeatedly interrelated tropes of making and (self-)destruction in Michelangelo's own poetry, the analogy between the deadly sling and an implement of sculpture implies a connection between creation, destruction, and the infliction of pain.[121] Elsewhere on the same sheet Michelangelo alludes to a parallel dialectic—that of the slowly accumulated rewards of labor and the instantaneousness of their loss—when he cites part of a beginning line from a Petrarchan sonnet: "Broken are the high Column and the green Laurel."[122] Lamenting the almost simultaneous deaths of Laura and Cardinal Giovanni Colonna, Petrarch concludes his muted protest against mortality with the following complaint: "Oh our life that is so beautiful to see, how easily it loses in one morning what has been acquired with great difficulty over many years!" (*Rima* 269).[123] Perhaps an unrelated poetic musing or perhaps related to the self-identification with David and his weapon, the phrase emphasizes the almost simultaneous destruction of what is done; when read in relationship to the comparison with carving David, the phrase gives a poetic dimension to a largely physical endeavor of art that surfaced only as criticism of sculpture in so-called *paragone* literature or that was aestheticized through the terminology of style and technique and, somewhat later, through elegant, abstract personifications.[124] The oft-repeated phrase in Renaissance art theory that art is the hiding of art's presence encompasses the predominant Renaissance approach to labor and its signs.[125] Michelangelo similarly affirms the subjugation of the hand to the intellect,[126] but he also describes the mess, the physical distress and unease, of art: complaining of his work on the Sistine Ceiling, he writes, "the brush that is always above my face, by dribbling down, makes [my breast] an ornate pavement."[127] Art, with all of its physical properties and demands, its constructive and destructive aspects, functions as a metaphor in Michelangelo's poetry for the making and unmaking of the self.

Titian's later paintings explore the related expression of subjectivity through corporeality in figures such as the flayer and Jerome, but also in his own independent self-portraits. When, in the mid-sixteenth century, Titian turned his attention to self-portraiture, he creatively interpreted the genre with his unconventional representations of himself as though represented by another. Turned away from the viewer in both his Prado and Berlin self-portraits (figs. 3 and 4), Titian offered views of himself that were not obviously taken from the mirror—even if he accomplished the portraits with a series of mirrors—which suggests that these images figure a view from memory or from a less visually reflective experience of oneself.[128] The Berlin *Self-Portrait* enacts this on the surface of the canvas itself: the varied thickness and thinness of the pigment convey a sense of physicality and presence from the accumulated layers of paint or, unexpectedly, from the weave of the exposed canvas. Thick brushstrokes work to create the texture of his shirt and fur vest, but the most obviously worked areas are those of the hands, which Titian created by dragging his hand through the tacky surface of paint.[129] The painter engages in an action of making, which simultaneously endows the represented hands with a physical substance and effaces their resemblance to hands: making and unmaking are inextricably connected in their principal instruments.[130] These strokes can be read simply as the sign of the artist's presence—appropriate for a self-portrait—but such a reading overlooks the importance of human embodiment in registering such presence and as the basis for semiosis in general. Although (literally) authoritative, these marks are, above all, contingent, and register a projection of the painter's body in the world.

Titian moves away from figuring an awareness of himself through gestures and a direct visual address and turns to a more personal, embodied process that does not involve just vision but centers around the extension and projection of his entire body into the world. This is not the autonomous self that observes the world as a detached object. According to this paradigm, being and existence are located in the body, expressed through that same body, and affected and shaped by the world the body inhabits. Hence Boschini's notion of the painter as fencer and as surgeon—activities that depend on a connection between bodies—and Titian's own physical connection to his depicted body.

This notion of embodied subjectivity could explain the proliferation of "disguised" self-portrait identifications in cinquecento paintings. Artists might or might not actually represent themselves more often in the guise of a historical or legendary figure in the sixteenth century, but certain pictorial situations of embodiment—whether created through subject matter, pictorial structure, and/or technical execution—involve an observer—whether depicted or actual—so directly, so physically, that the experience seems explained entirely by the painter's presence, which in turn heightens expectations that the painter will figure his presence through physical resemblance. The *Flaying* interferes with this reflexive interpretive gesture by associating an iconographic tradition of artistic creativity with a figure who, although bearing a resemblance to depictions of the aged painter, could not be more unworthy of the association, and by figuring the punishment of Marsyas as a pictorial act. But in doing so the painting itself compares two modes of making that paradoxically invert the very dialectic of this musical competition: Midas, in the pose of meditation and thought among the satyrs, appears as the figuration of an inferior, even foolish, approach to making, whereas Apollo, physically involved in the thickness of Marsyas, figures the chosen and divine mode of making. The *Flaying* establishes a dialectic between two paradigms—one, the melancholic Midas, framed as pictorially archaic, and the other, the destructive Apollo, as unfolding in the horrifying present—that reminds us of a comparative situation in another painting, the *School of Athens* (fig. 33), which addresses the different pictorial modes of quattrocento geometry and cinquecento inspiration. By extension, then, painting no longer seems to be exclusively an intellectual or even divine art, but rather one of the body, with all of its vulnerabilities and disfigurations.

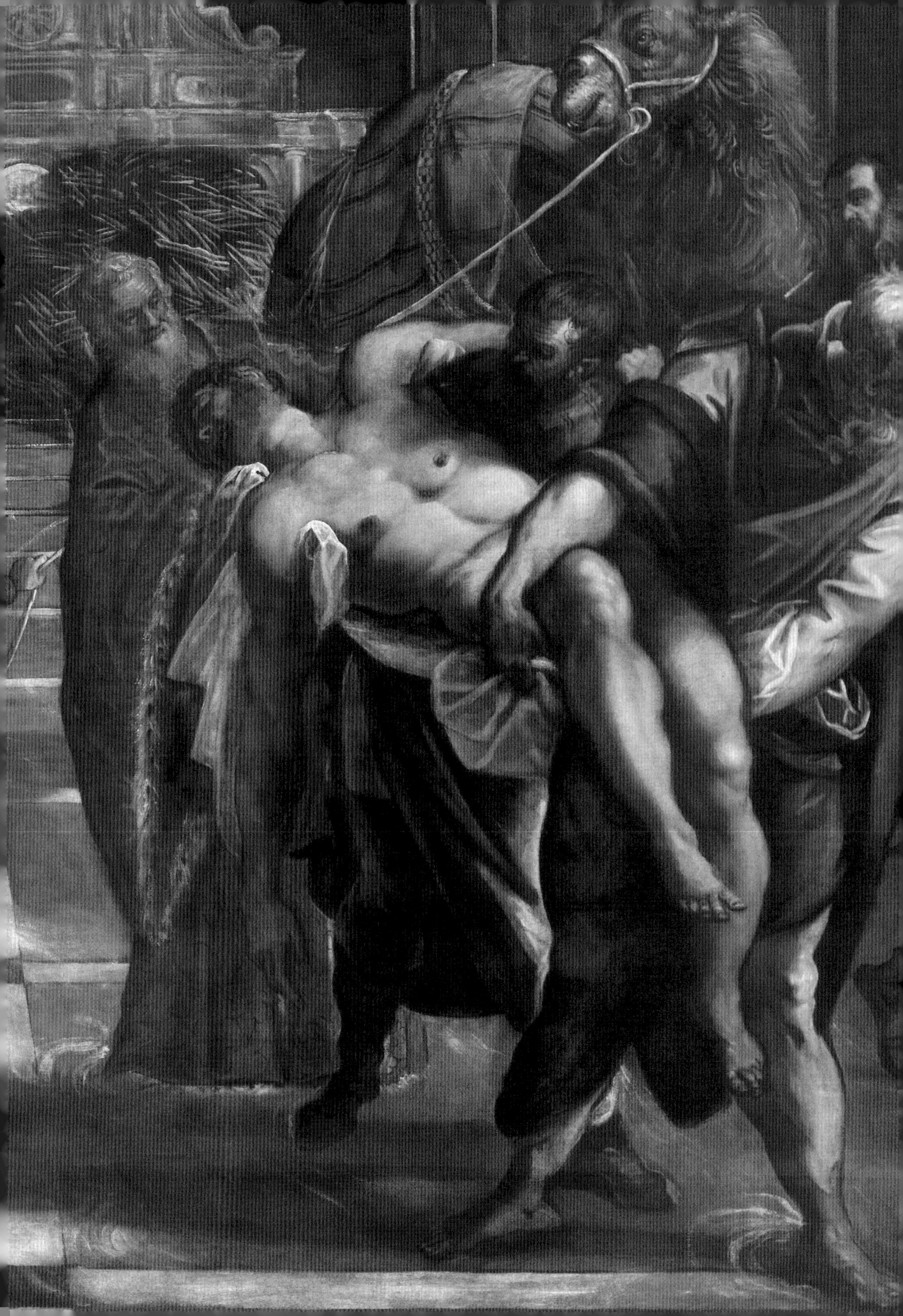

3

Violence and Retrospection

At the same time that new questions about the art of painting arise in Titian's painting, the compositional types employed in many of these paintings unexpectedly return us to those more frequently used in quattrocento and early cinquecento painting. The *Flaying of Marsyas,* our most recent example of this situation, turns to frontal devotional image-types, which must have been notably archaic by the 1570s. Other later paintings by Titian return to the half-length narrative composition (fig. 8; plates 1, 14, 15, and 18), which also had asserted its popularity during the careers of earlier northern Italian painters as Andrea Mantegna, Giovanni Bellini (fig. 32), and Giorgione.[1] Like these earlier devotional half-lengths, Titian's later examples depict events from the Passion; however, their active brushwork disrupts the stasis of the quattrocento compositions and recalls the even earlier cultic and mystical associations with bodily presence and materiality found in their source, the *imago pietatis* (fig. 38). Titian's devotional half-lengths also remind us of the earliest Renaissance theorization of painting that first developed out of these image-types and that shaped the direction of other image-types, such as the Albertian *istoria.* These theoretical concepts, all of which find their central underpinning in the principle of mimesis, include the empathic connection with the viewer created through gaze and gesture and the indexical relationship between the body and the mind.[2] Venetian painting was not as strictly committed to Albertian or humanist principles of the visual arts as was central Italian painting.[3] Similarly, these later paintings under consideration in this chapter reveal a critical dimension to their deviation from a humanist model and to their retrospectiveness that the violent subject matter reinforces.[4]

This simultaneous presence and operation of seemingly contradictory modes has been noted by other art historians, and even defined Titian's later style and *Spätstil* in general for Panofsky: "Titian's latest style—like the latest style of most great masters—

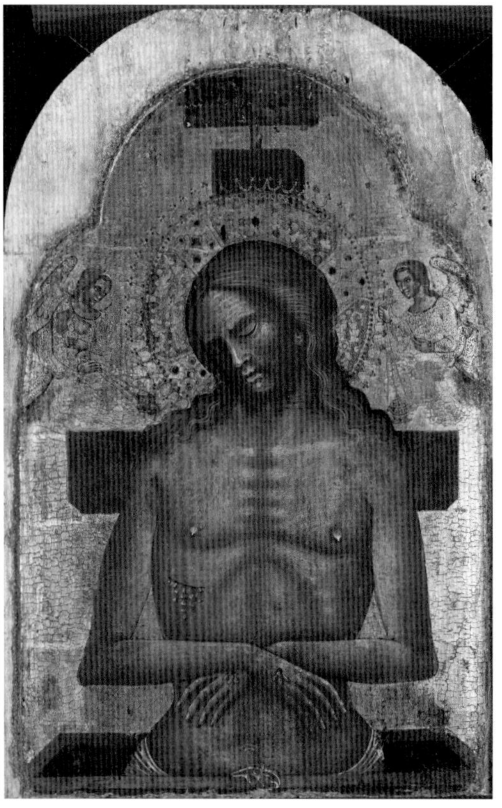

Fig. 38 Venetian School, *The Dead Christ*, National Gallery, London

amounts to a coincidence of opposites: intense emotion and outward stillness, color and non-color, the broadest and apparently almost chaotic technique of execution and the most rigid order and density of composition."[5] This chapter seeks to understand the broader significance and circumstances of these contradictions in and for Renaissance painting.

Friendship and Aggression

Those slightly distanced from Renaissance pictorial ideals, such as seventeenth-century writers, articulated the potentially violent impact on viewers of Titian's later paintings without being concerned that he challenged the Renaissance humanistic ideals. One of these, the Bolognese writer Virgilio Malvezzi, who spent some time in the Spanish court of Philip IV and possibly absorbed the generally positive assessment by Spanish theorists of Titian's later work,[6] reframed the discussion away from tropes of viewing distance and old age in his commentary on Plutarch's *Life of Coriolanus* (1648).[7]

> Titian, perhaps the most famous of painters, and certainly among the most famous, painted at times with so many and such diligent brushstrokes that it almost seemed as if he wished to make each and every hair countable; and at times he was content to rough in his paintings with few and very rough strokes ["di pocchi, e rozzissimi colpi"]. The intelligent observer of such diverse styles will recognize in the one the charm of the feminine ["il vago della femina"], in the other robust masculinity ["il robusto maschile"]. The former will be given passing praise; the latter will hold one fast in admiring contemplation ["si fermarà con ammiratione"]: one will feel oneself gently attracted by the delicate, violently seized upon by the crude ["sentirassi dalla delicate soavemente inclinare, dalla rozza violentemente rapire"].[8]

This passage, noteworthy for its accepting recognition of the different affects and effects of different styles, appears after a lengthy discussion of the benefits and disadvantages to society of educating men of both refined and rough stock. Far preferable to overeducating a good-natured man is leaving a rougher one virtually untilled.

> Let not an evil nature be too much tilled, nor fed with feed; it is offended by being fed, and too much tillage offends it; either the feed doth not . . . take root there or it turns to poison. Let an indifferent nature have a great deal of education, and a good one but a little, if you will not have it grow weak and effeminate. The ancient Romans, while the excellent soil lasted did not tenderly till it with learning, because they would not weaken the sturdiness of their citizens, nor cause their corn to lie upon the ground through too much rankness, but did educate them rustically in a military way, and so they brought forth a plentiful generation of heroic persons. The curious dressing of a garden is fit for tulips and such kinds of flowers, which for the most part delight the eye, but are without savor, scent, or substance; and such are those men, who brought up in music, singing, and dancing serve for ornament, but are fruitless and vain in a Commonwealth.[9]

Malvezzi develops his protracted advice from a brief analogy in Plutarch's text between agricultural husbandry and the training of youths. Titian's painting, more than Titian himself, notably serves as a non-ancient, non-Roman example of the sweetness and roughness found in agriculture and in societal behavior. Rather than addressing Titian's character, Malvezzi focuses his attention on the affective power of Titian's images on viewers and avoids the issue of subject matter altogether. The shifting terms of the analogy become obvious in the passage that follows Malvezzi's remarks on Titian:

> What was Cato (whom antiquity was never weary of commending) but a plant growing in an excellent soil, a picture drawn with rough strokes? And the two brutes, one of which expelled the tyrant and the other slew him, who will not say but they were trees of the forest? The second was inferior to the first in fortune, because he exceeded him in knowledge. He knew the defect after he had been hurt by it; and when he lay dying, he styled all sciences vain. Lucius, hardened by the savageness of the forest, killed his own children. Marcus, softened with the delicacy of tillage, suffers Caesar's friends to live, losing that Commonwealth with his learning, which the other had built up with his ignorance. The people of Rome who hoped for liberty through Marcus' valor, feared he would lose the beauty of his horridness of the forest by means of manuring; Caesar almost assured himself that he had lost it. They were both deceived, for with that part of savageness which remained, he could kill Caesar and ruin the Commonwealth with that softness which he had acquired.[10]

Rough, untilled men commit acts of violence and savagery, which, in the end, strengthen society—especially if they occupy leadership positions—whereas softer, learned men paradoxically cause more destruction.

But how do Titian's paintings relate to a discussion that seems to be more political than pictorial in subject? Philip Sohm, who first brought attention to this text, considers Malvezzi's comments within a larger trend of gendering style.[11] Paintings with high finish and detail exhibited feminine charm; those with rougher strokes suggested masculine strength. As Sohm observes, Malvezzi drew upon the rhetorical division between a delicate, ornate style that pleases immediately and a rough style that endures.[12] But Malvezzi makes an even stronger distinction than these rhetorical categories had offered by describing poles of loving affection and violence in viewer response.[13] The viewer, we read, will be seduced or will be "violently seized by the rough." The murderous and savage actions of the "rough" men discussed in Malvezzi's text imply through analogy the possible severity of the violent attacks by the rough on bystanders, or, in this pictorial case, the viewers. However casual and unprogrammatic Malvezzi's arguments on the arts might seem to be, his text suggestively offers ways of thinking about the experience of viewing these rougher, looser paintings by Titian.

One consequence of Malvezzi's text is that the "rapacious" experience of viewing Titian's paintings challenges the dominant Renaissance viewer-response model of empathy and friendship—even as these states exist alongside this violent possibility in Malvezzi's text. Beginning with Alberti's commentary *On Painting* (Latin, 1435; Italian, 1436), art theorists expected painting to elicit an emotional response or reaction that mirrored the represented passions. Following ancient writers on poetics, Alberti advises that painting follow our natural predilections to "mourn with the mourners, laugh with those who laugh, and grieve with the grief-stricken" by depicting figures who clearly demonstrate their emotions.[14] This imitative paradigm appears earlier in Alberti's text in his analogies of painting with friendship and with the reflective exchange of Narcissus.[15] And it survived into at least the mid-sixteenth century with the publication of Lodovico Dolce's treatise on painting. Dolce, following Horace, expanded the imitative emotional relationship to include the painter.

> What is needed is that the figures should stir the spectators' souls—disturbing them in some cases, cheering them in others, in others again inciting them to either compassion or disdain, depending on the character of the subject matter. . . . Nor can the painter stir emotion unless he already experiences in his own being, while executing the figures, those passions—or shall we say "states of mind" ["affetti"]—which he wishes to imprint on the mind of another.[16]

Dolce, like Alberti and most Renaissance theorists writing after the Florentine humanist, included the full range of emotional response, from joy to grief, in his recommendations, but the dominant theoretical relationship between painting and viewer was amorous—implying its imitative quality and structure, the pleasure derived from it, and, in the case of Dolce, the subject matter. Paintings, according to Dolce, "inflame" beholders with love, and even children "point their fingers at [painting]; and it appears in this way that their babyish hearts are chock-full of sweetness."[17] Given the predominance of Petrarchan poetry in cinquecento literary and visual culture, the favoring of sensuous paintings capable of inspiring amorous feelings in the beholder should not be surprising.[18] Malvezzi's reiteration of this idea only demonstrates its longevity.

His pendant claim of the viewer being "violently seized" could be an extreme expression of the imitative structure of beholding, especially since most of these roughly executed paintings have violent subject matter; or, the aggressive relationship ("rapire") could register the failure of the imitative model for paintings that deviate from the expected standard of resemblance. These pictures, in their difference, assault the viewer. Alberti, following the advice given to ancient rhetoricians and dramatists, founded his theory of painting on the human figure and presumed that facial expressions and gestures would be legible and easily interpreted. He advised that "motions of the mind" should be clearly demonstrated through the body.[19] Renaissance viewers trained both by this and other texts and by extant paintings were in no way prepared to look at paintings that challenged a preexisting representational standard; one could assert, given Vasari's and subsequent writers' recommendations of viewing Titian's painting from a distance, that they understandably would have expected diligent brushstrokes that rendered every hair.[20]

Titian's later paintings overturned these expectations not only through their rough execution but through the very structure of the compositions. Frontal and balanced compositions predominate, and yet gestures and facial expressions, when they appear, often fail to convey the passions of the depicted figures. We recall Panofsky's observation of "intense emotion and outward stillness" cited at the outset of this chapter. David Rosand notes this paradoxical quality specifically in Titian's *Christ Crowned with Thorns* (ca. 1570–76; plate 16): "Gestures no longer carry the immediate conviction of physical application, and the entire action assumes the quality of a ritualized performance. . . . Christ . . . seems hardly to feel his earthly torment; his nearly expressionless head now contrasts with and relates to the flaming lamps above."[21] Other arguably more finished paintings—such as the *Flaying*—include figures that exhibit an unexpected calm and absence of expression given the subject matter or that limit the rhetorical energy to a single distraught figure (such as the Magdalene in the Prado *Entombment* [plate 13] and the *Pietà* [plate 11]).[22] The active brushwork over the entire painting not only assumes the expressive energy once assumed by gestures and facial expressions, but, in muting and disfiguring the expected modes of registering emotion, also heightens the violence and loss implicit in the subject matter.[23]

Although many of these compositions move away from rhetorical empathic

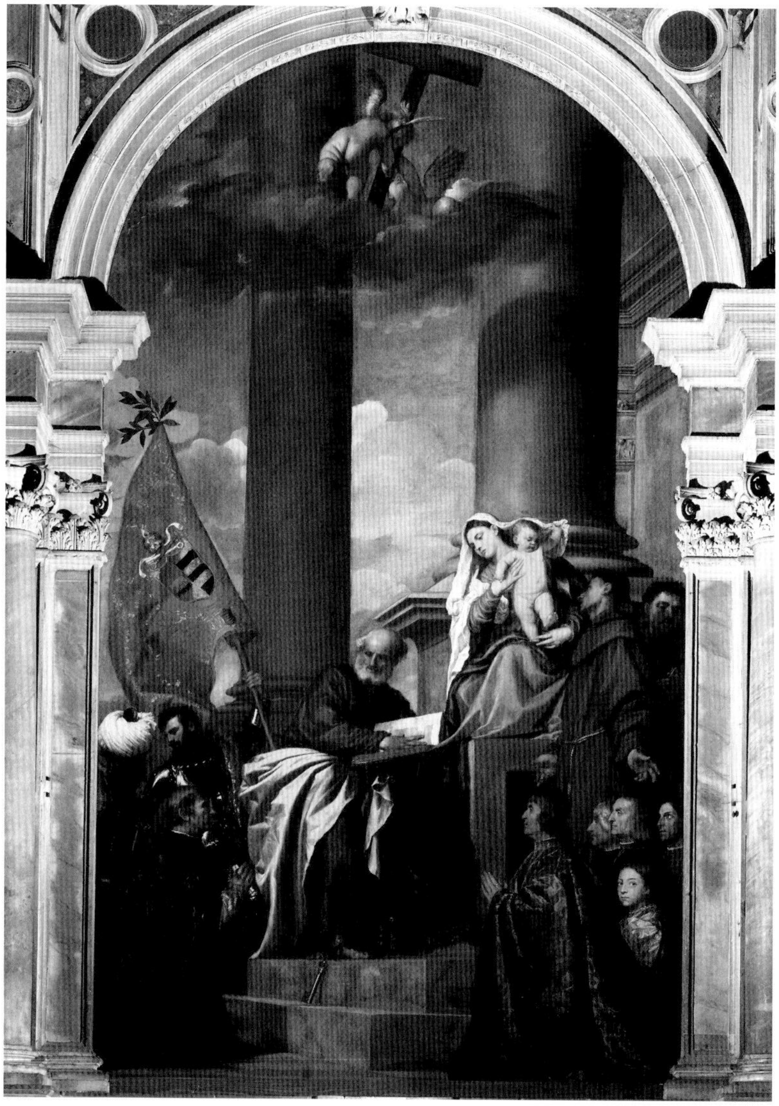

Fig. 39 Titian, *Madonna of the Pesaro Family,* Santa Maria Gloriosa dei Frari, Venice

structures central to figurative painting in the Renaissance, many of them unexpectedly adhere to the Albertian recommendation of including an interlocutor, that figure who "tells the spectators what is going on." A staple in quattrocento narrative and devotional painting, the interlocutor directed the viewer's attention and/or served as an index of the subject represented. Alberti elaborates: "I like there to be someone in the 'historia' who tells the spectators what is going on and either beckons them with his hand to look, or with ferocious expression and forbidding glance challenges them not to come near, as if he wished their business to be secret, or points to some danger or remarkable thing in

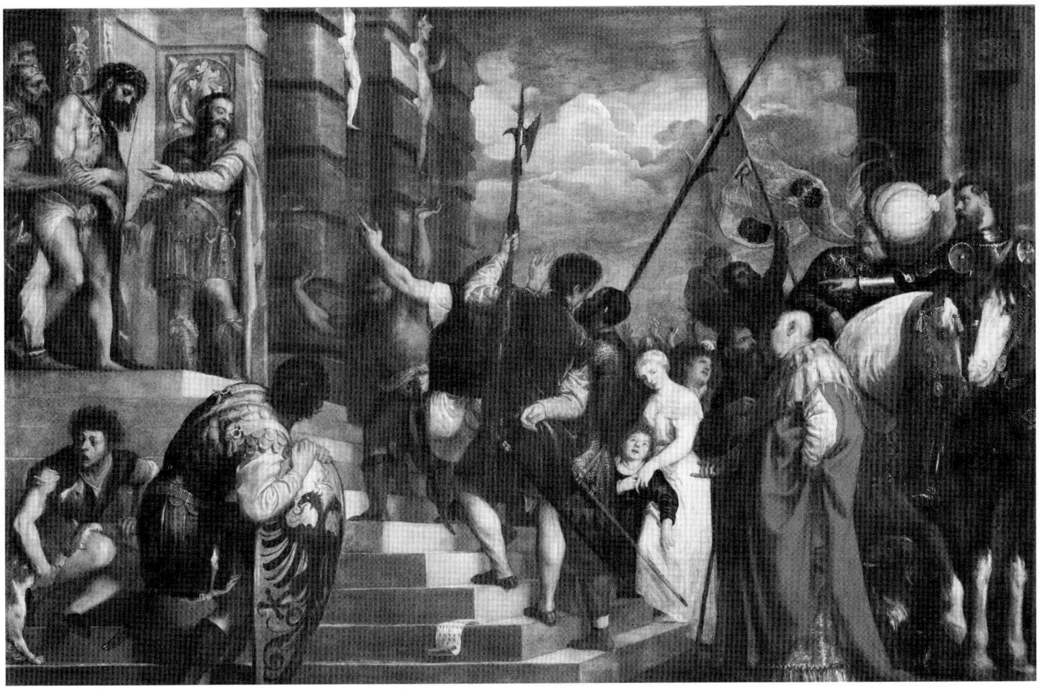

Fig. 40 Titian, *Ecce Homo,* Kunsthistorisches Museum, Vienna

the picture, or by his gestures invites you to laugh or weep with them."[24] The Virgin in Masaccio's *Trinity* enacts this function (and probably influenced Alberti's conception) in her visual address to the viewer to contemplate the crucified Christ (fig. 25).[25] The dialogic figure, appearing as an affirmation of the beholder's presence, encouraged the viewer to consider the interlocutor positively. Even when Alberti describes the interlocutor's role of excluding the viewer, a situation rarely explored in Renaissance painting, the interlocutor belongs to the social network of the multifigured *istoria* and guides our response.[26] Cinquecento painters gradually abandoned the instructive, gesturing figure as compositions became less statically organized around a centric point, such as the *sacra conversazione* and narrative pictures constructed with perspective; although many sixteenth-century paintings retained traces of the Albertian concept with the inclusion of a figure who gazes directly at the beholder. When such figures appear in Venetian painting, and most commonly among the rhetorical gestures of the *scuole* pictures, they usually indicate a portrait likeness or suggest a generalized intimacy and recognition of the viewer's presence. They, like their central Italian counterparts, function positively, often isolated by their radiance, appearing to be trustworthy in their didactic aim and affirming our role as, for example, witnesses to a scene of divine presentation (figs. 39 and 40).[27]

Around midcentury, when Titian's contemporaries had largely abandoned the reflexive figure and his own paintings returned to earlier compositions, the function of the interlocutor figure underwent a creative reinterpretation in his work. Children and animals assume the role that originally conveyed authority and control over the signification of the painting. At first these naïve beings seem like sympathetic, even blameless indicators; however, their placement in scenes of martyrdom complicates their role as our guide. Consider, for example, the youth holding the reeds in the *Christ Crowned with Thorns* (plate 16). The devout viewer would rather not acknowledge and be acknowledged by him. A similar unease occurs with the *satirino* and the fearsome dog that together fulfill the role of the interlocutor in Titian's *Flaying of Marsyas* (plate 3): the devotional visual source suggests that we should feel compassion for the martyred and his affected intimates, and yet the mythological story affirms the righteousness of the gods.[28] The satyr's restraint of the dog echoes the fatal curbing of impulses at the center, but the situation of a half-beast reining in beast also parodies the Apollonian action.[29] These figures, with placid expressions despite the gravity of both scenes, elicit some confusion over whether to emulate and trust them—which, of course, becomes appropriate given their compromised status as torturer and half-beast, respectively, and given the subjects of the paintings.[30] These paintings complicate the foundations of Renaissance figurative painting even as they signify according to them.[31]

In doing so, the interlocutory roles of these naïve beings unexpectedly refocus our attention from the enactment of a narrative to the immediacy and bestiality of the martyrdom. The animals and children indicate the physical savagery of the event by emphasizing martyrdom as a base and thoughtless act of man against man, which they, as naïve, impulsive beings, are capable of performing but without the same persecutory intent. Consider, for example, the interlocutory horse, dog, and child in the Escorial *Martyrdom of Saint Lawrence* (1564–67; plate 17).[32] The beasts, turned in opposing directions, form a *contrapposto* of threat: the horse responds to and the dog embodies the horror of mutilating the body. The turning child with crossed hands at the center of the group of soldiers enacts a similar conflict as our guide: he fulfills the compositional and thematic roles of isolating the martyred body that both allows the martyrdom to continue and maintains the sanctity of the sacrifice.[33]

In altering the discursive identity of the interlocutor, these figures introduce a less rational and more immediately responsive dimension to our experience of painting. An analogous situation occurs in the roughly contemporary series of paintings by Tintoretto (1562–66) involving another martyr, in which the body of Saint Mark performs miracles in a depicted perspectival space:[34] his body either obstructs or defies the spatial configuration he inhabits, either crossing over the orthogonals (fig. 41) or concealing with his gesturing hand the vanishing point (fig. 42). In doing so, the irrational workings of the saintly body within the calibrated, organized space emphasize the presence of his true body.

Fig. 41 Tintoretto, *Transport of the Body of Saint Mark*, Accademia, Venice

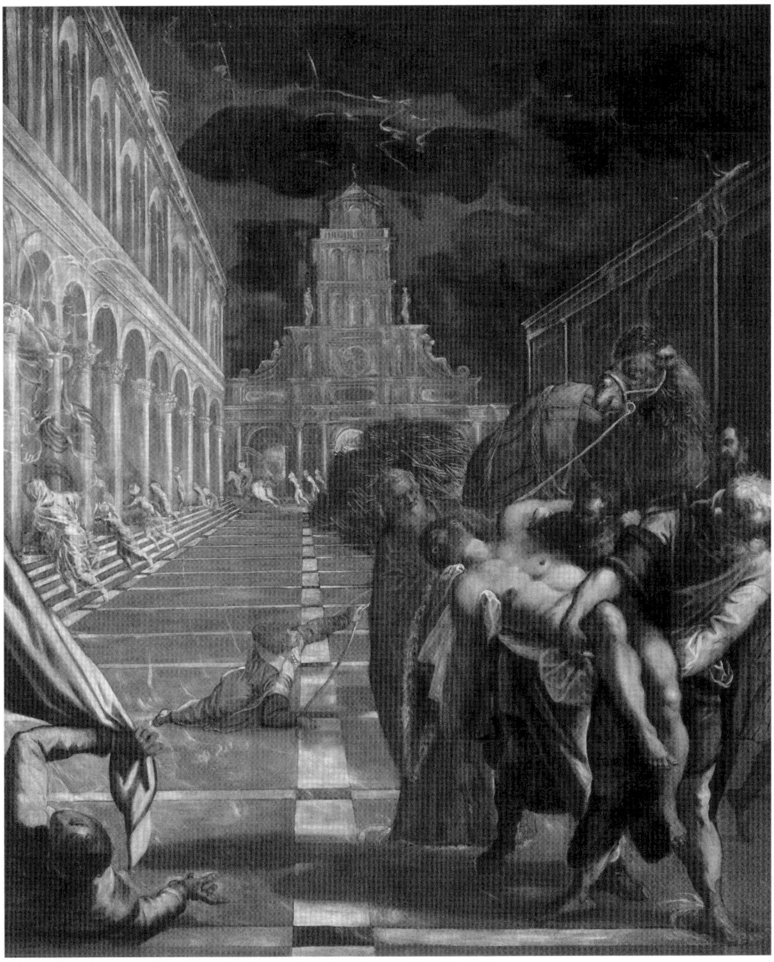

The Cinquecento Culture of Violence

Later Italian Renaissance art theory, especially those treatises written in the wake of religious reform, focused on precisely this conflicting relationship between a hermeneutic and an embodied experience of the visual arts. Many of these texts, in defending and warning against charges of idolatry, emphasized the distinction between the materials of art and the subject represented and recommended an exegetical (intellectual) reading of the devotional subject.[35] But, as we will soon see, we find lapses of this firm division woven throughout these texts at crucial moments when the suffering devotional body overwhelms the faithful viewer and the described experience evokes situations of embodiment similar to those that had led to charges of idolatry in the first place. Regardless of whether these texts bear any direct relation-

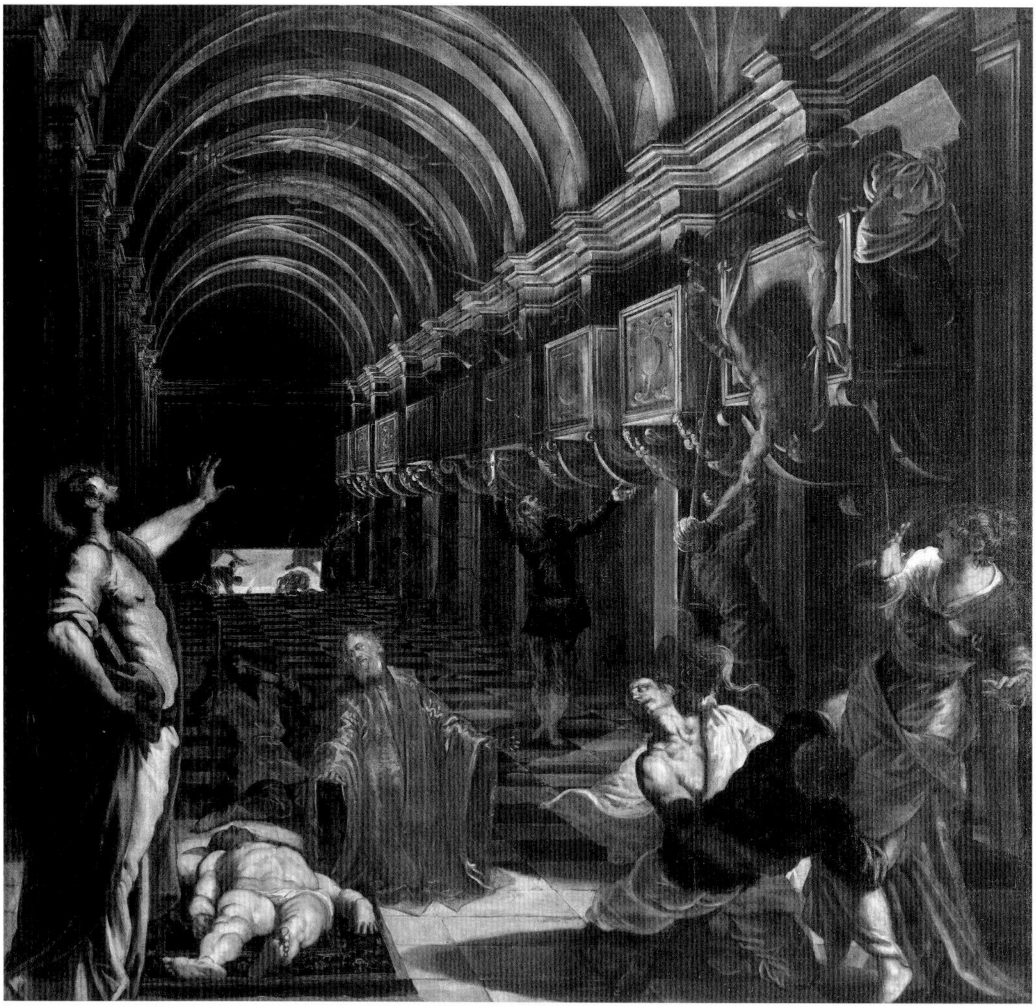

Fig. 42 Tintoretto, *Discovery of the Body of Saint Mark*, Pinacoteca di Brera, Milan

ship to specific works of art, including Titian's, they contribute to a mid-cinquecento culture occupied with the intersection of violence, devotion, and materiality.[36]

In defending the validity of the image, reformatory writers focused on how to stimulate piety in viewers. They recommended not only that painters emulate earlier iconic compositions, as though returning to simpler times, but that artists should also depict with the greatest verisimilitude those subjects capable of engaging viewers in devotion.[37] Foremost among these was the violence done to the body of Christ during the Passion and the recognition of his tortured body as an affirmation of faith.[38] One of these reformatory texts, Giovanni Andrea Gilio's *Dialogo nel quale si ragiona degli errori e degli abusi dei pittori* (1564), addressed such issues in a larger discussion of Michelangelo's *Last Judgment.* Painters, according to Gilio, should depict the body afflicted "in such a way that it no longer has the form of a man."[39] Scenes of the Passion of Christ should show him "bloody, ugly, deformed, afflicted, consumed, and dead."[40] These depictions do not violate decorum, as some might claim, but will spur viewers to feel more reverence and charity; they, in contradistinction to Christ's torturers, who revel in the signs of the humanity of Christ at the expense of His divinity, will "stop with marvel to contemplate the lowness."[41]

Guarding against idolatry, these texts carefully described a limited affective impact of the violent images on viewers. Beholders, we are reminded, should see the images with an intellectual eye and refrain from involving their senses since paintings are just representations and not the thing itself. But this ideal response weakened somewhat when viewing violent scenes, and especially those involving Christ. Gabriele Paleotti writes of this situation in his *Discorso intorno alle imagini sacre e profani* (1582): "To hear the narration of the martyrdom of a saint, the zeal and constancy of a virgin, the passion of Christ, are things that touch on the true; but to see with vivid colors the martyred saint, the struggling Virgin, and Christ nailed, it is true that devotion swells and deeply strikes ['compugne'] the viscera; and who does not recognize this is made of wood or of marble."[42] In an unexpected alteration of reformatory prescriptions, Paleotti criticizes unfeeling beholders by comparing them to inanimate materials, which have receded in his description of affective response. A depiction does not merely move viewers; it penetrates their physical and emotional recesses. Often, as Paleotti clarifies in the same pages, it does so violently. "If spoken or read words have the ability to transmute our senses, with how much more violence do depicted figures penetrate us and inspire pity, modesty, sanctity, and devotion, according to Saint Gregory. . . . As much as our imagination receives impressions, there is no doubt that there is no stronger and more efficacious instrument than images made from life ['imagini fatte al vivo'] which violate our incautious senses ['violentano i sensi incauti']."[43] For Paleotti, the violence experienced in the viewing process reflected the efficacy of devotional images and the openness of the beholder to identify physically and emotionally with the horrors and atrocities suffered by Christ and other martyrs. A visceral response, even though contradicting Paleotti's favoring of an intellectual understanding, would result in a hatred of sin and depravity and, consequently, a swelling of faith and belief.[44]

The tension between an intellectual and an embodied experience of Christ's suffering found expression in Vittoria Colonna's spiritual poetry through pictorial metaphors with a similar dialectical relationship, *disegno* and *colore*.[45] At the center of reform-minded intellectual circles associated with Michelangelo, Colonna articulated the intellectual comprehension of Christ's suffering and salvation with *disegno* and the corporeal dimension with *colore*.

> *With divine words He makes the*
> *beautiful* disegno
> *Of the true life, and then He gives* colore
> *With his blood, and so that love might be*
> *the cause*

Of this work, He gives Himself to it in
forfeit.
The soul is alive with flames, and the
intellect
Content with light, and with both
The purged desire rises and grows stronger.
Hot marks from the harsh wounds came
To me by the thousands, so that I with true
effect
Gain immortal life from His death.[46]

Colore stands in this sonnet as a metaphor for the direct corporeal experience of Salvation; and elsewhere in her poetry it broadens to signify mortal sinning flesh. Colonna repeats the common pictorial trope that associated *colore* with the material rather than the intellectual, and, in doing so, she simultaneously animates the materials of art (*colore* becomes blood) and objectifies the body of Christ (blood becomes the material of art). Her words recall a phrase written by Boschini to describe Titian's painting technique: "with a smear of red paint, almost like a drop of blood." Neither text describes the collapsing of signifier and signified nor the identity of artwork as object and the object represented—which were, of course, the central reformatory concerns. Instead, Colonna, much like Boschini would a century later, developed a phenomenological experience of materiality, violence, and devotion that goes well beyond Michelangelo's disparaging comments, spoken in Francisco de Hollanda's dialogue, that such art elicits tears in women and the elderly.[47] In another of her sonnets, Colonna imagines the transcendence of this embodied experience.

When our thought returns to itself,
And then the mind rises above itself,
So that, made strong by another power
It sees the Lord alive on the harsh Cross,
It rises to such ardor that it not only
believes
Itself to be His dear limb, but even feels
The thorns, the nails, the flagel and in part
His burning flame, only by means of his
living faith.[48]

Vittoria Colonna's poetic experience of the suffering body of Christ reflects an approach also taken by a writer close to Titian, Pietro Aretino. Best known for his satirical and lewd texts, Aretino also penned a prose account of the passion of Christ, *I quattro libri de la humanita di Cristo* (1539), in which he focused on the tortures brought upon the body of Christ.[49] Aretino did not rely upon explicit pictorial metaphors, as he did, for example, when describing in a letter to Titian a view of Venice at sunset; he instead created a smoky, heavy landscape for these sufferings—"a world that changes into fog"—that barely parts and allows the light from torches and a severe brutality and grief that overwhelms the senses.[50] At one point, the author, moved past the point of empathy, forgets his subject matter and his ideas abandon his materials of writing—the pen, the ink, the paper. The environment of Christ's suffering feels as thick as the suffering itself. In this text the world obscured by substantial conditions signifies, rather than conceals, the savagery unfolding within it. We find ourselves plunged into the layers and matter of violated humanity, not unlike our experience of Titian's later paintings.

The beholder's experience of violence and embodiment occurs, these texts imply, when the subject matter encompasses both situations and when materiality and embodiment assert their presence through one another. Reformatory writings often turned to the objecthood of artworks—the paint, the panel, the marble—as a way to minimize the ontological confusion of the object for the thing represented; an understandable approach given the illusionism of Renaissance painting and the long heritage of topoi—the speaking portrait, Zeuxis's grapes, etc.—that praise the artist for transcending the materials of art to give us the depicted thing itself. The poetic texts discussed above, involved in metaphors and not limited to replicating the natural world, seem to be describing a different kind of object of devotion. This object, defined by a coexistence of materiality and embodiment in creating presence, complicates the fundamental assumptions of the image as a perfect copy since affectivity obscures, and nearly overwhelms, the object.

The experience of Titian's later paintings evokes these textual descriptions of embodiment—without necessarily reflecting or participating in a reformatory agenda—because of the similar relationship established between materiality and affectivity. One of the clearest demonstrations occurs, following Boschini's own observations, in the depiction of blood, which, as Boschini observed, nearly collapses signifier and signified.[51] Blood flows down the upper body of Marsyas, following the planarity of the picture more than the contours of the body. Elsewhere, in the Munich *Christ Crowned with Thorns* (plate 16), red paint stains the beaten body of Christ without consistently responding to its depicted form;[52] and red paint functions as a highlight on a rock and a tree in the Escorial *Saint Jerome,* but gives more of a sense of a substance applied to a surface than of immaterial illumination.[53] The treatment of skin—whether suggested through exposed canvas or thick impasto—evokes the thing itself through the texture and thickness of the materials and not through illusion. This relationship between materiality and affectivity, although not limited to blood and flesh in Titian's work, evokes some of the same ontological issues at stake in relics and in contemporary debates over the Real Presence in the Eucharist.[54] In eliciting comparisons with the structure of experience of devotional artifacts, but without explicitly engaging in the reformatory debates, these later paintings assert themselves at the farthest reaches of the art of painting as defined in the Renaissance.[55] Titian's *impresa* of the bear licking her unformed cub reflects as much.[56]

The Violent Materiality of Sculpture

This association between violence and materiality and the embodied mode of reading that resulted were not without precedents in the visual arts, despite their apparent modernity and novelty for mid-sixteenth-century painting. Sculpture had long explored and elicited the affective dimensions and significance of different materials and textures. In Renaissance sculpture, these investigations usually were directed toward the imitation of surfaces and forms found in the natural world—the rotundity of an arm, the curled roughness

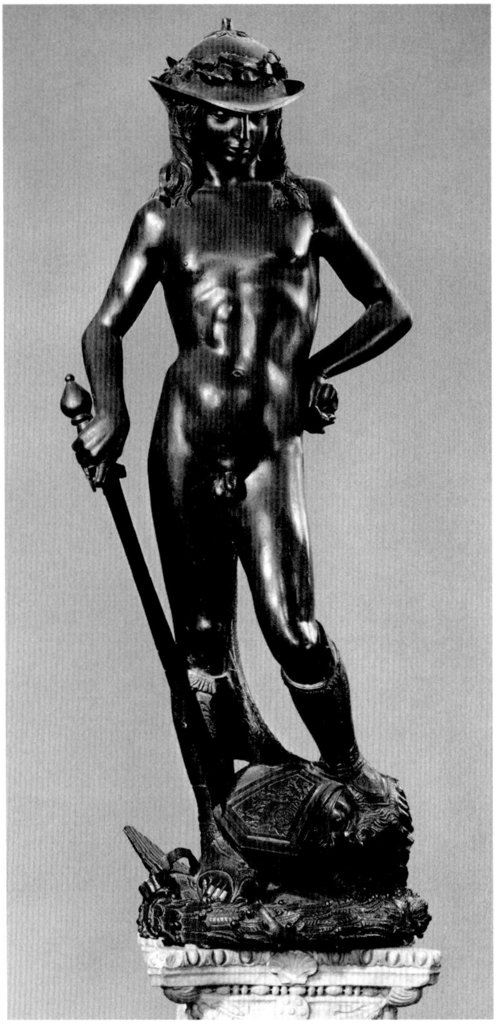

Fig. 43 Donatello, *David,* Museo nazionale del Bargello, Florence

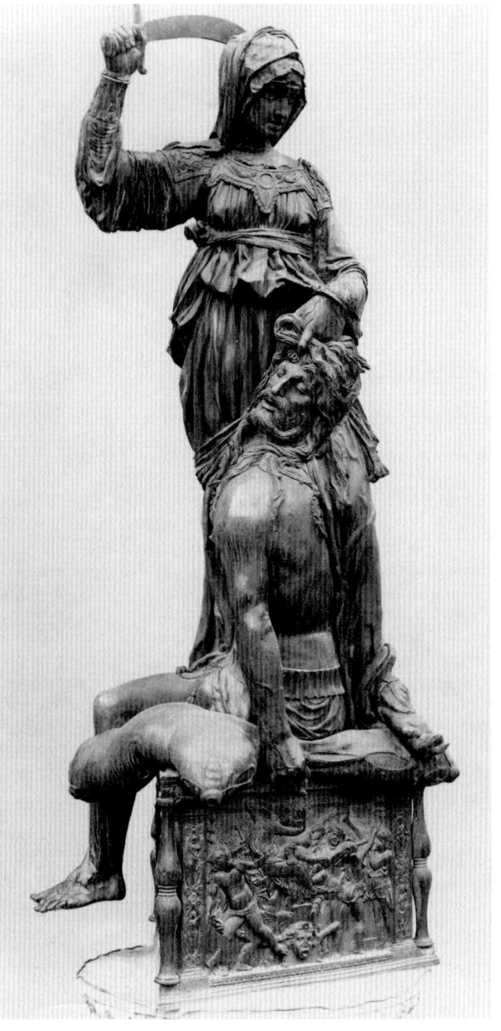

Fig. 44 Donatello, *Judith and Holofernes,* Piazza della Signoria, Florence

of a beard, for example. Such replication limited, at least in the minds of painting theorists, the intellectual ambitions of the art. Sculpture could only represent that which is, they claimed, whereas painting could represent that which seems to be.[57] But what these painting advocates overlooked—or suppressed—was that both arts always bore some relationship to the physicality of the medium, regardless of the degree of mimesis—whether in the polishing of originally rough materials or in the denial of those materials through the verisimilitude of the figure, for example.[58] Not every sculpture drew attention to this fundamental property of the art; but when Italian Renaissance sculptures developed this self-conscious relationship between process, materials, and subject matter, they almost invariably connected these aspects to some thematic of violence.[59]

The Florentine sculptor Donatello produced several sculptures and reliefs that explore this interrelationship of ideas. His bronze statue of the biblical hero David (ca. 1430–32; fig. 43) represents the youth's triumphant decapitation of Goliath, whose head rests beneath the hero's feet; but, as scholars have often remarked, the execution of the group, especially the boy, in shiny, polished bronze, endows the sculpture with an unexpected sensuality for figures just involved in aggressive combat.[60] The areas of contact between victor and defeated extend this suggestion of sensuality: the eagle wing on Goliath's helmet caresses David's thigh, and the curls of Goliath's hair nestle between David's toes.[61] Several art historians have convincingly explained the seemingly amorous relationship with the poetic identity of David as the beloved.[62] Even without the specific interpretative framework, the close association between violence and sensuality often surfaces in situations of deadly aggression.[63] The aggressor and victim interact with an intimacy, however hostile and deadly, that parallels the familiarity of the bodily relationship between lovers—whether or not the assault involves some kind of seduction. We find a similar, although less pronounced, interaction among figures in Donatello's *Judith and Holofernes* (fig. 44), which also establishes a relationship between the violent decapitation and sensuality with the entwining of the two bodies, the entangling of Holofernes' hair around the heroine's fingers, and her foot pressing against the victim's turned hand.[64]

At the other end of the continuum from smooth bronze is the rough, unrefined materiality that invokes not the sensuality of violence but the profound trauma, chaos, and vulnerability that swell in the wake of such savagery.[65] A later series of reliefs executed by Donatello for two pulpits in San Lorenzo depicts episodes from the passion of Christ and the martyrdom of the titular saint with a coarseness and lack of refinement that endow the crowded scenes of brutality with tragic fury (fig. 45).[66] Details such as the facial expressions retain a sketchy, abstract aspect—much like those in Titian's later paintings—and the figures lose any sense of solidity within the thin net of swirling draperies. Contemporaries of Donatello, not unlike those of the Venetian painter, noted the coarseness of the reliefs and attributed the lack of finish to Donatello's old age and failing eyesight rather than to an expressive idiom with a possibly earlier heritage in the artist's career.[67] Many early twentieth-century art historians followed suit and developed their definitions of old-age style on precisely these unexpected formal qualities in Donatello's art.[68]

One of Donatello's great admirers, Michelangelo, appears to have responded to the roughness and apparent incompleteness of his predecessor's work in some of his own earliest sculptures.[69] In the last decade of the fifteenth century, Michelangelo explored the expressive range of sculptural treatment and the affective dimension of different textures by varying such treatment according to the

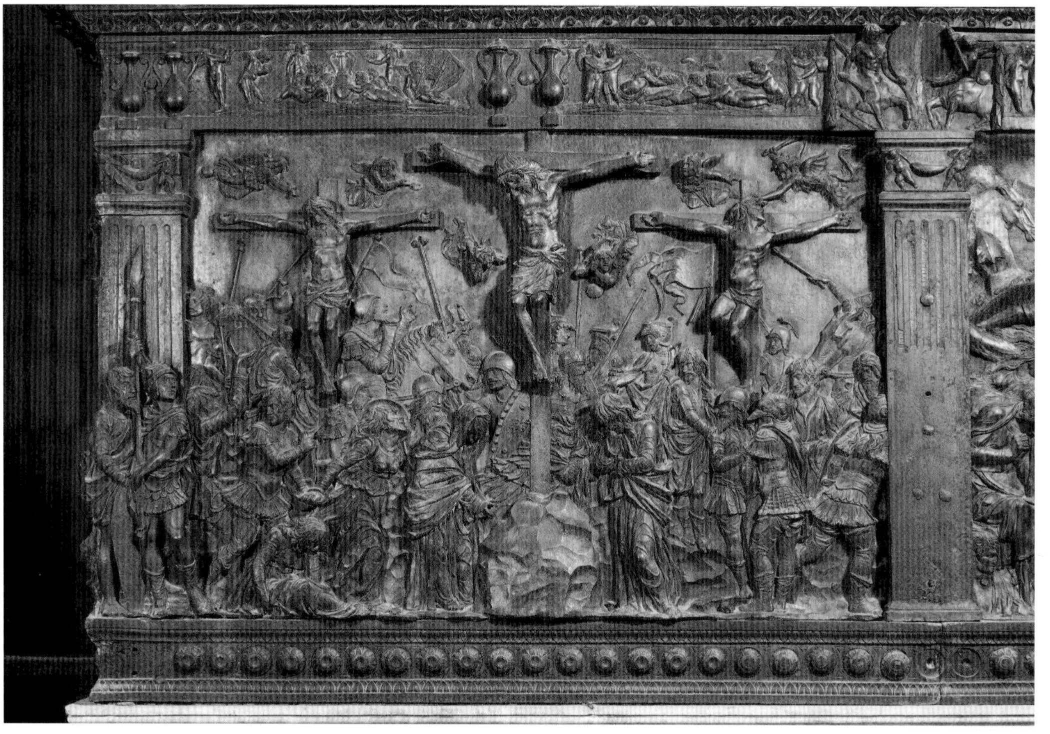

Fig. 45 Donatello, *Crucifixion,* detail of pulpit, San Lorenzo, Florence

subject matter. A scene of violence such as the *Battle of Lapiths and Centaurs* (ca. 1492; fig. 46) shows writhing bodies, some with undifferentiated faces and hands that barely emerge from the abraded block of marble. By contrast, the smooth, polished finish of the nearly contemporary *Bacchus* (ca. 1496–97; Bargello, Florence) and his *Pietà* (ca. 1498–1500; Saint Peter's, Vatican) convey respectively the fleshiness appropriate for the androgynous god and the sweetness and sanctity of a mother contemplating the death of her son and of the devotional moment of the death of Christ.[70] When we consider this early stylistic, textural calibration, the varied handling of statues for other projects, including the slaves for the massive tomb project of Julius II (figs. 47 and 48), bears thematic significance relating to the process of sculpture rather than indicating solely the degree to which these sculptures are finished. The slaves, all of whom remain quite literally connected to sections of their roughly combed marble blocks, embody the violence of their captive situation most obviously through their contorted poses, but also through their enactment of enslavement by means of the materials and techniques of sculpture. The stuff and process of sculpture function as a metaphor for entrapment and release, as has often been noted by viewers who move beyond the restrictive *nonfinito* arguments and by readers of his poetry;[71] but such particularizing of this reading to a neo-Platonic ideal, as routinely happens in such interpretations, limits the relevance of Michelangelo's work to a broader Renaissance tradition—one with apparent quattrocento roots and with significance for Titian's later paintings.

The association between violence and sculptural process in the work of Donatello and Michelangelo clarifies our role as viewers of sculpture by making the medium more obviously performative and experiential. Well into the sixteenth century, sculpture remained an art that, despite its three-dimensionality, was generally thought in terms of planarity. Even though many sculptors executed works "in the round," these statues were often placed against a wall or in a niche and largely seen from one vantage point. There are notable exceptions, such as equestrian monuments in *piazze* and, more significant to this argument, freestanding figure groups, including Donatello's *David and Goliath* and his *Judith,* which are meant to be walked around, with the changing vantage point of the moving spectator contributing to the unfolding of a complex event in which, for example with the *Judith,* seduction leads to death.[72] Donatello transfers this phenomenology of viewing to the San Lorenzo reliefs with the coarseness

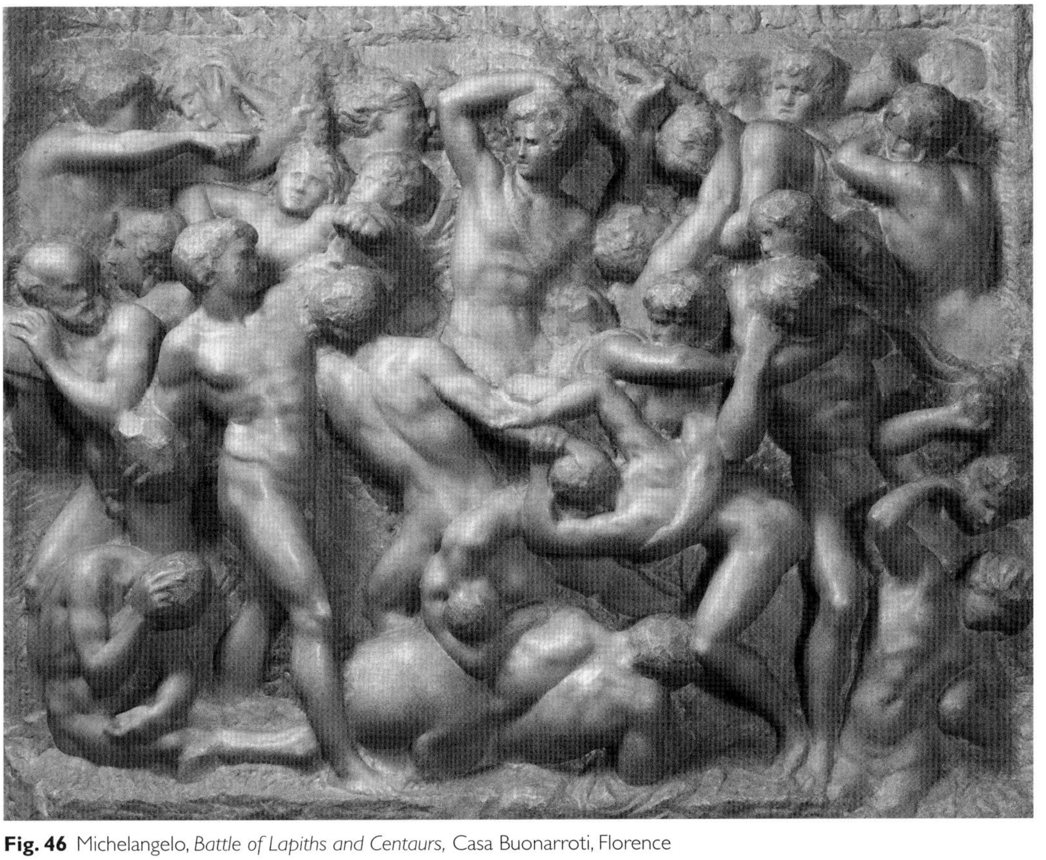

Fig. 46 Michelangelo, *Battle of Lapiths and Centaurs,* Casa Buonarroti, Florence

of their execution. The seemingly simultaneous emergence and disappearance of the figures endow the scene with a spatial and temporal extension that parallels the experience of walking around a freestanding work of art.[73] Michelangelo develops this phenomenology further by also relating this spatial and temporal extension to the act of carving itself. Every aspect of the slaves is directed toward some sense of a process; whether the imagined, continued movement of their struggle or that of the chisel, they embody simultaneously the idea of coming into being and of the elimination of that being.[74]

In an exchange of sonnets involving "Night" from the Medici Tombs, Michelangelo himself emphasizes how his sculpture relies on the bodily experience of the viewers. Speaking for the figure, he writes, "Don't disturb me, please, speak softly," and indicates through her avoidance the possibility of the antidiscursive work of art,[75] the work of art that, rather than narrate itself or convince the beholder of the possibility for dialogue, will not speak of itself to anyone. Although the conception of an antisocial image corresponds to an equally antisocial historical persona associated with the sculptor, it also suggests a shift to an experience of viewing not mediated by language.[76] Turning our interpretative attention to a change in the subjectivity elicited by these sculptures allows us to move away from the change in the subjectivity of

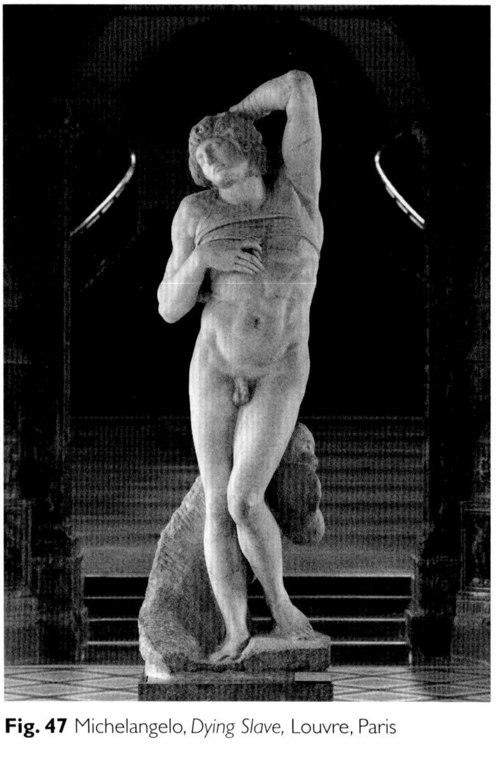

Fig. 47 Michelangelo, *Dying Slave*, Louvre, Paris

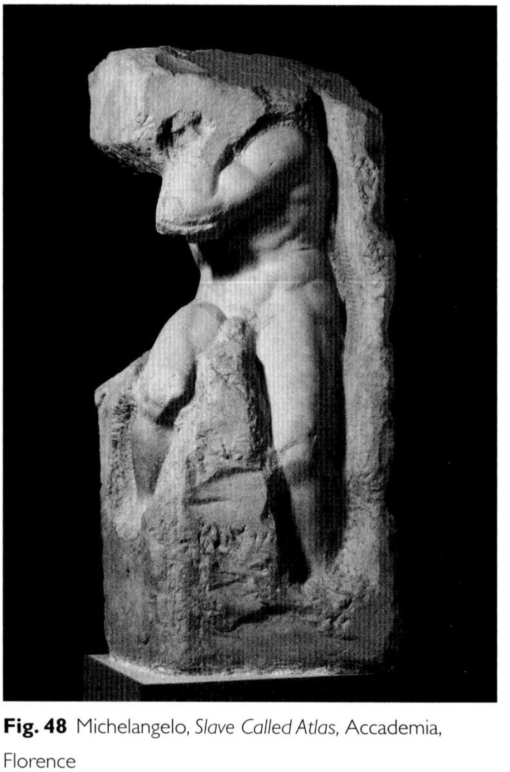

Fig. 48 Michelangelo, *Slave Called Atlas*, Accademia, Florence

the artist assumed in accounts of old-age style.

Subjectivity and Old-Age Style

The figures represented in these sculptures lack the perfect integrity and self-control advanced in contemporary texts on the arts and those closely related texts on behavior and comportment.[77] And yet, as slaves, as victims, as aggressors compromised by savagery, these figures appropriately embody the underside of the ideal. Bakhtin accounts for these figures that extend beyond the societal controls and boundaries as the "grotesque body," in contrast to the "classical body."[78] But this dialectic, although appealing for thinking about the ideal and what the ideal represses, overlooks a complexity in viewing these rougher works and more general complexities in Renaissance subjectivity: the notion of a mutable self and a profound awareness of the potential for a slippery continuum between subject and object.[79] Portraits and half-length images visualized the possibility of this slippage when they addressed beholders directly through gaze and gesture. Such images situated viewers in an "I-thou" exchange in which either participant could inhabit either role.[80] These sculptures push this subjectivity beyond the idea of a shifting with another to the physical, even violent, reality of experience. This could be a manifestation of what Malvezzi means to be "violently seized by the crude."[81]

We find this violent dynamic and dynamic of violence working itself into an image-type invested with the notion of selfhood, Titian's portrait of Doge Andrea

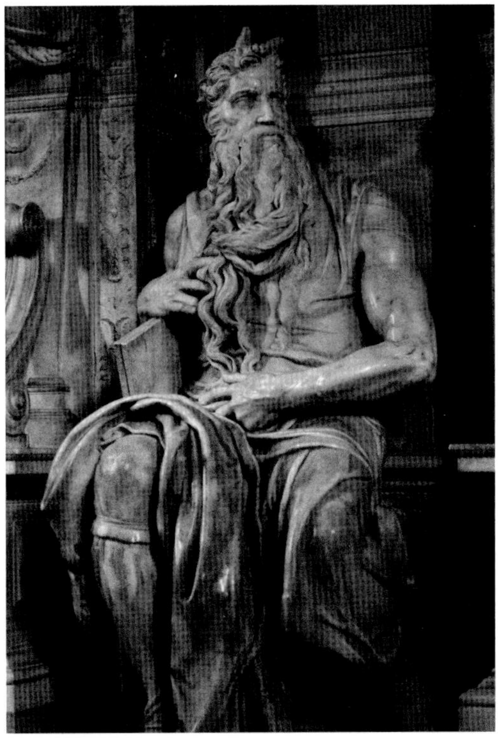

Fig. 49 Michelangelo, *Moses*, San Pietro in Vincoli, Rome

Gritti from the mid-1540s (plate 9).[82] The ample sitter poses with fearsomeness, a *terribilità*—unusual but not entirely out of place for a state portrait—and the active, sometimes loose, brushwork reinforces these qualities.[83] Nothing appears to be able to contain the sitter; his belt, cloak, and cape spread open against his substantial bulk. At the lower edge of the canvas, the strained limits of his physical presence bear a thematic relevance to the presumed structural limits of painting: the overstretched belt and the cape drawn up in a fold establish a lower boundary of the picture that shows the limits of that very boundary. Most likely influenced by Michelangelo's *Moses* (fig. 49; the action of pulling the cape bears a close resemblance to the hand fingering the beard), this depiction shares the potential for breaking out of some form of containment.[84] In the portrait, the cape folded over the belt suggests the idea of an underneath, which the many layers of clothing emphasize. But this underneath, marked by the loosest brushwork in the painting, also suggests the actual layering of paint and canvas that predominates in this work and will continue in Titian's later work.[85]

The motifs of folding and straining—although directed toward the figuration of an historical persona—could be read as indicating a broader thematic in Titian's later conception of painting as being not an art of the surface, but a medium capable of actual, rather than just notional, depth. What makes the Gritti portrait an important moment for this shift is how the attention given to the lower edge reminds us of the now-absent

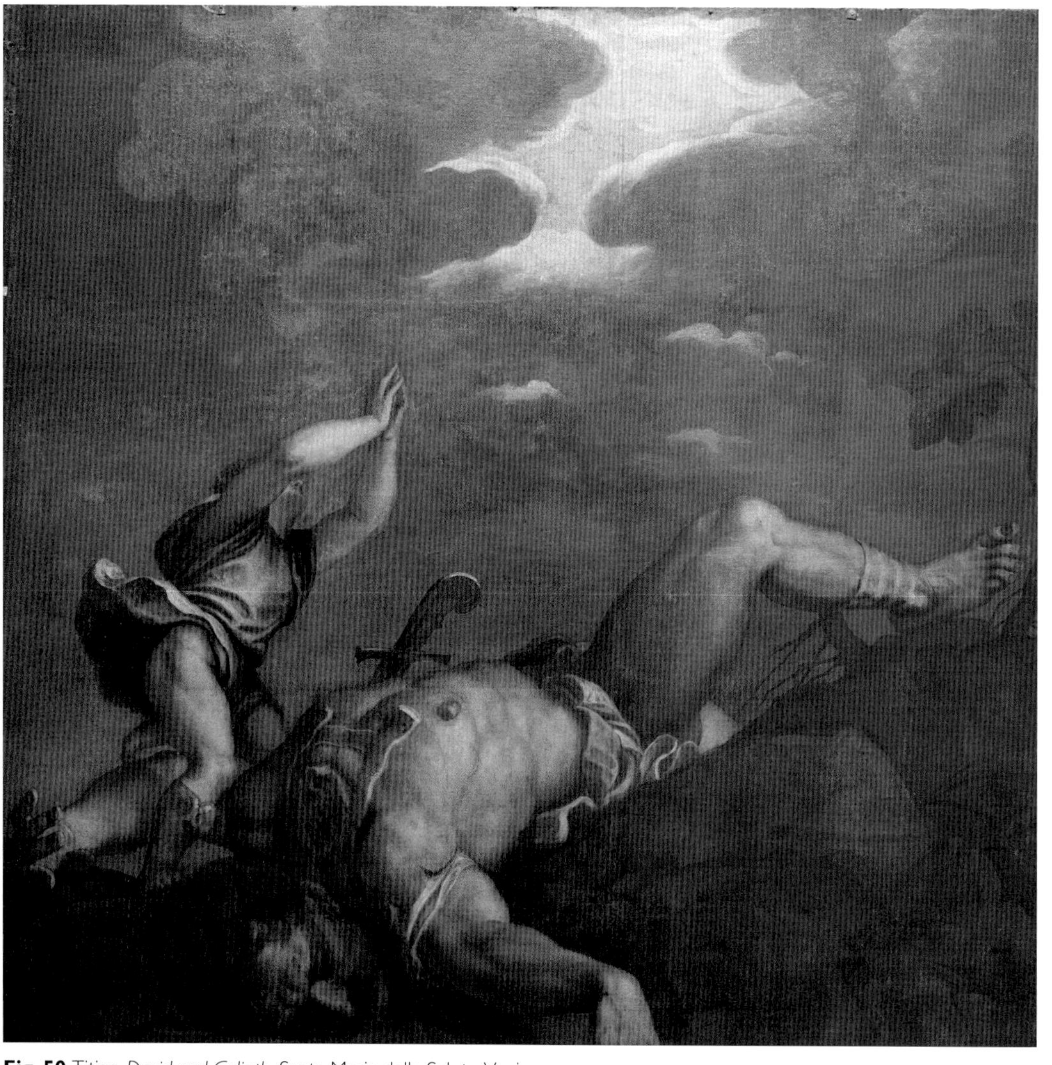

Fig. 50 Titian, *David and Goliath,* Santa Maria della Salute, Venice

formal inventions—such as the parapet—that were developed to delimit the outer boundary or surface of the picture plane at its lower edge.[86] Beholders of this painting establish a less controlled and calibrated relationship with the sitter than in portraits with more defined limits—an appropriate absence of division for those who are invested in and subservient to the authority of the doge. The representation of the doge spills out and collides with, if not overpowers, the viewer's sense of self on a level of imagined physical experience. The depicted and actual physicality of the painting develop the visceral impact that portraits reportedly had generated in antiquity and in the Renaissance.[87]

Deepening the parallels of this experience of painting with that of sculpture is the possibility of associating a lack of containment with the figuration of the real—which in painting also translates into the figuration of the abject.[88] The *Judith* (ca. 1550; plate 15), questionably attributed to Titian,[89] represents the horrific, yet triumphant moment when the Jewish heroine, with the help of her handmaid, hides the decollated head of the Assyrian Holofernes in a sack.[90] As in the portrait of Doge Gritti, the lower edge of the canvas presents a situation of ineffective containment: the heroine places the head, bruised by death, in a sack that appears both to issue from her own dress and to be an extension of the splotched mess of the head. The contrast with the shimmering refinement of execution in the figure of Judith (perhaps the misleading result of an unfortunate restoration) emphasizes the materiality of violence experienced.[91] Titian asserted a similar experience of materiality in another decapitation scene, the *David and Goliath* for the ceiling of Santo Spirito in Isola, now in Santa Maria della Salute (fig. 50).[92] Both situations rely on structural devices to make the viewer feel the impact more directly: in the ceiling painting, the head of Goliath appears, through foreshortening, to be poised to fall on the beholder; in the *Judith,* we wonder if she looks down at the decapitated body, which appears to be on our side of the picture. But unlike those earlier half-length narrative images that divided our space from that of the participants, regardless of their apparent physical involvement with us (fig. 51), here the fragmented sword and uncontained, abject head force an uncomfortable level of involvement.

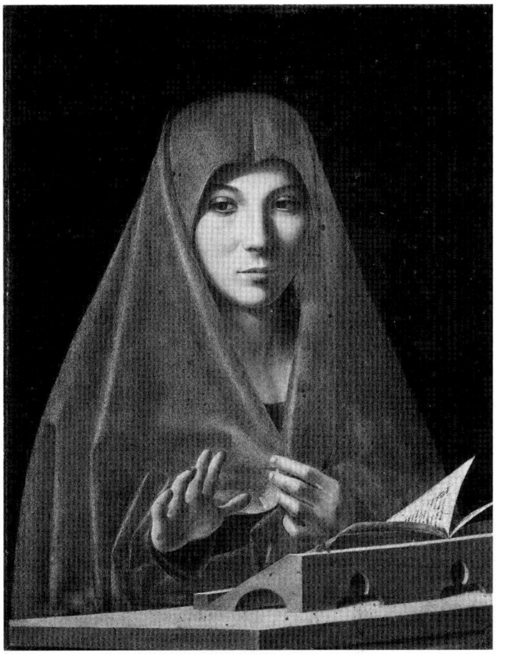

Fig. 51 Antonello da Messina, *The Virgin Annunciate,* Galleria nazionale della Sicilia, Palermo

The stylistic variations in these and Titian's other later works clarify the difference between a mode of painting that associates materiality and violence and one that binds together illusionism and the ideal. Connoisseurs and art historians explain the frequent stylistic discrepancies between different sections of later canvases as signs of studio involvement. Given the contemporary reports and physical evidence of Titian's active and large workshop, this could be a completely plausible explanation.[93] Perhaps studio hands skilled in particular specialties, such as the detailed representation of jewels that we see in the *Flaying* (plate 3), contributed to certain details of the paintings.[94] Or, just as likely, perhaps the stylistic variations in a single canvas reflect a consciousness of how styles mean and how viewers experience them differently. Malvezzi, as we have seen, articulated this for Titian's work and apparently recognized the simultaneity of different styles in a single canvas.[95]

The paintings themselves instruct us on how to interpret these different stylistic modes and, in some cases, on how certain kinds of interpretation fail. Both Donatello's *David* and the *Judith* associate heroism with a polished style and associate a deserved death with a materiality that moves away from illusionism—and the two modes gain significance because of their comparison with one another.[96] Even if the contrast within Titian's *Judith* results from a botched restoration, as some scholars have asserted, the restorer inadvertently heightened a contrast found in Titian's other paintings.[97] Consider the crown of Midas in the *Flaying* mentioned above. The one nearly perfect illusionistic area of the canvas represents a symbol of power, which, emptied of meaning in the case of our flawed judge, transports us to the level of ideas, of signs, rather than any physical reality or experience, such as the unmaking of Marsyas. A similar situation occurs in Titian's St. Louis *Ecce Homo* (ca. 1570–76; fig. 8), in which the jeweled brooch and patterned cloak of Pilate contrast with the roughly executed, nearly transparent drapery covering Christ, his vaporous, dissolving face, and the torch-streaked background.[98] Perfect illusionism, rather than some correction or addition to the loosely executed painting, could be seen as standing out in these examples as the aberration, as the foolish distraction that, in symbolizing something other than itself, unnecessarily diverts our attention from the morass of humanity, from the thickness of being.

Subject matter, and not just audience or other circumstantial contexts, affects how these stylistic variations mean and vice versa. So much of this discussion around Titian's later paintings understandably has concerned degrees of authorship and issues of patronage.[99] But these foci often infuse interpretation with some form of biography. A variation within a single composition or between compositions might relate to decorum of subject. Rhetoricians had long acknowledged and practiced this requirement of style—and even advocated a varied style for a single oration.[100] The concept of decorum, for all of its relevance, privileges subject matter, rather than recognizing that style and subject transform one another as they do in these later paintings. None of these readings supplants each other; but thinking about the violent affects of style rather than an old-age style focuses our attention back on the images themselves. This approach is not without history. It shifts the inquiry from a personal history to a broader history of art.

Retrospection and Materiality in Half-Length Narratives

Indications of the importance of the history of art for Titian's later work come in the relatively high number of compositions that return us to image-types developed and popularized in the early decades of Titian's career.[101] His *Flaying* (plate 3) and *Pietà* (plate 11), as discussed in the previous chapter, adopt a compositional structure similar to that of the static *sacre conversazioni* of quattrocento painting. The source for the *Mellon Venus* (plate 8), those sensuous half-length representations of beauty beholding itself, returns us to early cinquecento pictorial developments. In these returns, the temporal distance allows for a critical distance—sometimes in the form of distortion or undermining of the source—rather than straightforwardly endowing these later paintings with an aura of the past or of authenticity.

Some of Titian's late works encompass both critical and temporal operations when the archaic image-type already embeds within itself the associations of temporality, memory, and substitution. His Prado *Self-Portrait* (fig. 3), as I have argued elsewhere, demonstrates a retrospective impulse with significance for the genre of portraiture in adopting the long-outdated profile pose for his own depiction.[102] The *Self-Portrait* traces personal memory and mortality through the history of art—and specifically of portraiture—and vice versa.

In a related association, Titian's return to the half-length narrative image, a cognate of the portrait and the icon that was nearly archaic by the 1520s, deepens the already complex temporality of this image-type.[103] Early in his career, Titian, influenced by his Venetian and northern Italian predecessors and contemporaries, turned to the half-length narrative form for representations of biblical events (*Christ Carrying the Cross,* ca. 1510, Scuola di San Rocco, Venice;[104] *Tribute Money,* ca. 1516, Staatliche Gemäldegalerie, Dresden[105]) and, less frequently, of events from legendary and historical scenes of conflict, such as his so-called *Il Bravo* (ca. 1515; fig. 52) and *Tarquin and Lucretia* (ca. 1515, Kunsthistorisches Museum, Vienna).[106] Developed by adding figures to the iconic core of medieval cult images, notably the image of the Holy Face or of the Man of Sorrows (fig. 38), these half-length images present through their proximity to the beholder a heightened emotional impact and connection with, and a greater sense of the presence of, the depicted.[107] Often a fictive stone parapet mediates the relationship with the viewer, simultaneously connecting and dividing the structural and temporal dimension of the picture and offering a symbolic context for the collected figures.[108] The intimate experience of viewing involves and implicates the beholder directly, and,

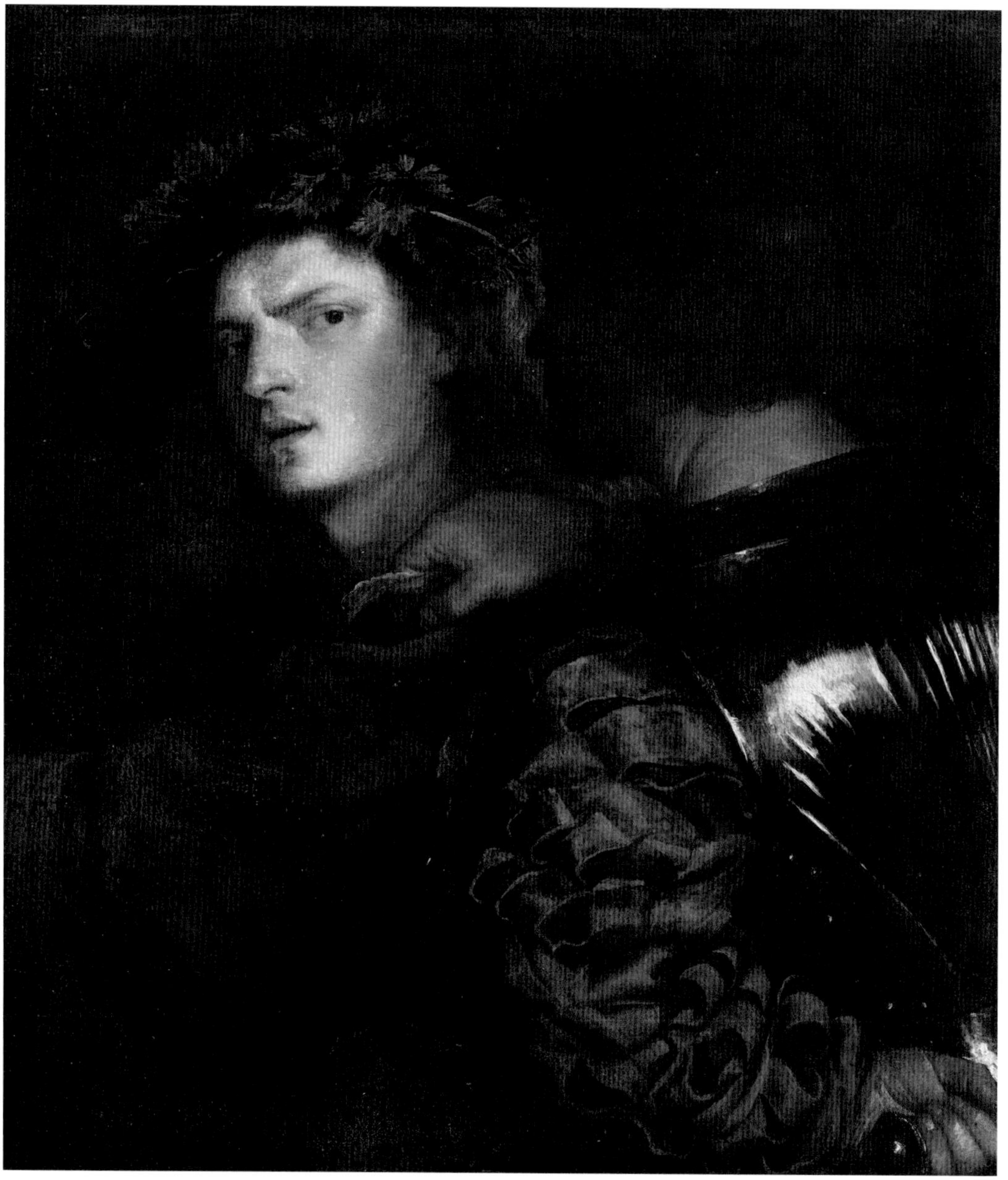

Fig. 52 Titian, *Il Bravo*, Kunsthistorisches Museum, Vienna

consequently, the emotional appeals and situations of the depicted are more deeply felt. Protagonists often appear at their most vulnerable, eliciting empathy and piety from the viewer.

The timeless quality of these half-length scenes, combined with their rich heritage in earlier icons and memorial sculpture and their circulation through multiple replicas, made these images seem archaic or anachronistic even when they were first produced.[109] Renaissance artists explored anachronism through a variety of subjects and mechanisms, especially through the idea of the antique and through icons, that offered a vague history of origins that Renaissance art self-reflexively staged.[110] This gave rise to the depiction of the so-called lost original, or the fictional replication of a historical artifact that never existed but seems as though it should have existed in the past.[111] Without any exact prototype, the half-length narrative creates a multifaceted sense of the past that lives on through the fictive contrast between sculpted monument and the presence of painting; the shared claim of portraits and icons to defy time through referential substitution; and the timelessness of the allusion to some narrative moment. Titian's return to the half-length nearly thirty years after his first involvement with the type adds another stage in this folded history.[112]

Titian's later cinquecento interest in early cinquecento half-length narratives aligns his later devotional paintings with the reformatory interest in archaism.[113] Although their re-emergence appears to conflict with the reformatory interest in dynamic narratives and full-length representations of saints, these abbreviated images could be seen as drawing upon the new ideals of devotional simplicity, directness, and piety. Most of these paintings were sent directly to the Spanish royal family or ultimately arrived and remained in Spain, suggesting that these focused images of suffering appealed to the pious ideals of those deeply committed to the Catholic faith.[114] Perhaps they reminded Spanish viewers of a simpler, more devout past exemplified by earlier devotional half-lengths, especially those by Northern painters—one of which in Venetian possession in the sixteenth century, the *Ecce Homo* by Quentin Massys, in all likelihood served as an influential source for Titian's Prado and St. Louis *Ecce Homo* (plate 18 and fig. 8).[115] Rather than explicitly supporting the Church's agenda, if at all, these paintings explore the abjection, violence, and embodiment that attended the passion of Christ and that a minority of reform writers discussed, as we have seen, but that had been suppressed in art by the Renaissance valorization of perfect likeness found in instances of the *acheiropoetoi,* the "images not made by human hands" (fig. 53).

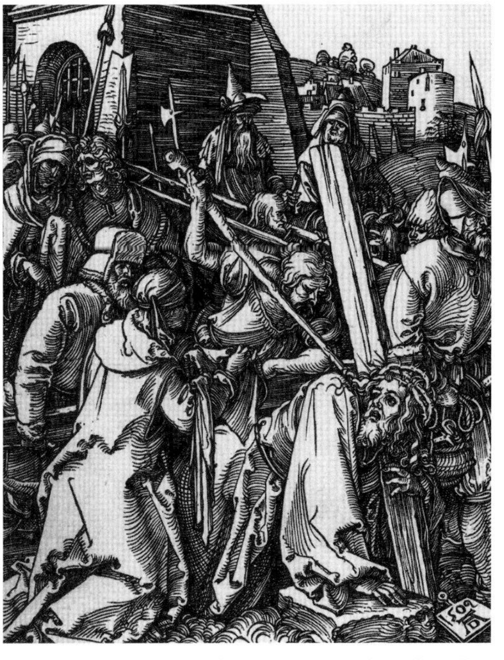

Fig. 53 Albrecht Dürer, *Christ Bearing the Cross,* from *The Small Passion,* British Museum, London

Titian's later half-length images appear to conflict in every detail with these miraculous images. Obviously made with human hands and not limited to the face of Christ, the half-length images contrast with the acheiropoetic circumstances and the isolation of the Holy Face. Renaissance artists focused on the image and the episode as incidents of the perfect copy, oftentimes by acknowledging the inadequacy of their attempts to replicate that perfect copy or by celebrating the potential of new media, such as oil paint, to approach the miraculous type (as in the case of Jan van Eyck and Dürer [fig. 35]).[116] The self-created, autonomous *vera icon,* with its divine perfection, also embeds within itself associations with the corporeal and the incarnate Christ, especially through the Western Church's most famous example of the *sudarium* of Saint Veronica: the direct contact with his body and his bodily secretions—the sweat, blood, and tears—produced the image of the Holy Face on Saint Veronica's veil (fig. 53).[117] It registers an imprint of Christ's body through the abjection of his body. The idea of the image as imprint and trace—and not its actual appearance—evokes the active brushwork in Titian's later depictions of Christ's body, especially when framed by the historical conditions of archaism.[118] The brushstrokes register an instance of contact that appears both to be happening and to have already happened, figuring a simultaneity of opposing temporal conditions which the image-type itself reflects in its affirmation of presence distilled through the past.[119] As indexes both in the present and seemingly at one remove from their moment of creation, the brushstrokes figure situations of contact that emphasize the materiality of devotion and violence and not just the presence of the maker.

For all of the structural similarities between the fifteenth-century half-lengths and Titian's later versions, the loose brushwork in the latter brings to the surface the associations with embodiment and materiality embedded, but not necessarily explicitly developed, in the cultic source. In those earlier examples, viewers beheld the body of Christ, in all of its physiognomic detail, and reflected on his sacrifice. Even when circumstantial figures later filled out the single-figure composition, the attention given to the body by those figures remained largely meditative and reverential. As the surrounding figures expressed more extreme emotional reactions to the figure of Christ, the wounded body of Christ appealed more directly to the viewer by extending illusionistically into the space of the viewer. In Giovanni Bellini's Brera *Pietà* (fig. 32), the wounds in the extremities appear to project beyond a delimiting barrier—to which is appended a fictive *cartellino* with an affective appeal—for the viewer to see and to imagine feeling.[120] This development of implied contact and outreach in half-length narratives parallels that occurring contemporaneously in portraiture. But in both image-types—the portrait and the half-length—this connection with the depicted remains arrested on or limited by the surface. Foreshortening and formal inventions, such as the parapet, encourage and facilitate a shifting between subject and object. The beholder imagines alternating between these two roles—

as suggested by the many written responses to Renaissance portraits.[121] The emergence of a mode of painting such as Titian's encourages, by contrast, a conflation or a merging between subject and object through the thickness of materials and the lack of resemblance. The intimacy of the half-length type actually pulls us closer to the images,

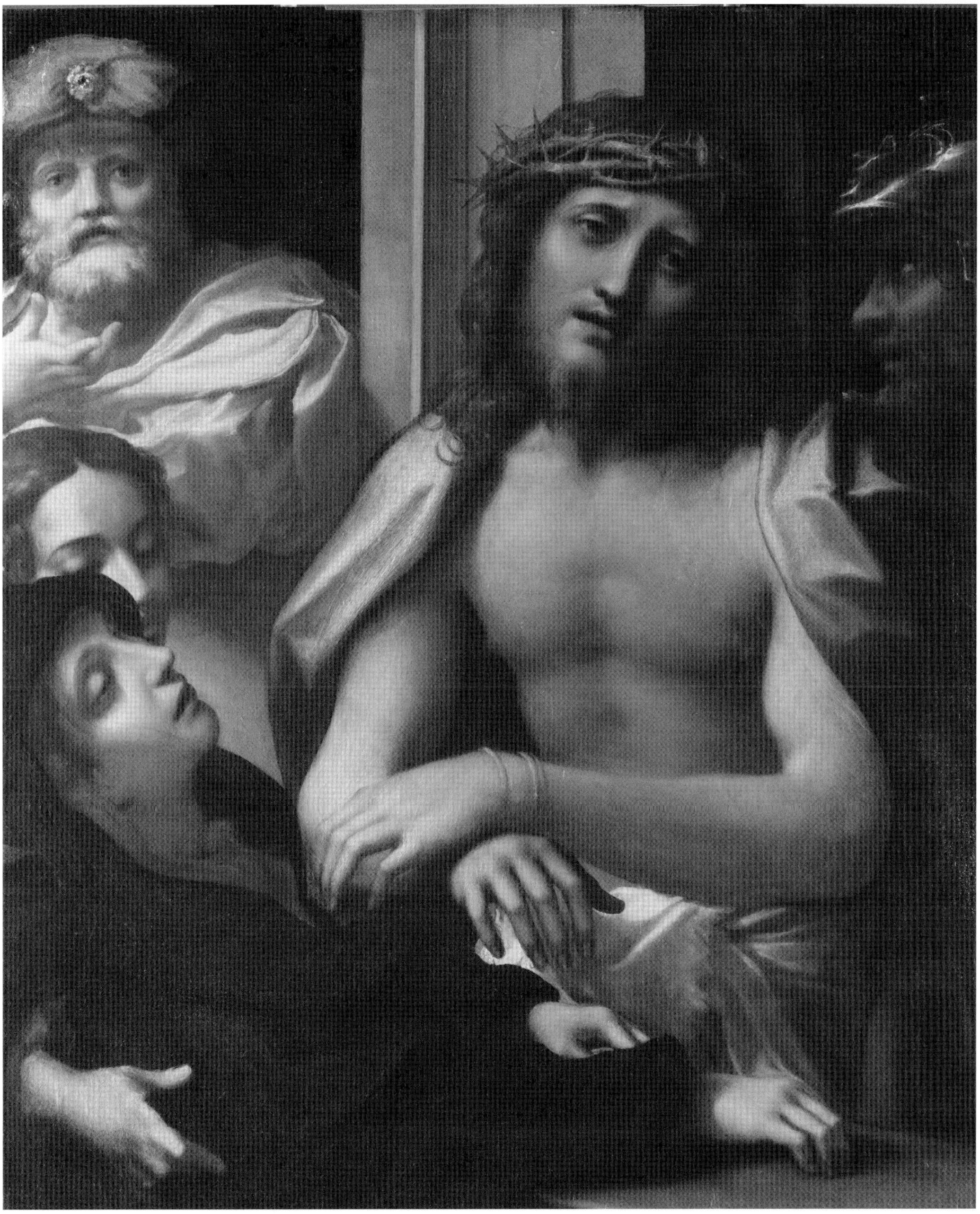

Fig. 54 Correggio, *Ecce Homo,* National Gallery, London

and the materiality of the devotional figure is conveyed through the thickness of painting rather than solely through the depiction of facial expressions or tears (fig. 8 and plate 18).

The depiction of weight, labor, and contact in these half-lengths also contributes to an empathy developed through the body. The cross in *Christ Carrying the Cross* (plate 14)—not merely an accessory as in earlier representations, despite its symbolism as the weight of sin—requires effort to move it, as the flattened beard of Simon of Cyrene suggests.[122] Another scene from the Passion, the Prado *Ecce Homo* (plate 18), emphasizes the physical presence of Christ's body at a moment associated with visual display, when Pilate presents Christ to the Jews and Romans.[123] An awkward figure not usually present in the half-length abbreviation of the narrative turns his back to us and touches the left forearm of Christ while he looks at Pilate. He recalls one of the figures from the crowd that appears somewhat isolated in an earlier narrative version of the event (fig. 40).[124] Similarly dressed and also seen from behind, the earlier figure leads us to the vision of suffering and, with his unseen face, forms a *contrapposto* with the screaming youth who receives instinctive consolation from his dog. The half-length figure, by contrast, crowds the scene, appearing too close to the displayed body not to be noticed by Pilate and the executioner. He reminds us—especially in the Prado version, in which he gazes directly at Christ—of awkward figures involved in a visionary experience, which seems thematically proximate to a story of beholding according to Correggio's *Ecce Homo* (fig. 54).[125] Only Titian's figure links his viewing to touching, reminding us of the material presence of Christ's human body through the parallel post-Passion encounter between Thomas and the resurrected Christ but also the torturers' base interest in body as proof of the absence of divinity. Titian's later version of the *Ecce Homo* (fig. 8) omits the searching figure and offers us the experience of the beaten, marked, and disappearing body of Christ.

Regardless of whether we consider these later half-lengths to be executed by Titian and/or his studio, the interest in the half-length type appears to be a deliberate return to the history of Renaissance art.[126] But this historical interest, while a central part of reformatory directives in the arts, pervades so many of Titian's later works—sacred and profane—and finds itself so changed in the final works that the past seems present, only to be left behind for something different. Panofsky appears to sense a similar operation when he observes: "Just as Titian's last religious painting, the *Pietà* in the Accademia, is in a sense a farewell to the antique and Michelangelo, so is his last mythological painting, the *Nymph and Shepherd* in the Vienna Museum—likewise unfinished—a farewell to the antique and Giorgione."[127] In their farewells, the paintings do not artificially demarcate history, as Panofsky's analysis and broader investment in linear time would imply; but, as we have seen, they make use of history as a means to create something immediate that compels the viewer to exist in the now, with all of its threatening changeability. The viewer "violently seized by the rough" can, it seems, only experience the attack in the present moment. In representing the immediacy of the perils and vulnerabilities of humanity, Titian's later painting significantly strays from the humanist ideals advocated for Renaissance painting. The idealized, perfect body appropriated from the ancient past has finally been sacrificed for the body that unmakes itself again and again in the present.

NOTES

Introduction

1. "Ell'è, dunque, un piano coperto di campi di colori, in superficie o di tavola o di muro o di tela, intorno a' lineamenti detti di sopra, i quali per virtù di un buon disegno di linee girate circondano la figura." Giorgio Vasari, *Le vite de' più eccellenti pittori, scultori, ed architettori: Nelle redazioni 1550 e 1568,* ed. Paola Barocchi, 6 vols. (Florence: Sansoni, 1966–69 [vols. 1–3, 5, 6]; Florence: Studi per edizione scelte, 1967 [vol. 4]), 1:113. Vasari's definition generalizes and makes more practical the metaphorical association of the mirror with painting, which Alberti, in his *On Painting,* implied in his naming Narcissus as the inventor of the art. Leon Battista Alberti, *On Painting,* ed. and trans. Cecil Grayson (London: Penguin, 1991), ¶26, p. 61. Paolo Pino, a painting theorist contemporary with Vasari, repeats the Tuscan's emphasis on the flatness of the picture through the metaphor of the mirror. See Pino, *Dialogo di pittura* (1548), in *Trattati d'arte del Cinquecento fra manierismo e Controriforma,* ed. Paola Barocchi (Bari: G. Laterza, 1960–62), 1:100.

2. Pliny the Elder, *Natural History,* 35.64–66. Renaissance art theorists cited these stories as exemplary of different aspects of the art, whether the universality of painting (Benedetto Varchi, "Della maggioranza delle arti—Disputa II," in Barocchi, *Trattati d'arte del Cinquecento,* 1:37–38), the vividness of color (Lodovico Dolce, *Dialogo della pittura* [1557], in *Dolce's "Aretino" and Venetian Art Theory of the Cinquecento,* ed. and trans. Mark W. Roskill [New York: New York University Press, 1968], 150–51), or the honor in practicing the art (Pino, *Dialogo di pittura,* 112).

3. For the invention of perspective and recessional motifs, see, as an introductory survey, Samuel Y. Edgerton, *The Renaissance Rediscovery of Linear Perspective* (New York: Basic Books, 1975). On the significance of *rilievo,* especially in the Tuscan tradition, and its relationship to Pliny's stories, see David Summers, *Michelangelo and the Language of Art* (Princeton: Princeton University Press, 1981), 41–55. Stephen Bann considers more generally the role in Western art of the story of Zeuxis's painting of grapes in *The True Vine: On Visual Representation and the Western Tradition* (Cambridge: Cambridge University Press, 1989).

4. Dolce (*Dialogo della pittura,* 130–31) warns against solely relying on direct experience, especially in the representation of beautiful women.

5. The phrase first appears in Cennino Cennini's *Il Libro dell'arte,* where he writes: "And this is an art called painting, for which one ought to have fantasy and skill of hand, to find things not seen, hidden in the shadow of natural ones, and retrace them with the hand, thus demonstrating that that which is not is [quello che non è, sia]." Cennini, *Il Libro dell'arte,* ed. Franco Brunello (Vicenza: N. Pozza, 1971), 3–4. The translation cited here is given by Mary Pardo, "The Subject of Savoldo's *Magdalene,*" *Art Bulletin* 71 (1989): 84; the work has also been translated by Daniel V. Thompson Jr. as *The Craftsman's Handbook: The Italian "Il Libro dell'Arte"* (New York: Dover, 1960). Closer to the time period under consideration in this study is Paolo Pino's statement in his *Dialogo di pittura* that "painting is poetry itself, that is to say invention, which makes that which is not, appear to be" (115). See also Summers, *Michelangelo,* 41–55.

6. Vasari articulated the role of *maniera* and *licenza* in cinquecento art when comparing artists of the "modern manner" to those of the quattrocento in his preface to the third part of his *Lives,* 4:3–13. On Vasari's conception, see Patricia Rubin, *Giorgio Vasari: Art and

History (New Haven: Yale University Press, 1995), 236. *Maniera* referred to an artist's manner or style and not necessarily to a stylistic mode that we think of as mannerism. Philip Sohm clarifies this distinction in his study *Style in the Art Theory of Early Modern Italy* (Cambridge: Cambridge University Press, 2001), 87–100. For a discussion of *licenza* in architecture, see Alina Payne, *The Architectural Treatise in the Italian Renaissance: Architectural Invention, Ornament, and Literary Culture* (Cambridge: Cambridge University Press, 1999), 13–33. Excessive *dimostrazioni dell'arte* received criticism from painting theorists and religious reformers who were concerned with decorum. See, for example, Giovanni Andrea Gilio da Fabriano, *De gli errori, a degli abusi dei pittori . . .* (1564), in *Trattati d'arte del Cinquecento,* 2:5–115. But such criticisms of the extreme in the visual arts had Alberti as their source. See Alberti, *On Painting,* esp. book 2, ¶44, p. 80; and also Summers, *Michelangelo,* 90–92.

7. Gabriele Paleotti, *Discorso intorno alle immagini sacre e profane* (1582), in Barocchi, *Trattati d'arte del Cinquecento,* 2:171–72. Consequently, there was a rise in popularity of archaism and of pictures within pictures as way to isolate the image as object. On archaism, see Stuart Lingo, "The Capuchins and the Art of History: Retrospection and Reform in the Arts in Late Renaissance Italy" (Ph.D. diss., Harvard University, 1998); Alexander Nagel, *Michelangelo and the Reform of Art* (Cambridge: Cambridge University Press, 2000), esp. 1–24. On metapictorial motifs, see Hans Belting, *Likeness and Presence: A History of the Image Before the Era of Art,* trans. Edmund Jephcott (Chicago: University of Chicago Press, 1994), 458–90; Victor I. Stoichita, *The Self-Aware Image: An Insight into Early Modern Meta-painting,* trans. Anne-Marie Glasheen (New York: Cambridge University Press, 1997), 67–102; originally published as *L'instauration du tableau: Mètapeinture à l'aube des temps modernes* (Paris: Méridiens Klincksieck, 1993).

8. Until the mid-cinquecento, painting theorists suppressed any discussion of the practice of painting in order to elevate the art and to compete with poetry. Pino (1548), who was sensitive to the northern Italian, and especially Venetian, mode of painting, acknowledged the work of painting by comparing the physical gestures of the painter to those performed by musicians in the making of their art. See Pino, *Dialogo di pittura,* 107. Pino might have been thinking about Plato's differentiation of imitation in the *Republic,* 10.595c. Dolce (*Dialogo della pittura,* 150–55), in including *colorito* (verb) rather than *colore* (noun) in his tripartite division of painting, implicitly recognized the importance of handling.

9. Translated in David Rosand, "Titian and the Critical Tradition," in *Titian: His World and Legacy* (New York: Columbia University Press, 1982), 22. Vasari writes: "Ma è ben vero che il modo di fare che tenne in queste ultime è assai diferente dal far suo da giovane: con ciò sia che le prime son condotte con una certa finezza e diligenza incredibile, e da essere vedute da presso e da lontano, e queste ultime, condotte di colpi, tirate via di grosso e con macchie, di maniera che da presso non si possono vedere e di lontano appariscono perfette. E questo modo è stato cagione che molti, volendo in ciò immitare e mostrare di fare il pratico, hanno fatto di goffe pitture: e ciò adiviene perché, se bene a molti pare che elle siano fatte senza fatica, non è così il vero e s'ingannano, perché si conosce che sono rifatte, e che si è ritornato loro addosso con i colori tante volte che la fatica vi si vede. E questo modo sì fatto è giudizioso, bello e stupendo, perché fa parere vive le pitture e fatte con grande arte, nascondendo le fatiche" (*Le vite,* 6:166).

10. Vasari's allusion to Horace returns us to the *locus classicus* of the comparison between painting and poetry: "Poetry is like painting. There is a kind which appeals to you more when you stand near and others when you step back farther" (*Ars poetica,* 361–62). Gombrich discusses both Horace's passage and Vasari's description of Titian's later style in his *Art and Illusion: A Study in the Psychology of Pictorial Representation* (Princeton: Princeton University Press, 1960), 191–95. Both passages support Gombrich's own approach to illusion and materiality as inversely related.

11. Mary of Hungary advised Mary Tudor to look at the portrait of Philip II (now in the Prado) from a distance. Philip remarked of his own portrait that he had hoped for more finish. See Miguel Falomir, *Tiziano,* exh. cat. (Madrid: Museo Nacional del Prado, 2003), 218.

12. For the full text of Aretino's 1545 letter to Cosimo, see *Lettere sull'arte di Pietro Aretino,* ed. Fidenzio Pertile and Ettore Camesasca (Milan: Edizione del Milone, 1957), cclxv, 107–8. The portrait is in the Palazzo Pitti, Florence.

13. Diego Guzmán de Silva and the marquis of Ayamonte voiced concerns over Titian's limited ability in his old age, but still thought of Titian as a superior artist. For the correspondence between the two, see Matteo Mancini, *Tiziano e le corti d'Asburgo nei documenti degli archivi spagnoli* (Venice: Istituto

veneto di scienze, lettere ed arti, 1998), 409–14; Luigi Ferrarino, *Tiziano e la corte di Spagna nei documenti dell'Archivio Generale di Simancas* (Madrid: Istituto italiano di cultura, 1975), 125. Many art historians have interpreted these documents as confirmation that these later paintings were unfinished, or in some way falling below Renaissance standards. References to these studies appear throughout this book; however, one of the most vocal supporters of this view is Charles Hope. See his *Titian* (New York: Harper and Row, 1980); and somewhat in the same vein, see Hans Ost, *Tizian-Studien* (Cologne: Böhlau, 1992). By contrast, Rodolfo Pallucchini, *Tiziano* (Florence: G. C. Sansoni, 1969), 1:151–57, summarizes positive assessments of Titian's later work. For the influence of modern painting on concurrent interpretations of Titian's work, see especially Theodor Hetzer, *Tizian: Geschichte seiner Farbe* (Frankfurt am Main: V. Klostermann, 1935). Most influential for a consideration of Titian's later work outside of the "finito-nonfinito dialectic" has been that of David Rosand, who drew a connection between materiality, represented corporeality, and the presence of the painter. See his *Titian* (New York: H. N. Abrams, 1978); "Titian and the Eloquence of the Brush," *Artibus et Historiae* 2, no. 3 (1981): 85–96; *The Meaning of the Mark: Leonardo and Titian* (Lawrence: Spencer Museum of Art, University of Kansas, 1988); and "La mano de Tiziano," in *Tiziano: Técnicas y restauraciones, Actas del Simposium Internacional celebrado en el Museo Nacional del Prado* (Madrid: Museo Nacional del Prado, 1999), 127–38. Other recent considerations of Titian's later work include Sylvia Ferino-Pagden, ed., *L'ultimo Tiziano e la sensualità della pittura* (Venice: Marsilio Editori, 2008), and especially Bernard Aikema, "Pittura di macchia: Tiziano e gli altri fra Venezia e l'Europa," 89–99; Falomir, *Tiziano;* Daniela Bohde, *Haut, Fleisch und Farbe: Körplicherkeit und Materialität in den Gemälden Tizians* (Emsdetten: Edition Imorde, 2002); Valeska von Rosen, *Mimesis und Selbstbezüglichkeit in Werken Tizians* (Emsdetten: Edition Imorde, 2001); Una Roman D'Elia, *The Poetics of Titian's Religious Painting* (Cambridge: Cambridge University Press, 2005), esp. 128–30; Thomas Puttfarken, *Titian and Tragic Painting: Aristotle's Poetics and the Rise of the Modern Artist* (New Haven: Yale University Press, 2005); Rebecca Zorach, "Despoiled at the Source," *Art History* 22, no. 2 (1999): 244–69; Paula Carabell, "Image and Identity, Two Case Studies: Michelangelo and Titian" (Ph.D. diss., Columbia University, 1994), and "*Finito* and *Non-finito* in Titian's Last Paintings," *Res* 28 (1995): 77–93.

14. This unresolved relationship is noted in another context by Michael Baxandall, *The Limewood Sculptors of Renaissance Germany* (New Haven: Yale University Press, 1980), 123.

15. For the interrelationship between medium and subject matter, which Gombrich separates in his arguments in *Art and Illusion,* see Michael Podro, "Fiction and Reality in Painting," in *Funktionen des Fiktiven,* ed. Dieter Henrich and Wolfgang Iser, Poetik und Hermeneutik 10 (Munich: Wilhelm Fink, 1983), 225–37; and more recently, in Podro's *Depiction* (New Haven: Yale University Press, 1998), 6–8.

16. Marco Boschini, *La carta del navegar pitoresco: Edizione critica con la "Breve instruzione" premessa alle "Ricche minere della pittura veneziana,"* ed. Anna Pallucchini (Venice: Istituto per la collaborazione culturale, 1966). Philip Sohm offers an invaluable analysis of the often confusing texts in his *Pittoresco: Marco Boschini, His Critics, and Their Critiques of Painterly Brushwork in Seventeenth- and Eighteenth-Century Italy* (Cambridge: Cambridge University Press, 1991).

17. Paolo Berdini, *The Religious Art of Jacopo da Bassano* (Cambridge: Cambridge University Press, 1997), 27–29, 103–20.

18. Translation mine. "Vedendolo tutto abbagliato ed incomprensibile, non discernendo più né forma né sostanza, di modo che, quasi temendo d'aversi inavertentemente troppo avicinato a quella rappresentante Divinità." Boschini, *Breve instruzione,* 726–27.

19. "Chè non se puol tocar Dio con le man" (ibid., 202). For the entire description of the painting, see 200–204.

20. Paolo Berdini (*Religious Art of Jacopo da Bassano,* 27–29, 34–35) interprets this passage in relationship to the painter's visualization of textual expansion and to Jacopo's selective brushwork.

21. In articulating a formalism of technique, I am following the materialist formalism articulated by Yve-Alain Bois, which incorporates into a formalist analysis aspects of painting such as facture and its dissolution of form that traditionally have been excluded from formalism more generally. See *Painting as Model* (Cambridge, Mass.: MIT Press, 1990), xviii–xix, 249–52, and "Whose Formalism?" *Art Bulletin* 78 (1996), 9–12. Other scholars whose work (interestingly on Manet, whose paintings engage related questions of facture and illusion) bridges the domain of formalism and its exclusions include Carol Armstrong (*Manet Manette*

[New Haven: Yale University Press, 2002]) and Jean Clay ("Ointments, Makeup, Pollen," *October* 27 [1983]: 3–44).

22. For the consideration of the role of the "index" in art history, see Mieke Bal and Norman Bryson, "Semiotics and Art History," *Art Bulletin* 73, no. 2 (1991): 190; Rosalind E. Krauss, "Notes on Index," in *The Originality of the Avant-Garde and Other Modernist Myths* (Cambridge, Mass.: MIT Press, 1985), 196–216. Most considerations of the indexicality of facture foreground the presence of the painter. James Elkins addresses the failure of semiotics in interpreting individual visual marks as part of his larger project of asserting the irreducibility of paintings to texts and text-based methods. "Marks, Traces, *Traits,* Contours, *Orli,* and *Splendores:* Nonsemiotic Elements in Pictures," *Critical Inquiry* 21 (Summer 1995): 822–60. An exchange between Elkins and Mieke Bal resulted from this article. Mieke Bal, "Critical Response I: Semiotic Elements in Academic Practices," *Critical Inquiry* 22 (Spring 1996): 573–89; James Elkins, "Critical Response II: What Do We Want Pictures to Be? Reply to Mieke Bal," *Critical Inquiry* 22 (Spring 1996): 590–602. See, by contrast, Hubert Damisch, *A Theory of /Cloud/: Toward a History of Painting,* trans. Janet Lloyd (Stanford: Stanford University Press, 2002), 2–37.

23. Boschini, *Breve instruzione,* 712.

24. David Rosand, *Painting in Sixteenth-Century Venice: Titian, Veronese, Tintoretto* (Cambridge: Cambridge University Press, 1997), 10–25. See also Sohm, *Pittoresco,* 3–5. Recent technical examinations have revealed the multiple textures given to different layers of Venetian paintings, including stippling and fingerprints. See Elke Oberthaler and Elizabeth Walmsley, "Technical Studies of Painting Methods," in *Bellini, Giorgione, Titian, and the Renaissance of Venetian Painting,* ed. David Alan Brown and Sylvia Ferino-Pagden, exh. cat. (New Haven: Yale University Press, 2006), 286–300; and Carmen Garrido, "Aproximaciones a la técnica de Tiziano," in Falomir, *Tiziano,* 93–109.

25. Light and its diffusion became important themes in earlier oil painting. For this and the introduction of oil paint to Italy, see Millard Meiss, "Jan van Eyck and the Italian Renaissance," in *Venezia e l'Europa (Atti del XVIII Congresso internazionale di storia dell'arte)* (Venice: Arte veneta, 1956), 58–69; reprinted in Meiss, *The Painter's Choice: Problems in the Interpretation of Renaissance Art* (New York: Harper and Row, 1976), 19–35. See also Rosand, *Painting in Sixteenth-Century Venice,* 11–12. Vasari (*Le vite,* 1:132–34) credits Hubert and Jan van Eyck with developments in oil painting and claims that Antonello da Messina introduced these methods to Italian painting from his travels to the Netherlands. Antonello most likely gained familiarity with these methods through Netherlandish paintings in Naples. See Joanne Wright, "Antonello da Messina: The Origins of His Style and Technique," *Art History* 3 (1980): 41–60.

26. Vasari (*Le vite,* 4:41–47) criticizes Giorgione for this elimination of drawing. Recent exhibitions on Venetian painting have demonstrated that these painters relied on drawings more than previously thought by scholars. See Brown and Ferino-Pagden, *Bellini, Giorgione, Titian,* 286–300.

27. Michael Baxandall describes an "intentional flux" in painting that contradicts the idea of a fixed intention in *Patterns of Intention: On the Historical Explanation of Pictures* (New Haven: Yale University Press, 1985), 62–63.

28. Most of these situations, which are discussed more fully in chapter 1, affirm the imposition of form on formless matter or the recognition of form within matter. See, for example, Leonardo da Vinci, *Treatise on Painting [Codex Urbinas Latinus 1270],* trans. A. Philip McMahon (Princeton: Princeton University Press, 1956), para. 256, 38v; para. 261, 62r. For the image made by chance, see H. W. Janson, "The 'Image Made by Chance' in Renaissance Thought," in *De Artibus Opuscula XL: Essays in Honor of Erwin Panosfky,* ed. Millard Meiss (New York: New York University Press, 1961), 254–66. Vasari (*Le vite,* 1:111) introduces and then restricts the idea that chance was the father of the arts.

29. On *sprezzatura* and color, see Dolce, *Dialogo della pittura,* 156–57. For the rhetoric of the amorphousness of color, consult Jacqueline Lichtenstein, *The Eloquence of Color: Rhetoric and Painting in the French Classical Age,* trans. Emily McVarish (Berkeley and Los Angeles: University of California Press, 1993). More generally on color in Venetian arts, see Paul Hills, *Venetian Colour: Marble, Mosaic, Painting and Glass, 1250–1550* (New Haven: Yale University Press, 1999). Pino includes in his *Dialogo di pittura* (134) a humorous example of formlessness of color and its complication of illusion when he describes a mother who, upon seeing a portrait of her daughter, complains that the black spot (*macchia*) depicted under the nose deviated from the actual appearance of her child.

30. Vasari, *Le vite,* 1:133; and 4:42, where he associates Giorgione with love. See also Pino, *Dialogo di pittura,* 120.

31. Stephen J. Campbell discusses the significance of de-composition in "'Fare una cosa morta parer viva': Michelangelo, Rosso, and the (Un) divinity of Art," *Art Bulletin* 84, no. 4 (2002): 596–620.

32. With an interest in the figurative and materiality, the current project follows the approach of Georges Didi-Huberman. Most relevant for this project is his *Fra Angelico: Dissemblance and Figuration,* trans. Jane Marie Todd (Chicago: University of Chicago Press, 1995). On the distinction between Didi-Huberman's concept of deformation in a figurative tradition and the *informe* in modernism, see Yve-Alain Bois, "Figure," in *Formless: A User's Guide,* by Yve-Alain Bois and Rosalind E. Krauss (New York: Zone Books, 1997), 79–81.

33. Martin Kemp, "The 'Super-Artist' as Genius: The Sixteenth-Century View," in *Genius: The History of an Idea,* ed. Penelope Murray (Oxford: Basil Blackwell, 1989), 32–53; David Rosand, "Raphael's *School of Athens* and the Artist of the Modern Manner," in *The World of Savonarola: Italian Elites and Perceptions of Crisis,* ed. Christine Shaw and Stella Fletcher (Aldershot: Ashgate, 2000), 212–32; Campbell, "Fare una cosa morta," 596–620.

34. Vasari (*Le vite,* 1:117) describes drawing as an action that gives us the "furor dell'artefice." For the history and significance of the sketch in Renaissance art, see David Rosand, *Drawing Acts: Studies in Graphic Expression and Representation* (Cambridge: Cambridge University Press, 2002), 50–54. Summers (*Michelangelo,* 60–70) gives an impressive history of the idea and its significance.

35. For these devices generally, see Stoichita, *Self-Aware Image,* 198–267; and in Venetian painting, see Rona Goffen, "Signatures: Inscribing Identity in Italian Renaissance Art," *Viator* 32 (2001): 303–70; Louisa C. Matthew, "The Painter's Presence: Signatures in Venetian Renaissance Pictures," *Art Bulletin* 80, no. 4 (1998): 616–48.

36. Many contemporaries—including Vasari—criticized Tintoretto for his speed: "Ha costui alcuna volta lasciato le bozze per finite, tanto a fatica sgrossate, che si veggiono i colpi de'pennegli fatti dal caso e dalla fierezza, piuttosto che dal disegno e dal giudizio" (*Vite,* ed. G. Milanesi [Florence, 1878–85], vol. 7, 452). For the relevance of speed for cinquecento literary culture, see Tom Nichols, *Tintoretto: Tradition and Identity* (London: Reaktion Books, 1999), 68–99; Una Roman D'Elia, "Tintoretto, Aretino, and the Speed of Creation," *Word and Image* 20 (2004), 206–18. On the interpretation of Tintoretto's brushwork, see David Rosand, "Tintoretto e gli spiriti nel penello," in *Jacopo Tintoretto nel quarto centenario della morte,* ed. Paola Rossi and Lionello Puppi (Padua: Il Poligrafo, 1996), 133–38.

37. Boschini, *Breve instruzione,* 730–32.

38. Ibid., 711–12; trans. in Rosand, "Titian and the Critical Tradition," 24.

39. Boschini, *Breve instruzione,* 712.

40. Michael Leja discusses the abstract expressionist ego in his *Reframing Abstract Expressionism: Subjectivity and Painting in the 1940s* (New Haven: Yale University Press, 1993), 249–74.

41. On the gendering of form and matter, from its ancient heritage to contemporary thought, see David Summers, "Form and Gender," *New Literary History* 24 (1993): 243–71; Judith Butler, *Bodies That Matter: On the Discursive Limits of "Sex"* (New York: Routledge, 1993).

42. For the trope of the artist as divine, see Ernst Kris and Otto Kurz, *Legend, Myth, and Magic in the Image of the Artist: A Historical Experiment,* trans. Alastair Lang (New Haven: Yale University Press, 1979), 38–59; Patricia A. Emison, *Creating the "Divine" Artist: From Dante to Michelangelo* (Leiden: E. J. Brill, 2004); Campbell, "Fare una cosa morta," 596–605.

43. Harold E. Wethey, *The Paintings of Titian* (London: Phaidon, 1969–75), 2.143–44, cats. 104 and 105; Jodi Cranston, *The Poetics of Portraiture in the Italian Renaissance* (Cambridge: Cambridge University Press, 2000), 98–126.

44. Compare, for example, with Michael Fried's approach to Courbet's subjectivity in the painter's self-portraits and other depictions, in which, according to Fried, Courbet strives to reduce all distance between himself and representation. See Fried, *Courbet's Realism* (Chicago: University of Chicago Press, 1990).

45. On this interaction of subject matter and medium, see Podro, *Depiction,* 5–28.

46. Representative of this approach are Baxandall, *Limewood Sculptors,* and Hills, *Venetian Colour.*

47. A selection of recent titles exploring materialist interests includes Peter Stallybrass and Ann Rosalind Jones, *Renaissance Clothing and the Materials of Memory* (Cambridge: Cambridge University Press, 2000); Patricia Fumerton and Simon Hunt, *Renaissance Culture and the Everyday* (Philadelphia: University of Pennsylvania Press, 1998); Lena Cowen Orlin, *Material London, ca. 1600* (Philadelphia: University of Pennsylvania Press, 2000).

48. Michael Cole, *Cellini and the Principles of Sculpture* (Cambridge: Cambridge University Press, 2002); Gridley McKim-Smith, Greta Andersen-Bergdoll, and Richard Newman, *Examining Velázquez* (New Haven: Yale University Press, 1988). Although slightly outside of the time period of interest to this book, see also Svetlana Alpers, *Rembrandt's Enterprise: The Studio and the Market* (Chicago: University of Chicago Press, 1988); Ernst van de Wetering, *Rembrandt: The Painter at Work* (Amsterdam: Amsterdam University Press, 1997).

49. For this second approach, see Cole, *Cellini and the Principles of Sculpture,* 13.

50. For a recent consideration of the poststructural interest in that which exceeds discourse, and its specific manifestations—such as the confusion between figure and ground—in Renaissance visual culture, see Rebecca Zorach, *Blood, Milk, Ink, Gold: Abundance and Excess in the French Renaissance* (Chicago: University of Chicago Press, 2005), esp. 18–19. Susan Sidlauskas addresses the significance of figure-ground dissolution in nineteenth-century painting. See her *Body, Place, and Self in Nineteenth-Century Painting* (Cambridge: Cambridge University Press, 2000), 2–13.

51. Rona Goffen, "Icon and Vision: Giovanni Bellini's Half-Length Madonnas," *Art Bulletin* 57 (1975), 487–514; Mary Pardo, "Artifice as Seduction in Titian," in *Sexuality and Gender in Early Modern Europe: Institutions, Texts, Images,* ed. James Grantham Turner (Cambridge: Cambridge University Press, 1993), 55–89.

52. Wethey, *Paintings of Titian,* 3.166–67, 182–84, cats. 27 and 36; Ferino-Pagden, *L'ultimo Tiziano,* 230.

53. Aby Warburg, *The Renewal of Pagan Antiquity,* ed. Gertrud Bing, trans. David Britt (Los Angeles: Getty Research Institute, 1999), 271–72, 553–58.

54. Koerner (*Moment of Self-Portraiture,* 199–200) articulates how Dürer explored the conceptual and regional split between the closed body and the materiality of flesh.

55. Patricia A. Emison, *Low and High Style in Italian Renaissance Art* (New York: Garland, 1997).

56. The work of Pietro Aretino readily comes to mind as an example of this deviance. See Patricia H. Labalme, "Personality and Politics in Venice: Pietro Aretino," in *Titian: His World and His Legacy,* 119–32; D'Elia, *Poetics of Titian's Religious Paintings,* 16–18, 58, 95–97, 159–60. For parodies of Petrarchan poetry, see Patrizia Bettella, "Discourse of Resistance: The Parody of Feminine Beauty in Berni, Doni, and Firenzuola," *Modern Language Notes* 113 (1998): 192–203. On cinquecento tragedy, see Bernard Weinberg, *A History of Literary Criticism in the Italian Renaissance* (Chicago: University of Chicago Press, 1961); Marvin Theodore Herrick, *Italian Tragedy in the Renaissance* (Urbana: University of Illinois Press, 1965); Louise George Clubb, *Italian Drama in Shakespeare's Time* (New Haven: Yale University Press, 1989); Salvatore di Maria, *The Italian Tragedy in the Renaissance: Cultural Realities and Theatrical Innovations* (Lewisburg: Bucknell University Press, 2002).

57. William Kerrigan and Gordon Braden, *The Idea of the Renaissance* (Baltimore: Johns Hopkins University Press, 1989); Cynthia Marshall, *The Shattering of the Self: Violence, Subjectivity, and Early Modern Texts* (Baltimore: Johns Hopkins University Press, 2002); Allison M. Levy, *Re-membering Masculinity in Early Modern Florence: Widowed Bodies, Mourning, and Portraiture* (Burlington, Vt.: Ashgate, 2006).

58. Alberti (*On Painting,* 40–59) articulates this relationship in his exposition on perspective.

59. The study of the inclusion of the spectator in Renaissance art has a long history, beginning with Jacob Burckhardt and Alois Riegl. For a selected bibliography of related studies, in addition to a more recent account of the device, see John Shearman, *Only Connect . . . : Art and the Spectator in the Italian Renaissance* (Princeton: Princeton University Press, 1992), 6n3.

60. Daniel Arasse, "The *Venus of Urbino,* or the Archetype of a Glance," in *Titian's "Venus of Urbino,"* ed. Rona Goffen (Cambridge: Cambridge University Press, 1997), 91–107; Pardo, "Artifice as Seduction," 55–89.

61. "Il senso de le cose ha nel pennello" (Pietro Aretino, letter to Boccamazza, 1553, in *Lettere sull'arte di Pietro Aretino,* 436). For modern responses, see David Rosand, "*Ermeneutica amorosa:* Observations on the Interpretation of Titian's Venuses," in *Tiziano e Venezia: Convegno internazionale di studi, Venezia, 1976* (Vicenza: N. Pozza, 1980), 375–81; Katya Berger Andreadakis and John Berger, *Nymph and Shepherd* (Munich: Prestel, 1996), 55.

62. I explored the temporality of these staring figures in "Close Looking in Titian's Later Paintings," a paper delivered at Drawing Inspiration: A Symposium in Honor of David Rosand, Columbia University, October 17, 2008. A Festschrift that will include this paper is forthcoming.

63. For Petrarch's sonnets on the portrait of Laura, see *Petrarch's Lyric Poems: The "Rime sparse" and Other Lyrics,* trans. and ed. Robert M. Durling (Cambridge, Mass.: Harvard University Press, 1976), *Rime* 77–78, 176–79. The ancient heritage of the topos is collected in James Hutton, *The Greek Anthology in Italy to the Year 1800* (Ithaca: Cornell University Press, 1935). For the role of the topos in Renaissance painting, see Fredrika H. Jacobs, *The Living Image in Renaissance Art* (Cambridge: Cambridge University Press, 2005), esp. 109–10; Shearman, *Only Connect,* 112–14; Cranston, *Poetics of Portraiture,* 50–55.

64. On Pygmalion, see Ovid, *Metamorphoses,* trans. Frank Justus Miller (London: William Heinemann; Cambridge, Mass.: Harvard University Press, 1968), 10.247, 253. On the *Cnidian Venus,* see Pliny the Elder, *Natural History,* trans. H. Rackham (Cambridge, Mass.: Harvard University Press, 1952), 36.21. See also Lucian, *Eikones,* trans. A. M. Harmon (London: William Heinemann; New York: G. P. Putnam and Sons, 1925), 4.263.

65. Leonardo da Vinci, *Treatise on Painting,* 1:147–48. Referred to in Zorach, *Blood, Milk, Ink, Gold,* 21–22.

66. Jacobs, *Living Image,* esp. 1–4.

67. David Summers, *The Judgment of Sense: Renaissance Naturalism and the Rise of Aesthetics* (Cambridge: Cambridge University Press, 1987), 32–110.

68. Leonardo, *Treatise on Painting,* 1:32–45; Varchi, "Della maggioranza delle arti—Disputa II," 43. I discuss both senses in relation to the trope of vividness in "The Touch of the Blind Man: The Phenomenology of Vividness in Italian Renaissance Art," in *Sensible Flesh: On Touch in Early Modern Culture,* ed. Elizabeth D. Harvey (Philadelphia: University of Pennsylvania Press, 2003), 224–42.

69. Boschini, *La carta,* 47, 191, 204, 206, 221, 576.

70. "Sono infinite le cose appertinenti al colorire, et impossibil è isplicarle con parole" (Pino, *Dialogo di pittura,* 117).

71. Dolce, *Dialogo della pittura,* 150–55.

72. Lichtenstein, *Eloquence of Color,* 37–54; Patricia L. Reilly, "The Taming of the Blue: Writing out Color in Italian Renaissance Theory," in *The Expanding Discourse: Feminism and Art History,* ed. Norma Broude and Mary D. Garrard (New York: Icon Editions, 1992), 87–99; Joanna Woodall, "Drawing in Colour," in *Peter Paul Rubens: A Touch of Brilliance* (Munich: Prestel, 2003), 11.

73. Una Roman D'Elia, "Drawing Christ's Blood: Michelangelo, Vittoria Colonna, and the Aesthetics of Reform," *Renaissance Quarterly* 59 (2006): 90–129.

74. Raymond Klibansky, Erwin Panofsky, and Fritz Saxl, *Saturn and Melancholy: Studies in the History of Natural Philosophy, Religion, and Art* (New York: Basic Books, 1964), 3–14; Nancy D. Siraisi, *Medieval and Early Renaissance Medicine: An Introduction to Knowledge and Practice* (Chicago: University of Chicago Press, 1990), 91–135.

75. Summers, *Judgment of Sense,* 71–109.

76. Siraisi, *Medieval and Early Renaissance Medicine,* 91–105; Gail Kern Paster, *The Body Embarrassed: Drama and the Disciplines of Shame in Early Modern England* (Ithaca: Cornell University Press, 1993), and *Humoring the Body: Emotions and the Shakespearean Stage* (Chicago: University of Chicago Press, 2004).

77. On the studio practice of making replicas, see Erika Tietze-Conrat, "Titian's Workshop in His Late Years," *Art Bulletin* 28 (1946): 76–88; Hans Tietze, "An Early Version of Titian's *Danaë:* An Analysis of Titian's Replicas," *Arte Veneta* 8 (1954): 199–208; Miguel Falomir, "Titian's Replicas," in *Tiziano,* 77–91. For a recognition of the creative possibilities in making replicas, see Paul Joannides, "Titian's Repetitions," in *Titian: Materiality, Likeness, "Istoria,"* ed. Joanna Woods-Marsden (Turnhout: Brepols, 2007), 37–51. Tintoretto's adoption of the style of earlier painters and other archaisms, particularly in his work of the 1550s, generated criticism from Vasari, who condemns the painter for changing styles to win commissions and refers to his paintings as "baie," or jokes, presumably for their tendency toward pastiche. Carlo Ridolfi writes in his *Life of Veronese* that Veronese made similar complaints. *Le maraviglie dell'arte,* ed. Detlev von Hadeln (Berlin, 1914), 1.349. Recently Tom Nichols (*Tintoretto,* 63–78, 122–37) has attributed these stylistic variations and archaisms to the Venetian conception of *restauro,* to tradition-bound patrons—including *scuole*—issuing commissions, and to Tintoretto's own marketing savvy in appealing to these local patrons. Nichols also connects Tintoretto's citation of well-known compositions and figures to mannerism. The present book argues that Titian's relationship to the history of art and of *his own* art operates within a metapictorial circuit that might parallel some of the operations found in "mannerist" painting and of Tintoretto's painting but that it

does so without the effect of parody and /or of formal disarray. On the formal and stylistic recursiveness of *scuole* paintings, including Titian's *Presentation of the Virgin* for the Scuola della Carità, see David Rosand, *Painting in Sixteenth-Century Venice,* 103–6. For Mansueti's imitation of the Bellinesque style of the Scuola Grande di San Marco paintings, see Peter Humfrey, "The Bellinesque Life of the St. Mark Cycle for the Scuola Grande di San Marco in Its Original Arrangement," *Zeitschrift für Kunstgeschichte* 48 (1985): 225–42.

78. Rosand, "*Ermeneutica amorosa,*" 375–81, and "So-and-So Reclining on Her Couch," in *Titian 500,* ed. Joseph Manca, Studies in the History of Art 45 (Washington: National Gallery of Art, 1993), 101–19. The latter essay is reprinted in Goffen, *Titian's "Venus of Urbino,"* 37–62.

79. Retrospection on one's work is often seen as an indication of old-age style. See Philip Sohm, *The Artist Grows Old: The Aging of Art and Artists in Italy, 1500–1800* (New Haven: Yale University Press, 2007); Herbert von Einem, "Zur Deutung des Altersstiles in der Kunstgeschichte," in *Album Amicorum J. G. van Gelder,* ed. J. Bruyn, J. A. Emmons, E. de Jongh, and D. P. Snoep (The Hague: Martinus Nijhoff, 1973), 88–92; Ost, *Tizian-Studien,* 1–29, esp. 8–9. More complete references to this critical phenomenon can be found in chapter 3 of this book.

80. Alberti, *On Painting,* ¶25, p. 60 (friendship); ¶¶40–41, pp. 75–77 (*concinnitas*).

Chapter 1

1. Most scholars date the *Mellon Venus* to ca. 1555. For this view, see Stephan Poglayen-Neuwall, "Titian's Pictures of the Toilet of Venus and Their Copies," *Art Bulletin* 16 (1934): 358–84; Hans Tietze, *Leben und Werk* (Vienna: Phaidon, 1936), 2:314; Francesco Valcanover, *Tutta la pittura di Tiziano* (Milan: Rizzoli, 1960), 2:15; Rodolfo Pallucchini, *Tiziano* (Florence: G. C. Sansoni, 1969), 143–44; Fern Rusk Shapley, "Titian's *Venus with a Mirror,*" *Studies in the History of Art* 4–5 (1971–72): 93–105; Harold E. Wethey, *The Paintings of Titian* (London: Phaidon, 1969–75), 3.200–203, 242–45, cats. 22 and 51; David Rosand, *Titian* (New York: H. N. Abrams, 1978), fig. 1; Rona Goffen, *Titian's Women* (New Haven: Yale University Press, 1997), 133–38. One exception, Charles Hope, dates the painting to 1565. *Titian* (New York: Harper and Row, 1980), 149–60. Also significant for the dating is the relationship between the *Mellon Venus* and the many painted variations on the subject. In addition to Poglayen-Neuwall, cited above, see Tamara Formicova, "Lo sviluppo compositivo della 'Venere allo specchio con due amorini' nell'opera di Tiziano e la copia dell'Ermitage," *Arte Veneta* 31 (1977): 195–99; and Irina Artemieva, "La *Venere allo specchio* Barbarigo e il *Dialogo della pittura* di Ludovico Dolce," in *L'ultimo Tiziano e la sensualità della pittura,* ed. Sylvia Ferino-Pagden (Venice: Marsilio Editori, 2008), 195–201.

2. For the "woman at her toilette" theme, see Petra Schäpers, *Die junge Frau bei der Toilette* (Frankfurt am Main: Peter Lang, 1997); Elise Goodman-Soellner, "Poetic Interpretations of the 'Lady at Her Toilette' Theme in Sixteenth-Century Painting," *Sixteenth Century Journal* 14 (1983): 426–42; Anne Christine Junkerman, "*Bellisima donna:* An Interdisciplinary Study of Venetian Sensuous Half-Length Images of the Early Sixteenth Century" (Ph.D. diss., University of California, Berkeley, 1988); Rona Goffen, "Bellini's *Nude with Mirror,*" *Venezia Cinquecento* 1 (1991): 185–99, and *Giovanni Bellini* (New Haven: Yale University Press, 1989), 252–57.

3. *Die strambotti des Serafino dall'Aquila,* ed. Barbara Bauer-Formiconi (Munich: Fink, 1967), 204.

4. Mary Pardo, "Veiling the *Venus of Urbino,*" in *Titian's "Venus of Urbino,"* ed. Rona Goffen (Cambridge: Cambridge University Press, 1997), 108–28, and "Artifice as Seduction in Titian," in *Sexuality and Gender in Early Modern Europe: Institutions, Texts, Images,* ed. James Grantham Turner (Cambridge: Cambridge University Press, 1993), 55–89; Goodman-Soellner, "Poetic Interpretations," 426–42; Goffen, *Titian's Women,* 133–37; John Shearman, *Only Connect . . . : Art and the Spectator in the Italian Renaissance* (Princeton: Princeton University Press, 1992), 227–29.

5. On the northern precedent for the Venus at her toilette, see Linda Seidel, *Jan van Eyck's Arnolfini Portrait: Stories of an Icon* (Cambridge: Cambridge University Press, 1993), 201–10.

6. For the designation of two cupids, see Erwin Panofsky, *Problems in Titian, Mostly Iconographic* (New York: New York University Press, 1969), 132–35, and "Blind Cupid," in *Studies in Iconology: Humanistic Themes in the Art of the Renaissance* (New York: Harper and Row, 1962), 95–128.

7. Titian most probably saw the Medici Venus, which assumes the same pose, during his travels to Rome in 1545–46. On this influence, see Goffen, *Titian's Women,* 302n86; Luba Freedman,

The Revival of the Olympian Gods in Renaissance Art (Cambridge: Cambridge University Press, 2003), 154; Rosand, *Titian,* 33.

8. Pardo, "Artifice as Seduction," 55–89; Elizabeth Cropper, "The Place of Beauty in the High Renaissance and Its Displacement in the History of Art," in *Place and Displacement in the Renaissance,* ed. Alvin Vos (Binghamton, N.Y.: Medieval and Renaissance Texts and Studies, 1995), 159–205.

9. Leon Battista Alberti, *On Painting,* trans. and ed. Cecil Grayson (London: Penguin, 1991), ¶26, p. 61. For a discussion of Narcissus and Venetian depictions of sensuous women, see Pardo, "Artifice as Seduction," 55–89.

10. Junkerman, "*Bellissima donna,*" 374–75.

11. Pallucchini, *Tiziano,* 143–44. The condition report (1989) issued by the National Gallery of Art makes no mention of the sketchy mirror. I am grateful to the curatorial records department for making available this report.

12. Most viewers of the painting tend to overlook the materiality of the mirror. Exceptions include J. A. Crowe and J. B. Cavalcaselle (*The Life and Times of Titian* [London: John Murray, 1881], 335), who note the "broad modeling," heavy impasto, and injuries of time; Pardo ("Veiling the *Venus of Urbino,*" 108–28); and Goffen (*Titian's Women,* 136), who interprets the difference in terms of different optical realities. The materiality of the entire canvas figures heavily in the later dating by Hope (*Titian,* 149–60).

13. The extensive bibliography on Titian's later style consistently notes these stylistic features of the paintings from the mid-sixteenth century, but scholars disagree on whether the paintings are finished and the extent to which studio hands participated in their execution. For a recent compilation and discussion of early modern criticism and more recent art historical scholarship, see Miguel Falomir, "El ultimo Tiziano [1551–1576]," in *Tiziano,* exh. cat. (Madrid: Museo Nacional del Prado, 2003), 243–47; David Rosand, "Titian and the Critical Tradition," in *Titian: His World and His Legacy,* ed. David Rosand (New York: Columbia University, 1982). Also helpful, although less recent, is the review of scholarship by Pallucchini, *Tiziano,* 151–57.

14. The number of extant "Venus at Her Toilette" paintings contributes to this opinion. For the X-ray and restoration report, see Shapley, "Titian's *Venus with a Mirror,*" 93–105. On Titian's studio and studio practice, see Erica Tietze-Conrat, "Titian's Workshop in His Late Years," *Art Bulletin* 28 (1946): 76–88.

15. Wolfgang Braunfels, "I quadri di Tiziano nello studio a Biri Grande (1530–76)," in *Tiziano e Venezia,* 407–10. After Titian's death, his Casa Grande was purchased with its contents by Cristoforo Barbarigo. On the provenance of the painting prior to its arrival at the National Gallery, Washington, D.C., see Wethey, *Paintings of Titian,* 3.201.

16. Michael Podro, *Depiction* (New Haven: Yale University Press, 1998), 5–9; Richard Wollheim, *Painting as an Art* (Princeton: Princeton University Press, 1987), 46–47.

17. Gustav Hartlaub, *Zauber des Speigels: Geschichte und Bedeutung des Spiegels in der Kunst* (Munich: R. Piper, 1951); Ritamary Bradley, "Backgrounds of the Title 'Speculum' in Medieval Literature," *Speculum* 29 (1954): 100–115; Frederick Robert Goldin, *The Mirror of Narcissus in the Courtly Love Lyric* (Ithaca: Cornell University Press, 1967); J. W. Fernandez, "Reflections on Looking into Mirrors," *Semiotica* 30 (1980): 27–39; Victor I. Stoichita, *The Self-Aware Image: An Insight into Early-Modern Meta-Painting,* trans. Anne-Marie Glasheen (Cambridge: Cambridge University Press, 1997), first published as *L'instauration du tableau: Métapeinture à l'aube des temps modernes* (Paris: Méridiens Klincksieck, 1993).

18. *Rima* 361. Cited and translated in *Petrarch's Lyric Poems: The "Rime sparse" and Other Lyrics,* trans. and ed. Robert M. Durling (Cambridge, Mass.: Harvard University Press, 1995), 570.

19. Jodi Cranston, *The Poetics of Portraiture in the Italian Renaissance* (Cambridge: Cambridge University Press, 2000), 140–56, with fuller bibliography for Parmigianino's picture.

20. For Titian's *Vanitas,* see Wethey, *Paintings of Titian,* 3.184–85, cat. 37.

21. Titian employed the *pudica* pose for his *Mary Magdalene* (Florence, Galleria Pitti). See Rosand, *Titian,* 106. For the recumbent nude and its thematic and formal significance in Titian's oeuvre, see David Rosand, "*Ermeneutica amorosa:* Observations on the Interpretation of Titian's Venuses," in *Tiziano e Venezia,* 375–81, and "So-and-So Reclining on Her Couch," in *Titian 500,* ed. Joseph Manca, Studies in the History of Art 45 (Washington: National Gallery of Art, 1993), 101–19. The latter essay is reprinted in Goffen, *Titian's "Venus of Urbino,"* 37–62.

22. First described by Bartholomaeus Facius in *De Viris*

Illustribus Liber (1456). For the English translation, see Michael Baxandall, "Bartholomaeus Facius on Painting: A Fifteenth-Century Manuscript of the 'De Viris Illustribus,'" *Journal of the Warburg and Courtauld Institutes* 27 (1964): 102–3; Seidel, *Jan van Eyck's Arnolfini Portrait,* 201–10. The trope of the painting of the bathing woman most certainly influenced the lost or legendary painting attributed to Giorgione of the armored Saint George standing by a stream and a mirror. For this Giorgionesque invention, consult Paolo Pino, *Dialogo di pittura* (1548), in *Trattati d'arte del Cinquecento fra manierismo e Controriforma,* ed. Paola Barocchi (Bari: G. Laterza, 1960–62), 1:131; Giorgio Vasari, *Le vite de' più eccellenti pittori, scultori, ed architettori: Nelle redazioni 1550 e 1568,* ed. Paola Barocchi, 6 vols. (Florence: Sansoni, 1966–69 [vols. 1–3, 5, 6]; Florence: Studi per edizione scelte, 1967 [vol. 4]), 1:113, 4:46.

23. For the prosthetic function of mirrors, see Umberto Eco, "Mirrors," in *Semiotics and the Philosophy of Language* (Bloomington: Indiana University Press, 1986), 202–26; Heinrich Schwarz, "The Mirror of the Artist and the Mirror of the Devout: Observations on Some Paintings, Drawings, and Prints of the Fifteenth Century," in *Studies in the History of Art, Dedicated to William E. Suida on His Eightieth Birthday* (London: Phaidon, 1959), 90–105.

24. Jaynie Anderson, "The Giorgionesque Portrait: From Likeness to Allegory," in *Giorgione: Atti del convegno internazionale di studio per il 5° centenario della nascita* (Castelfranco Veneto: Banco Popolare di Asolo e Montebelluna, 1979), 153–58; Jaynie Anderson, *Giorgione: The Painter of "Poetic Brevity"* (New York: Flammarion, 1997); Carlo Pedretti, "Ancora sul rapporto Giorgione-Leonardo e l'origine del ritratto di spalla," in *Giorgione: Atti del convegno,* 181–85; Wendy Steadman Sheard, "Giorgione's Portrait Inventions, c. 1500: Transfixing the Viewer (with Observations on Some Florentine Antecedents)," in *Reconsidering the Renaissance,* ed. Mario A. Di Cesare (Binghamton, N.Y.: Medieval and Renaissance Texts and Studies, 1992), 171–76.

25. Jodi Cranston, "Tropes of Revelation in Raphael's *Transfiguration,*" *Renaissance Quarterly* 56 (2003): 1–25, and "Desire and Gravitas in the Portraits of Bindo Altoviti," in *Raphael, Cellini, and a Renaissance Banker: The Patronage of Bindo Altoviti,* ed. Alan Chong, Donatella Pegazzano, and Dimitrios Zikos (Boston: Isabella Stewart Gardner Museum, 2003), 115–31.

26. *Rima* 143: "Her locks loosed to the breeze, I see her turning back"; and *Rima* 159: "He looks in vain for divine beauty who never saw her eyes, how sweetly she turns them." Translated in *Petrarch's Lyric Poems,* 288–89, lines 9–10, and 304–5, lines 9–11.

27. I will discuss the materiality of the entire painting later in this chapter.

28. This difference is not noted among the *pentimenti* or in the condition report issued in 1971–72. See Shapley, "Titian's *Venus with a Mirror,*" 93–105. Crowe and Cavalcaselle observe the thick impasto of the mirror. See note 12 of this chapter.

29. For reproduction of these copies after or studio versions of Titian's seated Venus, see Wethey, *Paintings of Titian,* vol. 3, plates 126–33. Anthony van Dyck, in his sketch of the so-called Crasso type (a seated Venus with two cupids who both look at the viewer), included only a stick-figure outline of the reflected goddess. However, Van Dyck's sketches do not accurately copy Italian paintings. See the various sketches in *A Description of the Sketchbook by Sir Anthony van Dyck* (London: G. Bell, 1902).

30. Crowe and Cavalcaselle, *Life and Times of Titian,* 335: "The surface is broadly modeled, and notwithstanding all the injuries of time and retouching, we still see that it was impasted repeatedly and with surprising skill before it received the finishing glaze, smirch, and touch."

31. For the provenance of painting, see Wethey, *Paintings of Titian,* 3.201, cat. 51. Even though the painting remained in Titian's house, he received many visitors there, according to Vasari (*Le vite,* 6:169).

32. Alberti, *On Painting,* ¶26, p. 61. Stephen Bann, *The True Vine: On Visual Representation and the Western Tradition* (Cambridge: Cambridge University Press, 1989), 105–26; Cranston, *Poetics of Portraiture,* 127–33, with fuller bibliography.

33. Leonardo da Vinci, *The Literary Works of Leonardo da Vinci,* ed. and trans. Jean Paul Richter (London: Phaidon, 1970), 1:320. For similar observations on the immateriality of mirrors, see Cranston, *Poetics of Portraiture,* 127–44.

34. Mary Pardo, "The Subject of Savoldo's *Magdalene,*" *Art Bulletin* 71 (1989): 67–91; Schwarz, "Mirror of the Artist."

35. Vasari, *Le vite,* 6:166.

36. The origin for this crossover comes from the close relationship between portraits and icons. See Hans Belting, *Likeness and Presence: A History of the Image Before the Era*

of Art, trans. Edmund Jephcott (Chicago: University of Chicago Press, 1994), 1–16; David Rosand, "Tiziano sacro e profano," *Studi tizianeschi* 3 (2005): 57–66; Cranston, *Poetics of Portraiture,* 15–23. Leonardo comments on the dangerous elision between the two types when he recounts the story of a patron who requested that the painter remove all devotional signs from a painting that elicited a sensual response. See Leonardo, *Literary Works,* Urb. 13v–r.

37. Wethey, *Paintings of Titian,* 1.143–44, cat. 120.

38. Rosand, *Titian,* 106; Goffen, *Titian's Women,* 171–92. Hope (*Titian,* 158–59) notes the similarly large output of both compositions by Titian's studio and attributes this to the interest in paintings of "pretty girls."

39. One such example is Svetlana Alpers, *Rembrandt's Enterprise: The Studio and the Market* (Chicago: University of Chicago Press, 1988).

40. Shearman, *Only Connect,* 227–29; Edward Snow, "Theorizing the Male Gaze: Some Problems," *Representations* 25 (1989): 30–41; Andreas Prater, *Venus at Her Mirror: Velásquez and the Art of Nude Painting* (Munich: Prestel, 2002).

41. Shearman (*Only Connect,* 227–29) describes the mirror reflection in the *Mellon Venus* as an unidealized portrait; Snow ("Theorizing the Male Gaze," 30–41) considers the mirror in the *Rokeby Venus* as a sign of mortality, incorporated maternal anima, and transfigured desire.

42. For desire and illusionism, see Pardo, "Artifice as Seduction," 55–89; Cropper, "Place of Beauty," 190–205.

43. Pietro Bembo, *Gli Asolani,* trans. Rudolf B. Gottfried (Freeport, N.Y.: Books for Libraries Press, 1971), 52.

44. Cesare Ripa, *Iconologia* (Rome, 1593), proem. The passage is discussed and translated by Prater, *Venus at Her Mirror,* 72–73; Hubert Damisch, *A Theory of /Cloud/: Toward a History of Painting,* trans. Janet Lloyd (Stanford: Stanford University Press, 2002), 53–55.

45. Pardo, "Savoldo's *Magdalene,*" 67–91; Cropper, "Place of Beauty," 201–5; Philip L. Sohm, *Style in the Art Theory of Early Modern Italy* (Cambridge: Cambridge University Press, 2001), 190–94; Paolo Alei, "'Intelligitur plus Semper quam Pingitur': The Renaissance Heritage of Timanthes' Veil" (Ph.D. diss., Oxford University, 2002).

46. Pliny the Elder, *Natural History,* trans. H. Rackham (Cambridge, Mass.: Harvard University Press, 1952), 9:367 (35.40.145–46).

47. H. W. Janson, "The 'Image Made by Chance' in Renaissance Thought," in *De Artibus Opuscula XL: Essays in Honor of Erwin Panosfky,* ed. Millard Meiss (New York: New York University Press, 1961), 254–66.

48. Alberti began his *De statua* with the accidental image found in nature as the origin of sculpture: "They probably occasionally observed in a tree-trunk or clod of earth and other similar inanimate objects certain outlines in which, with slight alterations, something very similar to the real faces of nature was represented." Translated in *On Painting and On Sculpture: The Latin Texts of "De pictura" and "De statua,"* ed. and trans. Cecil Grayson (London: Phaidon, 1972), 121.

49. "Non resterò però di mettere fra questi precietti una nova inventione di speculatione, la quale benchè paia piccola e quasi degnia di riso, nondimeno è di grande utilità a destrare lo ingegno a varie inventioni; e questa è se tu riguarderai in alcuni muri imbrattati di varie macchie o pietre di vari misti, se avrai a inventionare qualche sito potrai lì vedere similtudine di diversi paesi, ornate di montagnie, fiumi, sassi, albori, pianure, grandi valli e colli in diversi modi, ancora vi potrai vedere diverse battaglie e atti pronti di figure, strane arie di volti e abiti e infinite cose, le quali potrai ridurre in integra e bona forma" (Ash. I.13a, Leonardo, *Literary Works,* 1:311–12). For a discussion of this and similar passages in the development of the sketch, see David Rosand, *Drawing Acts: Studies in Graphic Expression and Representation* (Cambridge: Cambridge University Press, 2002), 50–54.

50. "E interviene in simili muri e misti come del suono di campane che ne'loro tochi vi troverai ogni nome e vocabolo che tu imaginerai" (Ash. I.13a, Leonardo, *Literary Works,* 1:312).

51. Leonardo da Vinci, *Leonardo on Painting,* ed. Martin Kemp, and trans. Martin Kemp and Margaret Walker (New Haven: Yale University Press, 1989), 201. "Fa com'il sono delle campane, nelle quali si pò intendere quelle dire quell ch'a te pare." Urb. 33v–34r, Leonardo da Vinci, *Libro di Pittura,* ed. Carlo Pedretti (Florence: Giunti Gruppo Editoriale, 1995), 1:174.

52. Leonardo, *Leonardo on Painting,* 222. "Le quali macchie, ancora che integralmente fussino in sé privato di perfezzione di qualonque membro, non mancavano di perfezzione nelli loro movimenti o altri azzioni" (Urb. 61v–62r, Leonardo, *Libro di Pittura,* 1:222).

53. Vasari, *Le vite,* vol. 4, proem to the third part.

54. Wethey, *Paintings of Titian,* 3.133–35, cat. 6. Of interest for this discussion is Lacan's reference to "stain" in his discussion of the gaze. See Jacques Lacan, *The Four Fundamental Concepts of Psycho-Analysis,* ed. Jacques-Alain Miller, trans. Alan Sheridan (New York: W. W. Norton, 1978), 96.

55. David Summers, "Form and Gender," *New Literary History* 24 (1993): 243–71; Judith Butler, *Bodies That Matter: On the Discursive Limits of "Sex"* (New York: Routledge, 1993), 27–34; Jacques Derrida, *Positions,* trans. Alan Bass (Chicago: University of Chicago Press, 1981), 60–65; Jonathan Culler, *On Deconstruction: Theory and Criticism After Structuralism* (Ithaca: Cornell University Press, 1982), 93–99. Caroline Bynum questioned the presumed body/spirit division with examples from medieval theology. See "Why All the Fuss About the Body? A Medievalist's Perspective," *Critical Inquiry* 22 (1995): 1–33.

56. Giovanni Battista Armenini, *On the True Precepts of the Art of Painting,* ed. and trans. Edward J. Olszewski (New York: Burt Franklin, 1977), 118. For the association of gender with *disegno* and *colore,* see Patricia L. Reilly, "The Taming of the Blue: Writing out Color in Italian Renaissance Theory," in *The Expanding Discourse: Feminism and Art History,* ed. Norma Broude and Mary D. Garrard (New York: Icon Editions, 1992), 87–99.

57. Fredrika H. Jacobs, *Defining the Renaissance Virtuosa: Women Artists and the Language of Art History and Criticism* (Cambridge: Cambridge University Press, 1997), 27–64; Erwin Panofsky, *Idea: A Concept in Art Theory* (Columbia: University of South Carolina Press, 1968), 27–29.

58. Reilly, "Taming of the Blue," 87–88.

59. The word *macchia* describes a sketch or painting only in the late fifteenth century. The moral association with stain appeared by the early fourteenth century. See *macchia* in *Il Nuovo Etimologico,* ed. Manilo Cortelazzo and Michele A. Cortelazzo (Bologna: Zanichelli, 1999), 901–2; *Grande Dizionario della lingua italiana,* ed. Salvatore Battaglia (Turin: Unione Tipografico, 1975), 9:349–53.

60. Sohm, *Style in the Art Theory,* 148, and *Pittoresco: Marco Boschini, His Critics, and Their Critiques of Painterly Brushwork in Seventeenth- and Eighteenth-Century Italy* (Cambridge: Cambridge University Press, 1991), 36–38. Sohm cites definitions for "macchia" from the *Vocabolario della Crusca* (1612) and from Filippo Baldinucci's *Vocabolario Toscano dell'arte del disegno* (1681). For a later use of "macchia" in art criticism, see Hans Sedlmayr, "Bruegel's 'Macchia' (1934)," in *The Vienna School Reader: Politics and Art Historical Method in the 1930s,* ed. Christopher S. Wood (New York: Zone Books, 2000), 323–76.

61. "Fermavasi talora a considerare un muro dove lungamente fusse stato sputato da persone malate, e ne cavava le battaglie de'cavagli e le più fantastiche città e più gran paesi che si vedesse mai; simil faceva de' nuvoli dell'aria" (Vasari, *Le vite,* 4:62). English translation: "Life of Piero di Cosimo," in *Lives of the Most Eminent Painters, Sculptors, and Architects,* trans. Gaston du C. de Vere (London: 1912–14), 4:127.

62. Vasari, *Le vite,* 4:61. See also Sharon Fermor, *Piero di Cosimo: Fiction, Invention, and "Fantasia"* (London: Reaktion Books, 1993), 13–40.

63. Boschini, *La carta del navegar pitoresco,* ed. Anna Pallucchini (Venice: Istituto per la collaborazione culturale, 1966), 361; Sohm, *Style in the Art Theory,* 146.

64. Georges Didi-Huberman, *Fra Angelico: Dissemblance and Figuration,* trans. Jane Marie Todd (Chicago: University of Chicago Press, 1995), and "The Index of the Absent Wound (Monograph on a Stain)," *October* 29 (1984): 63–81. The idea of disfiguration still maintains an ideal of form, especially compared to the *informe.* See Yve-Alain Bois and Rosalind Krauss, *Formless: A User's Guide* (New York: Zone Books, 1997).

65. Vasari, *Le vite,* 6:166. Dolce and Pino also acknowledge that paint is merely substance until handled by the painter. See Lodovico Dolce, *Dialogo della pittura* (1557), in *Dolce's "Aretino" and Venetian Art Theory of the Cinquecento,* ed. and trans. Mark W. Roskill (New York: New York University Press, 1968), 154–55.

66. Boschini, *La carta,* 750: "forma senza forma, anzi con forma difforme." Boschini here describes the formal distortions necessary for perspective, but disfiguration emerges as a central theme in his account of Venetian painting. See also Sohm, *Style in the Art Theory,* 145, and *Pittoresco,* 155–57.

67. Marco Boschini, *Breve instruzione,* in *La carta,* 711–12. For the English translation, see Rosand, "Titian and the Critical Tradition," 24.

68. For the significance of *faciebat* in this painting, see Goffen, "Bellini's *Nude with Mirror,*" 185–99, and *Giovanni Bellini,* 252–57.

69. Cropper, "Place of Beauty," 190–205, alludes to a similar

phenomenology of Renaissance aesthetics, particularly in the cinquecento. Much recent art-historical criticism acknowledges the importance of the body in visuality by relying, to varying degrees, on phenomenology, especially the work of Maurice Merleau-Ponty. Among the first American art historians to employ this approach were Rosalind Krauss (*Passages in Modern Sculpture* [New York: Viking Press, 1977]) and Michael Fried ("Art and Objecthood," *Art Forum* 5 [June 1967]: 12–23, reprinted in *Art and Objecthood* [Chicago: University of Chicago Press, 1998], 148–72), who turned to phenomenology in discussions of minimalist sculpture. For a fuller consideration of phenomenology and sculpture, see Alex Potts, *The Sculptural Imagination: Figurative, Modernist, Minimalist* (New Haven: Yale University Press, 2000). Following the lead of Fried (*Courbet's Realism* [Chicago: University of Chicago Press, 1990]), scholars have structured their approach to painting with a similar framework, including viewers of early modern painting and drawing. See, most recently, Rosand, *Drawing Acts.*

70. Summers, "Form and Gender," 243–71.

71. Drawing upon psychoanalytic approaches, Rebecca Zorach considers abjection in some of Titian's *poesie.* "Despoiled at the Source," *Art History* 22 (1999): 244–69.

72. Mary Pardo, "Paolo Pino's 'Dialogo di Pittura': A Translation with Commentary" (Ph.D. diss., University of Pittsburgh, 1984), 360ff.

73. Benedetto Varchi, *Lezzione sopra il sottoscritto sonetto di Michelagnolo Buonarroti,* in *Le rime di Michelangelo Buonarroti,* ed. Cesare Guasti (Florence: Monnier, 1863), xcix. For a discussion of the passage and its translation, see David Summers, *Michelangelo and the Language of Art* (Princeton: Princeton University Press, 1981), 209–11. Related bibliography is included in Jodi Cranston, "The Touch of the Blind Man: The Phenomenology of Vividness in Italian Renaissance Art," in *Sensible Flesh: On Touch in Early Modern Culture,* ed. Elizabeth D. Harvey (Philadelphia: University of Pennsylvania Press, 2003), 224–42. Barocchi links Pino to Varchi via the argument of universality, not this union of form and matter. See her editorial comments in *Scritti d'arte del Cinquecento* (Milan: Riccardo Ricciardi Editore, 1971), 1:548n3.

74. Cranston, "Touch of the Blind Man," 224–42.

75. Lorenzo Ghiberti, *I commentari,* ed. Ottavio Morisani (Naples: Riccardo Ricciardi, 1947), 55; cited in Pardo, "Artifice as Seduction," 62.

76. Giovan Giorgio Trissino, *La poetica* (1529), in *Trattati di Poetica e Retorica del Cinquecento,* ed. Bernard Weinberg (Bari: Giuseppe Laterza and Figli, 1970), 1:38.

77. Richard Krautheimer, *Lorenzo Ghiberti* (Princeton: Princeton University Press, 1970), 2:372, doc. 52.

78. Baldassare Castiglione, *The Book of the Courtier,* trans. Charles S. Singleton (London: Doubleday, 1959), 144; Dolce, *Dialogo della pittura,* 115.

79. Cited in Robert Baldwin, "'Gates Pure and Shining and Serene': Mutual Gazing as an Amatory Motif in Western Literature and Art," in *The Language of Gesture in the Renaissance,* ed. Konrad Eisenbichler and Philip L. Sohm, Renaissance and Reformation, n.s. 10, no. 1 (Toronto: Canadian Society for Renaissance Studies, 1986), 23–48.

80. "Trovolla assisa in letto fuor del limbo, / pur mo' di Marte sciolta dale braccia, / il qual roverso li giacea nel grembo, / pascendo gli occhi pur della sua faccia" (I. 122). For the Italian text and the English translation, see Angelo Poliziano, *The Stanze of Angelo Poliziano,* trans. David Quint (University Park: Pennsylvania State University Press, 1993), 62–63.

81. Baldwin, "'Gates Pure and Shining,'" 25.

82. For a selection of these dialoghi, see Giuseppe Zonta, ed., *Trattati d'amore del Cinquecento* (Bari: G. Laterza, 1967). See also P. Lorenzetti, "La bellezza e l'amore nei trattati del Cinquecento," *Annali della Scuola Normale Superiore di Pisa: Filosofia e Filologia,* 1st ser., 28 (1914): 1–175; Benedetto Croce, "Trattati d'amore del Cinquecento," in *Poeti e scrittori del pieno e del tardo Rinascimento* (Bari: Laterza, 1945), 187–97.

83. Charles Nelson, *Renaissance Theory of Love: The Context of Giordano Bruno's "Eroici Furori"* (New York: Columbia University Press, 1958). For the role of sight in representations of the recumbent nude, see Maria Ruvoldt, *The Italian Renaissance Imagery of Inspiration: Metaphors of Sex, Sleep, and Dreams* (Cambridge: Cambridge University Press, 2004), 90–126.

84. Ruvoldt, *Italian Renaissance Imagery of Inspiration,* 77–79.

85. Rosand, "*Ermeneutica amorosa,*" 375–81.

86. "I sensi sono via alla ragione. Onde chiunque è così sciocco in amore ch'egli non curi i loro appetiti, ma come semplice intelligenzia cerchi solo di satisfarne la mente, egli è simile a colui il

quale, tranguggiando alcun cibo senza toccarlo co'denti, più s'inferma che si nutrichi." Sperone Speroni, "Dialogo d'amore," in *Trattatisti del Cinquecento,* ed. Mario Pozzi (Milan: Riccardo Ricciardi Editore, 1978), 1:517.

87. Bembo, *Gli Asolani,* 115. "Perciò che sì come il dipintore bene potrà come che sia la bianchezza dipignere delle nevi, ma la fredezza non mai, sì come cosa il giudicio della quale, al tatto solamente conceduto, sotto l'occhio non viene, a cui servono le pitture, similemente ho io testé quanto sia il giovamento d'Amore dimostrarvi pure in qualche parte potuto, ma le dolcezze che cadano in ogni senso et, come sorgevole fo[n]t[a]na assai più anchor anche la nostra, sopr'habondano in tutti loro, non possono nell'orecchia sola, per molto che noi ne parliamo, in alcuna guisa capire" (ibid., 155).

88. "Le cose, che soggiacciono al tatto; come sarebbe la freddezza della neve: o al gusto; come la dolcezza del mele" (Dolce, *Dialogo della pittura,* 96–97).

89. Ibid., 97.

90. "T'innamora ed è causa, che tutti li sensi insieme con l'occhio la vorrebbon possedere, e pare che a garra vogliono combater con l'occhio, pare che la bocca se la vorebbe per se in corpo; l'orecchio piglia piacere d'udire le sue bellezze; il senso del tatto la vorrebbe penetrare per tutti gli suoi meati; il naso anchora vorebbe ricevere l'aria ch'al continuo di lei spira" (Leonardo, *Literary Works,* 1:61, Urb. 11a–12b, Trat. 23).

91. Elizabeth Cropper, "The Beauty of Woman: Problems in the Rhetoric of Renaissance Portraiture," in *Rewriting the Renaissance: The Discourses of Sexual Difference in Early Modern Europe,* ed. Margaret W. Ferguson, Maureen Quilligan, and Nancy J. Vickers (Chicago: University of Chicago Press, 1986), 175–90.

92. Durling, *Petrarch's Lyric Poems,* 102–3.

93. Daryl Hines, *Ovid's Heroines: A Verse Translation of the "Heroides"* (New Haven: Yale University Press, 1991), 116–17. A cinquecento Petrarchan commentator noted the Ovidian source and the jealousy of the poet. See Alessandro Vellutello, *Il Petrarcha con l'espositione d'Alessandro Vellutello* (Venice, 1547), 99.

94. Durling, *Petrarch's Lyric Poems,* 340–41.

95. Ibid., 342–43.

96. Ibid.

97. David Summers, "Aria II: The Union of Image and Artist as an Aesthetic Ideal in Renaissance Art," *Artibus et Historiae* no. 20 (1989): 15–31; Summers, *Michelangelo and the Language of Art,* 56–59.

98. Alberti, *On Painting,* ¶¶44–45, pp. 79–81.

99. Georges Didi-Huberman, "The Imaginary Breeze: Remarks on the Air of the Quattrocento," *Journal of Visual Culture* 2 (2003): 275–89.

100. Summers, "Aria II," 23–26.

101. Cranston, "Desire and Gravitas," 115–31; Cropper, "Place of Beauty," 174–205.

102. Rosand, "*Ermeneutica amorosa,*" 375–81, and "So-and-So Reclining on Her Couch," 101–18.

103. Daniel Arasse, "The 'Venus of Urbino,' or the Archetype of a Glance," in Goffen, *Titian's "Venus of Urbino,"* 91–107; Pardo, "Veiling the *Venus of Urbino,*" 108–28.

104. Panofsky, "Blind Cupid," 95–128.

105. Letter from Antonio Pérez to Philip II: "One day the ambassador Francisco de Vargas asked him [Titian] why he had turned to that style of painting . . . with broad brushstrokes, almost like careless *borrones,* . . . and not with the sweetness of the brushwork of the great painters of his time; Titian responded: 'Sir, I wasn't sure that I could succeed at the delicacy and beauty of the brushwork of Michelangelo, Raphael, Correggio and Parmigianino, and even if I were to succeed, I would be considered less than they, or considered their imitator.'" Translated in Gridley McKim-Smith, Greta Andersen-Bergdoll, and Richard Newman, *Examining Velázquez* (New Haven: Yale University Press, 1988), 24; *Epistolario español: Colección de cartas de españoles ilustres antiguos y modernos,* ed. Eugenio de Ochoa (Madrid: Impr. de la publicidad, 1850), 519. See also Falomir, *Tiziano,* 243. The repetition of this anecdote throughout seventeenth-century Spanish art theory—including in Palomino's description of the style of Velázquez—attests to its appeal. See *Examining Velázquez,* 25.

Chapter 2

1. Alberti credits Narcissus as the inventor of painting. See Leon Battista Alberti, *On Painting,* trans. Cecil Grayson (London: Penguin, 1991), ¶26, p. 61.

2. Harold E. Wethey, *The Paintings of Titian* (London: Phaidon, 1969–75), 3.91–93, 153–54, cat. 16. For the bibliography of the painting prior to 1990, see the catalogue entry by Paola Rossi for the *Flaying* in *Tiziano,* exh. cat. (Venice: Marsilio Editore, 1990), 370–72. Additions to the bibliography include Philipp Fehl, "Realism

and Classicism in the Representation of a Painful Scene: Titian's 'Flaying of Marsyas' at the Archiepiscopal Palace at Kromeríz," in *Czechoslovakia Past and Present,* ed. Miloslav Rechcígl (The Hague: Mouton, 1968), 2:1387–1415; Augusto Gentili, "Tiziano e il non finito," *Venezia Cinquecento* 2 (1992): 93–127; Hans Ost, *Tizian-Studien* (Cologne: Böhlau, 1992), 111–70; Alessandro Ballarin, *Le siècle de Titien: L'age d'or de la peinture à Venise* (Paris: Réunion des Musées Nationaux, 1993), 624; Paula Carabell, "*Finito* and *Non-finito* in Titian's Last Paintings," *Res* 28 (Autumn 1995): 79–93; Rona Goffen, *Titian's Women* (New Haven: Yale University Press, 1997), 279–86; Irene Tobben, *Die Schindung des Marsyas: Nachdencken über Tizian und die Gefährlichkeit der Künste* (Berlin: Das Arsenal, 1997); David Rosand, "La mano de Tiziano," in *Tiziano: Técnicas y restauraciones* (Madrid: Museo Nacional del Prado, 1999), 127–38; Daniela Bohde, *Haut, Fleisch, und Farbe: Körperlichkeit und Materialität in den Gemälden Tizians* (Berlin: Emsdetten, 2002), and "Skin and the Search for the Interior: The Representation of Flaying in the Art and Anatomy of the Cinquecento," in *Bodily Extremities: Preoccupations with the Human Body in Early Modern Culture,* ed. Florike Egmond and Robert Zwijnenberg (Aldershot: Ashgate, 2003), 10–47; Miguel Falomir, *Tiziano,* exh. cat. (Madrid: Museo Nacional del Prado, 2003), 292–95; and Sylvia Ferino-Pagden, "Supplizio de Marsia," in *L'ultimo Tiziano e la sensualità della pittura,* ed. Sylvia Ferino-Pagden (Venice: Marsilio Editori, 2008), 232–35.

3. Much of the debate in the scholarship on the *Flaying* circulates around the question of whether this painting is finished. A strong indication of its being finished is the signature in the lower right of the composition. Other scholars who share this opinion include Rossi (*Tiziano,* 370–72) and Rosand ("La mano de Tiziano," 127–38). Ost (*Tizian-Studien,* 111–78) considers the painting to be unfinished, whereas Gentili and Falomir think that the painting was retouched after Titian's death. Falomir, *Tiziano,* 293–95; Augusto Gentili, *Da Tiziano a Tiziano: Mito e allegoria nella cultura veneziana del Cinquecento* (Milan: Feltrinelli, 1980), 225–40. Erwin Panofsky (*Problems in Titian, Mostly Iconographic* [New York: New York University Press, 1969], 171n85) rejects the painting from Titian's oeuvre because of what Panofsky sees as uncharacteristic "gratuitous brutality" and the *horror vacui.*

4. Rosand ("La mano de Tiziano," 127–38) relates the flayer's knife to the palette knife of the painter. The history of the melancholic pose and its significance for this painting will be taken up later in this chapter.

5. The subject matter alone suggests this potential association. The myth also had relevance for Dantesque and neo-Platonic thoughts on divine inspiration and harmony. See Edgar Wind, *Pagan Mysteries in the Renaissance* (London: Faber and Faber, 1958), 142–46; Jaromir Neumann, *Titian: The Flaying of Marsyas,* trans. Till Gottheiner (London: Spring Books, 1962); Gentili, *Da Tiziano a Tiziano,* 225–40; J. Rapp, "Tizians Marsyas in Kremsier: Ein neu-platonisch-orphisches Mysterium vom Leiden des Menschen und seiner Erlösung," *Pantheon* 45 (1987): 70–89; Norbert Huse and Wolfgang Wolters, *The Art of Renaissance Venice: Architecture, Sculpture, and Painting, 1460–1590,* trans. Edmund Jephcott (Chicago: University of Chicago Press, 1990), 330; Edith Wyss, *The Myth of Apollo and Marsyas in the Art of the Italian Renaissance: An Inquiry into the Meaning of Images* (Newark: University of Delaware Press, 1996), 133–41. Una Roman D'Elia rightly questions the neo-Platonic readings of this painting and suggests that the approach seems foreign to Titian and his intellectual milieu. *The Poetics of Titian's Religious Paintings* (Cambridge: Cambridge University Press, 2005), 212n136.

6. Hal Foster, speaking of expressionism, inserts a rhetorical figure between the self and expression. "The Expressive Fallacy," *Art in America* (January 1983): 80–83, 137. The misleading assumption that brushstroke = artist's presence is what he terms the "expressive fallacy."

7. Much of our inherited idea of the artist as heroic genius developed in the Romantic period. However, in the sixteenth century a few artists, among them Titian and Michelangelo, were thought of as having attained near-immortal status. For this refinement of the idea of genius in the Renaissance, see Martin Kemp, "The 'Super-Artist' as Genius: The Sixteenth-Century View," in *Genius: The History of an Idea,* ed. Peter Murray (Oxford: Basil Blackwell, 1989), 32–53.

8. Herbert von Einem, "Zur Deutung des Alterstils in der Kunstgeschichte," in *Album Amicorum J. G. van Gelder* (The Hague: Martinus Nijhoff, 1973), 88–92; Ost, *Tizian-Studien,* 1–29; Philip L. Sohm, *The Artist Grows Old: The Aging of Art and Artists in Italy, 1500–1800* (New Haven: Yale University Press, 2007).

9. For the paintings in Titian's studio upon his death, see Wolfgang Braunfels, "I quadri di Tiziano nello studio a Biri Grande (1530–76)," in

Tiziano e Venezia: Convegno internazionale di studi, Venezia, 1976 (Vicenza: N. Pozza, 1980), 375–81, 407–10. The *Flaying* was acquired in 1620 by Althea Talbot, wife of Thomas earl of Arundel. Rembrandt most likely knew of the painting when it sold in Amsterdam in 1654. See David Rosand, "Titian's Dutch Disciple," in *Rembrandt and the Venetian Influence* (New York: Salander-O'Reilly Gallery, 2000), 19. After a series of transactions in the seventeenth century, the painting passed to the Episcopal Palace of Kromeríz in the eighteenth century. For the details of its provenance, see Rossi, *Tiziano,* 370.

10. Julia Kristeva, *The Powers of Horror: An Essay on Abjection,* trans. Leon S. Roudiez (New York: Columbia University Press, 1982), 3–4. Joseph Leo Koerner describes the relationship between abjection and selfhood in the prints of Hans Baldung Grien. *The Moment of Self-Portraiture in German Renaissance Art* (Chicago: University of Chicago Press, 1993), 267.

11. On the ancient sculpted sources for the dog, see Ost, *Tizian-Studien,* 155–61. He suggests, among others, the Dionysus sarcophagus in the Villa Medici in Rome, which Titian could have seen during his 1545–46 visit to the city.

12. Koerner (*Moment of Self-Portraiture,* 266–72) articulates a similar disfiguration of the Dürerian subject in the work of Hans Baldung Grien.

13. The myth also appears in Ovid, *Fasti* 6.695–710; Lucian, *Dialogi deorum* 16.2; Hyginus, *Fabulae* 165, 191; Fulgentius, *Mythologiae* 3.9.

14. Midas appears only in the accounts of the story by Hyginus and Fulgentius. Traditionally Midas participates in the judgment of another musical competition, the one between Apollo and Pan (Ovid, *Metamorphoses* 11.146–93).

15. For the numerous representations of the myth, see Wyss, *Myth of Apollo and Marsyas,* 113–27; and for the specific relationship between music and justice, see Gentili, *Da Tiziano a Tiziano,* 225–26.

16. Wethey, *Paintings of Titian,* 3.59–60, 188–89, cat. 40 (*Venus and Adonis*), 77, 172–75, cat. 32 (*Europa*); David Rosand, "*Ut Pictor Poeta:* Meaning in Titian's *Poesie,*" *New Literary History* 3 (1971–72): 527–46, and *Titian* (New York: H. N. Abrams, 1978), 132, 144; Jane C. Nash, *Titian's "Poesie" for Philip II* (Baltimore: Johns Hopkins University Press, 1980); Gentili, *Da Tiziano a Tiziano,* 167–82, 205–16. See also *Titian and Rubens: Power, Politics, and Style* (Boston: Isabella Stewart Gardner Museum, 1998).

17. Wethey, *Paintings of Titian, III,* 3.141, cat. 9.

18. Gentili, *Da Tiziano a Tiziano,* 244–46.

19. Neumann, *Flaying,* n.p., notes the similarity to images of sacrifice but, like Rapp, prefers to interpret the composition as suggestive of the liberation of the spirit according to neo-Platonic thought. Rosand ("La Mano," 135) notes the relationship to images of martyrdom.

20. On Masaccio's fresco, see Rona Goffen, ed., *Masaccio's "Trinity"* (Cambridge: Cambridge University Press, 1998). For the significance of the center of the picture field, see Meyer Schapiro, "On Some Problems in the Semiotics of Visual Art: Field and Vehicle in Image-Signs," in *Theory and Philosophy of Art: Style, Artist, and Society* (New York: George Braziller, 1994), 1–32. For the sense of presence suggested in the *sacra conversazione,* see Rona Goffen, "*Nostra Conversatio in Caelis Est:* Observations on the Sacra Conversazione in the Trecento," *Art Bulletin* 61 (1979): 198–221.

21. Sixten Ringbom, *Icon to Narrative: The Rise of the Dramatic Close-up in Fifteenth-Century Devotional Painting* (Doornspijk: Davaco, 1984).

22. For Michelangelo and Raphael specifically, see Alexander Nagel, *Michelangelo and the Reform of Art* (Cambridge: Cambridge University Press, 2000), 113–40. For Titian, see David Rosand, "Titian and the Challenge of the Altarpiece," in *Painting in Sixteenth-Century Venice* (Cambridge: Cambridge University Press, 1997), 35–61; Patricia Meilman, *Titian and the Altarpiece in Renaissance Venice* (Cambridge: Cambridge University Press, 2000).

23. Rosand, "Titian and the Challenge of the Altarpiece," 35–61.

24. E. H. Gombrich notes the influence of devotional images on Botticelli's mythological paintings. See "Botticelli's Mythologies: A Study in the Neo-Platonic Symbolism of His Circle" (1945), published in revised form in his collected essays, *Symbolic Images: Studies in the Art of the Renaissance II* (London: Phaidon, 1972), 31–81. For these and the other images cited, see Sarah Ellen Lawrence, "*Conversazioni profane:* In Dialogue with Pagan Gods" (Ph.D. diss., Columbia University, 1994).

25. Aby Warburg, "Der Eintritt des antikisierenden Idealstils in die Malerie der Frührenaissance," *Kunstchronik* 30 (1913–14); translated, "The Emergence of the Antique as a Stylistic Ideal in Early Renaissance Painting," in *The Renewal of Pagan Antiquity: Contributions to the Cultural History of the European Renaissance,* trans. David Britt (Los Angeles: Getty

Research Institute for the History of Art and the Humanities, 1999), 271–80.

26. Devon L. Hodges discusses a similar fragmentation of time in *King Lear. Renaissance Fictions of Anatomy* (Amherst: University of Massachusetts Press, 1985), 72–73. For a more specific discussion of the genre of tragedy and Titian, see D'Elia, *Poetics of Titian's Religious Paintings,* 56–83; and Thomas Puttfarken, *Titian and Tragic Painting: Aristotle's Poetics and the Rise of the Modern Artist* (New Haven: Yale University Press, 2005).

27. Frederick Hartt, *Giulio Romano* (New Haven: Yale University Press, 1958), 11.

28. Alberti, *On Painting,* ¶¶41–43, pp. 76–79.

29. On the presumed relationship between narrative and pictorial realism, including the use of perspective, see E. H. Gombrich, *Art and Illusion: A Study in the Psychology of Pictorial Representation* (Princeton: Princeton University Press, 1960), 129–36; Leo Bersani and Ulysse Dutoit, *Forms of Violence: Narrative in Assyrian Art and Modern Culture* (New York: Schocken Books, 1985), 41–46.

30. For a detailed description of how Titian painted the *Flaying,* see Gentili, *Da Tiziano a Tiziano,* 225–29. Bersani and Dutoit (*Forms of Violence,* 43–46) find similar significance in the emphasis on the background in paintings as different as those by Rembrandt, Monet, and Morandi. They write: "And in Rembrandt's later work . . . there is practically no distinction between the human body and *mere* background. The achievement of these paintings is not, it seems to us, in some realistic rendering of the discolorations, the asperities, and the cracking of aging skin surfaces. Much more interestingly, Rembrandt uses the effects of age on the body as an occasion for connecting the human to the nonhuman. He does not, however, *de*humanize his subjects. . . . Rembrandt paints what might be called the egalitarian effects of matter. He gives us much more than the particular physicality of individual human subjects; his work suggests the equal physicality of all substances in the world" (43–46).

31. Bersani and Dutoit, *Forms of Violence,* 46.

32. Peter Humfrey, *The Altarpiece in Renaissance Venice* (New Haven: Yale University Press, 1993), 62–70.

33. See the papers collected in Peter Humfrey and Martin Kemp, eds., *The Altarpiece in the Renaissance* (Cambridge: Cambridge University Press, 1990).

34. See Harold E. Wethey, *Paintings of Titian,* 1.34, 39, 122–23; Ferino-Pagden, *L'ultimo Tiziano,* 308–11; Laurie Schneider, "A Note on the Iconography of Titian's Last Painting," *Arte Veneta* 23 (1969): 218–19; David Rosand, "Titian in the Frari," *Art Bulletin* 53 (1971): 196–213; Jürg Meyer zur Capellen, "Uberlegungen zur Pietà Tizians," in *Münchner Jahrbuch der Bildenden Kunst* 22 (1971): 117–32; Vinzenz Oberhammer, "Gedanken zum Werdegang und Schicksal von Tizians Grabbild," in *Studi di storia dell'arte in onore di Antonio Morassi* (Venice: Alfieiri, 1971), 152–61; K. Dorment, "Tomb and Testament: Architectural Significance in Titian's *Pietà,*" *Art Quarterly* 35 (1972): 399–418; J. Bruyn, "Notes on Titian's *Pietà,*" in *Album Amicorum J. G. van Gelder* (The Hague: Martinus Nijhoff, 1973), 66–75; Herbert von Einem, *Tizians Grabbild,* Bayerische Akademie der Wissenschaften, Philosophisch-Historische Klasse, Sitzungberichte 5 (Munich: Verlag der Bayerische Akademie, 1979); A. Niero, "Pietà liturgica e pietà poplare nel 'Vesperbild' di Tiziano," in *Interpretazioni veneziane: Studi di storia dell'arte in onore di Michelangelo Muraro,* ed. David Rosand (Venice: Arsenale Editrice, 1984), 323–29; Rona Goffen, *Piety and Patronage in Renaissance Venice: Bellini, Titian, and the Franciscans* (New Haven: Yale University Press, 1986), 151–54; Rosand, *Painting in Sixteenth-Century Venice,* 57–61; Rossi, *Tiziano,* 373–74; Nicholas De Marco, "Titian's *Pietà:* The Living Stone," *Venezia Cinquecento* 2 (1992): 55–92.

35. For Maurice Merleau-Ponty's notion of the invisible, see his "Eye and Mind" (1961), in *The Merleau-Ponty Aesthetics Reader,* ed. and trans. Michael B. Smith (Evanston: Northwestern University Press, 1993), 121–50.

36. The same could not be said for depictions of the female body. Titian, following Giorgione's *Dresden Venus,* oriented the composition of the *Venus of Urbino* around the centric point of the female genitalia. Christ's genitalia occasionally structure and orient the center of Renaissance paintings. See Leo Steinberg, *The Sexuality of Christ in Renaissance Art and in Modern Oblivion* (Cambridge, Mass.: MIT Press, 1983).

37. Alberti, *On Painting,* ¶¶18–23, pp. 53–59; ¶¶41–43, pp. 76–80.

38. Ost, *Tizian-Studien,* 150–53.

39. For the postbiblical stories describing Peter's objection to a crucifixion like that of Christ, see Leo Steinberg, *Michelangelo's Last Paintings: The Conversion of Paul and the Crucifixion of St. Peter in the Cappella Paolina, Vatican Palace* (New York: Oxford University Press, 1975), 42–55.

40. On the semiotics of direction, see Schapiro, "Semiotics of Visual Art," 1–32. In Milton's *Paradise Lost,* for example, we find a similar emphasis on direction and the distinction between falling and remaining still in his account of the fall of the rebel angels.

41. Steinberg (*Michelangelo's Last Paintings,* 48) interprets this gaze as stern and as the center of the entire picture.

42. M. M. Bakhtin, *Rabelais and His World,* trans. Hélène Iswolsky (Bloomington: Indiana University Press, 1984).

43. "Tutte le tre favole superiori dinotano la temerita di coloro che troppo di se presumono in guisa che dovendo riconoscer cio che fanno, e posseggono da li Dij, il contrario facendo, sprezzano la divina potenza, e fanno idoli di se stessi." Lodovico Dolce, *Le trasformationi* (Venice: F. Sansovino, 1568), canto 13, p. 69.

44. Objecthood becomes important during the Reformation for the deflection of claims of idolatry. See Joseph Leo Koerner, *The Reformation of the Image* (Chicago: University of Chicago Press, 2004), esp. 19–26.

45. Ovid, *Metamorphoses,* trans. Mary M. Innes (London: Penguin Books, 1955), 145.

46. For a comparison of the structure of the weapon and the tool, see Elaine Scarry, *The Body in Pain: The Making and Unmaking of the World* (Oxford: Oxford University Press, 1985), 172–76. Other scholars have connected the flaying of Marsyas, in both its textual and depicted versions, to anatomies. See Bohde, "Skin and the Search for the Interior," 10–47; and Fredrika H. Jacobs, "(Dis)assembling: Marsyas, Michelangelo, and the Accademia del Disegno," *Art Bulletin* 84 (2002): 426–48, and *The Living Image in Renaissance Art* (Cambridge: Cambridge University Press, 2005), 62–104.

47. In the mid-sixteenth century, new anatomical practices gave rise to suspicion concerning dissection. See Katharine Park, "The Criminal and the Saintly Body: Autopsy and Dissection in Renaissance Italy," *Renaissance Quarterly* 47 (1994): 1–33. See also Hodges, *Renaissance Fictions of Anatomy,* chap. 1; Jonathan Sawday, *The Body Emblazoned: Dissection and the Human Body in Renaissance Culture* (London: Routledge, 1995). Both scholars, however, in contrast to Park, advance a Renaissance perception of dissection as consistently negative. See also the related discussion in William S. Heckscher, *Rembrandt's "Anatomy of Dr. Nicolaas Tulp"* (New York: New York University Press, 1958); Barbara Maria Stafford, *Body Criticism: Imaging the Unseen in Enlightenment Art and Medicine* (Cambridge, Mass.: MIT Press, 1991); Bohde, "Skin and the Search for the Interior," 10–47.

48. The designs for Vesalius's study originated in the circle of Titian. See David Rosand and Michelangelo Muraro, *Titian and the Venetian Woodcut* (Washington: Foundation, 1976), 211–35. For a recent challenge to the connection between Titian and Vesalius, see Patricia Simons and Monique Kornell, "Annibal Caro's After-Dinner Speech (1536) and the Question of Titian as Vesalius's Illustrator," *Renaissance Quarterly* 61, no. 4 (2008): 1069–97.

49. On dissections and *memento mori* images, see James Elkins, *Pictures of the Body: Pain and Metamorphosis* (Stanford: Stanford University Press, 1999), 109–49.

50. Bohde, "Skin and the Search for the Interior," 10–47; Jacobs, "(Dis)assembling," 426–48.

51. This reading contrasts with those neo-Platonic readings given to the *Flaying* by Wind (*Pagan Mysteries,* 142–46), Neumann (*Titian: The Flaying of Marsyas,* n.p) and Rapp (*Tizians Marsyas,* 70–89), in which the soul becomes liberated.

52. Lynn Enterline, *The Rhetoric of the Body from Ovid to Shakespeare* (Cambridge: Cambridge University Press, 2000), 1–20.

53. David Rosand, "Titian and the Critical Tradition," in *Titian: His World and His Legacy,* ed. David Rosand (New York: Columbia University Press, 1982), 1–39.

54. Cited in the introduction, 8. Marco Boschini, "Breve instruzione," in *La carta del navegar pitoresco: Edizione critica con la "Breve instruzione" premessa alle "Ricche minere della pittura veneziana,"* ed. Anna Pallucchini (Venice: Istituto per la collaborazione culturale, 1966), 711–12. Translated by Rosand in "Titian and the Critical Tradition," 24. See also Rosand, "La mano," 131.

55. See Philip L. Sohm, *Pittoresco: Marco Boschini, His Critics, and Their Critique of Painterly Brushwork in Seventeenth- and Eighteenth-Century Italy* (Cambridge: Cambridge University Press, 1991), 150–51, 154–55.

56. On the opacity of oil paint, see David Rosand, *The Meaning of the Mark: Leonardo and Titian* (Lawrence: Spencer Museum of Art, University of Kansas, 1988), 49–89. For the relationship between Titian's technique and metamorphosis, see Bohde, "Skin and the Search for the Interior," 44–45.

57. Steinberg (*Michelangelo's Last Paintings,* 53–54) makes a

distinction between symbolic self-portraits and certain self-portraits.

58. This iconography will be discussed later in the chapter. The seminal work on the iconography of melancholy remains Erwin Panofsky's analysis of Dürer's *Melancholia I* in *The Life and Art of Albrecht Dürer* (Princeton: Princeton University Press, 1955), 156–71. Panofsky later collaborated with Raymond Klibansky and Fritz Saxl on a broader project on melancholy, *Saturn and Melancholy: Studies in the History of Natural Philosophy, Religion, and Art* (New York: Basic Books, 1964).

59. This similarity with the Prado *Self-Portrait* initiates most of the identifications of Midas as a self-portrait. Neumann (*Titian,* n.p.) first advances the resemblance, which then features in all subsequent interpretations. These include Gentili, *Da Tiziano a Tiziano,* 236–40; and Goffen, *Titian's Women,* 282–86. Some scholars consider the aged figure to be exemplary of a standard type in Titian's later work. Fehl, "Punishment of Marsyas," 377n74; Bruce Cole, *Titian and Venetian Painting, 1450–1590* (Boulder, Colo.: Icon Editions, 1999), 194

60. For a comprehensive list and corresponding bibliography of these identifications, see Luba Freedman, *Titian's Independent Self-Portraits* (Florence: Leo S. Olschki Editore, 1990), 50. For his self-portrait as Nicodemus, see Augusto Gentili, "Tiziano e la religione," in *Titian 500,* ed. Joseph Manca, Studies in the History of Art 45 (Washington: National Gallery of Art, 1993), 147–65. Crowe and Cavalcaselle (*The Life and Times of Titian,* 2:412) identify the figure as Joseph of Arimathea. For the confusion between Nicodemus and Joseph of Arimathea, see Wolfgang Stechow, "Joseph of Arimathea or Nicodemus," in *Studien zur Toskanischen Kunst* (Munich: Prestel, 1964), 289–302. See also Wethey, *Paintings of Titian,* 1.33, 35–36, 90–91, cats. 37–38 (Entombment); 134–36, cats. 105, 108 (Jerome).

61. For the identification of the self-portrait *en décapité,* see Louis Hourticq, *La Jeunesse de Titien* (Paris: Hachette, 1919), 138; Lodovico Foscari, *Iconografia di Tiziano* (Venice: Edizioni Sormari, 1935); Panofsky, *Problems in Titian,* 43; Freedman, *Titian's Independent Self-Portraits,* 50; Creighton Gilbert, "Some Findings on Early Works of Titian," *Art Bulletin* 62 (1980): 62–68. Gilbert also identifies as a self-portrait the Pharisee in Titian's *Tribute Money.* For the Louvre *Entombment,* see Hourticq, *La Jeunesse,* 69, 192–96, 284–85.

62. Some of the self-portraits that Vasari includes in his *Lives* include Masaccio and Filippino Lippi in the Brancacci Chapel. For Vasari's identification, see L. M. Sleptzoff, *Men or Supermen? The Italian Portrait in the Fifteenth Century* (Jerusalem: Magnes Press, 1978), 111–13; Katherine T. Brown, *The Painter's Reflection: Self-Portraiture in Venice, 1458–1625* (Florence: Leo S. Olschki Editore, 2000), 58.

63. In a letter written by Vasari to Michelangelo's nephew, Leonardo Buonarroti (March 18, 1564), he mentions a figure in the *Pietà* as "un vecchio che egli ritrasse se." Condivi identifies this older man as Nicodemus. *The Life of Michelangelo,* ed. Helmut Wohl, trans. Alice Sedgwick Wohl (University Park: Pennsylvania State University Press, 1999), 87. On the tradition of self-portraits in the guise of Nicodemus, see Corine Schleif, "Nicodemus and Sculptors: Self-Reflexivity in Works by Adam Kraft and Tilman Riemenschneider," *Art Bulletin* 75 (1993): 599–626; and specifically on the self-portrait of Michelangelo and his presumed tendencies as a Nicodemist, see Valerie Shrimplin-Evangelidis, "Michelangelo and Nicodemism: The Florentine *Pietà,*" *Art Bulletin* 71 (1989): 58–66.

64. Supporters of this view of disguised self-portraits in general include Joanna Woods-Marsden, *Renaissance Self-Portraiture: The Visual Construction of Identity and the Social Status of the Artist* (New Haven: Yale University Press, 1998), 159–67; John Pope-Hennessy, *The Portrait in the Renaissance* (New York: Pantheon Books, 1966), 290–300; and Brown, *The Painter's Reflection,* 57–65. Koerner (*Moment of Self-Portraiture,* 112–14) articulates examples of the subversion of this idea of authorship.

65. The identification of the flayed skin as a self-portrait of Michelangelo was first made by Francesco La Cava, an Italian physician, in *Il volto di Michelangelo scoperto nel Giudizio finale* (Bologna: N. Zanichelli, 1925). The difference between the bearded figure of St. Bartholomew and the skin was first noticed in a letter from Miniato Pitti to Vasari, but was not explained as a self-portrait until the early twentieth century. For a review of the early historiography around this identification, see Carlo Angeleri, "L'autoritratto di Michelangiolo nel 'Giudizio universale,'" in *Michelangiolo Buonarroti nel IV centenario del "Giudizio universale"* (Florence: G. C. Sansoni, 1942), 231–51. Nagel (*Michelangelo,* 195–97) considers the hanging skin as an "abject self-portrait," "a brooding admission of failure" specific to the contemporary criticisms of the fresco.

66. Patricia Lee Rubin, *Giorgio Vasari: Art and History* (New Haven: Yale University Press, 1995), 359–401; Catherine M. Sousloff, "*Lives* of Poets and Painters in the Renaissance," *Word and Image* 6 (1990): 154–62; Philip L. Sohm, "Caravaggio's Deaths," *Art Bulletin* 84 (2002), 450–51. Later historians attempted a similar operation, including Jacob Burckhardt. For a discussion of this tendency, see Rudolf Wittkower and Margot Wittkower, *Born Under Saturn: The Character and Conduct of Artists: A Documented History from Antiquity to the French Revolution* (New York: W. W. Norton, 1969), 281–93.

67. Vasari, *Le vite,* 4:155–217.

68. Ibid., 473–93.

69. Ernst Kris and Otto Kurz, *Legend, Myth, and Magic in the Image of the Artist: A Historical Experiment* (New Haven: Yale University Press, 1979); and Catherine M. Soussloff, *The Absolute Artist: The Historiography of a Concept* (Minneapolis: University of Minnesota Press, 1997).

70. Martin Kemp, "Lust for Life: Some Thoughts on the Reconstruction of Artists' Lives in Fact and Fiction," in *L'art et les révolutions: Actes XXVIIe Congrès international d'histoire de l'art* (Strasbourg: Société alsacienne pour le développement pour l'histoire de l'art, 1990–92), 7:167–86.

71. For the terminology of the self-portrait "in assistenza," see W. Wätzoldt, *Die Kunst des Porträts* (Leipzig: Hirt, 1908), 315. See also Victor Stoichita, *The Self-Aware Image: An Insight into Early Modern Meta-painting,* trans. Anne-Marie Glasheen (New York: Cambridge University Press, 1997), 200–206; Koerner, *Moment of Self-Portraiture,* 112–14; Woods-Marsden, *Renaissance Self-Portraiture,* 43–62; Freedman, *Titian's Independent Self-Portraits,* 34–46; Brown, *Painter's Reflection,* 57–65; Sletpzoff, *Men or Supermen?* 101–13; Pope-Hennessy, *Portrait in the Renaissance,* 257–300.

72. Vasari, *Le vite,* 4:167 . Bibliographies on the fresco can be found in *Raffaello nell'Appartamento di Giulio II e Leone X* (Milan: Electa, 1993), 349–50; and Marcia Hall, ed., *Raphael's "School of Athens"* (Cambridge: Cambridge University Press, 1997), 171–75.

73. Vasari (*Le vite,* 4:159, 331) identified the balding Euclid as Bramante. Following Vasari, D. Redig de Campos suggested other artistic identities in the fresco. See "La firma sigilata di Raffaello nella Scuola d'Atene," *Arti figurative* 1 (1945): 151, and "Il concetto platonico-cristiano della Stanza della Segnatura," in *Raffaello e Michelangelo: Studi di storia e d'arte* (Rome: G. Bardi, 1956), 15–16.

74. Freedman, *Titian's Independent Self-Portraits,* 46. One exception is Bronzino's self-portrait in the *Martyrdom of Saint Lawrence* (San Lorenzo, Florence), a painting that cites figures from Michelangelo's work. See Stephen J. Campbell, "Counter Reformation Polemic and Mannerist Counter-aesthetics," *Res* 46 (2004): 99–119. Another possible self-portrait could be the possible identification of the male figure looking directly at the beholder as Pontormo in his *Deposition* (Santa Felicita, Florence).

75. Venetian scuola cycles included portraits of historical figures well into the cinquecento. Dolce criticizes this practice: "I should not refrain from saying that, as regards historical subject matter, the man who painted in the Sala I mentioned before, next to Titian's battle picture, the history of the excommunication of the Emperor Frederick Barbarossa by Pope Alexander, and included in his invention a representation of Rome, exceeded the bounds of propriety in a serious way—in my opinion—when he put in so many Venetian senators, and showed them standing there and looking on without any real motivation. For the fact is that there is no likelihood that all of them should have happened to be there simultaneously in quite this way, nor do they have anything to do with the subject" (*Dialogo della pittura,* 124–25). Sometimes these historical figures had a close relationship to the art of painting: Veronese, for example, included portraits of his fellow artists in his *Marriage at Cana* (Louvre, Paris).

76. This is the convincing argument presented by David Rosand, "Raphael's *School of Athens* and the Artist of the Modern Manner," in *The World of Savonarola: Italian Elites and Perceptions of Crisis,* ed. Stella Fletcher and Christine Shaw (Aldershot: Ashgate, 2000), 212–32.

77. Jodi Cranston, *The Poetics of Portraiture in the Italian Renaissance* (Cambridge: Cambridge University Press, 2000), 98–126.

78. Again, the terminology of "disguised" self-portrait derives from Wätzoldt's classification, *verkapptes Selbstbildnis.* See his *Die Kunst des Porträts,* 317. See also Freedman, *Titian's Independent Self-Portraits,* 49–57; Brown, *Painter's Reflection,* 69–76.

79. Schleif, "Nicodemus and Sculptors," 599.

80. On the relationship between the self-image and narrative in which it appears, especially in regard to Michelangelo, see Ernst Steinmann, *Die Portraitdarstellungen des Michelangelo* (Leipzig: Klinkhardt and Biermann, 1913), 429.

81. Cranston, *Poetics of Portraiture,* 85–97.

82. The discussion around Titian's possible "disguised" self-portraits and portraits exemplifies this phenomenon. See Freedman, *Titian's Independent Self-Portraits,* 50; Gilbert, "Some Findings," 65–66.

83. Neumann, *Titian,* n.p.; Goffen, *Titian's Women,* 282–86.

84. Paul De Man, "Autobiography as De-Facement," in *The Rhetoric of Romanticism* (New York: Columbia University Press, 1984), 67–81.

85. Soussloff, *Absolute Artist,* 73–158; John Christie and Fred Orton, "Writing on a Text of the Life," *Art History* 11 (1988): 545–64; Nicholas Green, "Stories of Self-Expression: Art History and the Politics of Individualism," *Art History* 10 (1987): 527–32. There was, of course, opposition to this biographical impulse in art history through formalist criticism. See, for example, the critique of Freud's essay on Leonardo in Meyer Schapiro, "Freud and Leonardo: An Art Historical Study," in *Theory and Philosophy of Art: Style, Artist, and Society* (New York: George Braziller, 1994), 153–92.

86. One of the seminal works that discusses the elimination of the author is Roland Barthes, "The Death of the Author," in *Image, Music, Text,* ed. and trans. Stephen Heath (New York: Hill and Wang, 1977), 142–48. Michel Foucault also criticized the Romantic idea of the artist by articulating a historically variable subjectivity. See Michel Foucault, "What Is an Author?" in *Language, Counter-Memory, Practice: Selected Essays and Interviews,* ed. Donald Bouchard, trans. Donald Bouchard and Sherry Simon (Ithaca: Cornell University Press, 1977), 113–18, 120. Despite the interest in these essays, art history has retained an ongoing interest in the individual artist, even for movements usually detached from biography. See Anna C. Chave, "Minimalism and Biography," *Art Bulletin* 86 (2000): 149–63; Green, "Stories of Self-Expression," 527–28. On the notion of authorship and art history specifically, see Keith Moxey, *The Practice of Theory: Poststructuralism, Cultural Politics, and Art History* (Ithaca: Cornell University Press, 1994), 51–61.

87. For a summary of the reception to La Cava's identification, see Leo Steinberg, "The Line of Fate in Michelangelo's Painting," in *The Language of Images,* ed. W. T. J. Mitchell (Chicago: University of Chicago Press, 1980), 95–109.

88. Wind, *Pagan Mysteries,* 186–89; Leo Steinberg, "Michelangelo's *Last Judgment* as Merciful Heresy," *Art in America* (1975): 52–53, and "Line of Fate," 95–110; Marcia B. Hall, "Michelangelo's *Last Judgment:* Resurrection of the Body and Predestination," *Art Bulletin* 58 (1976): 85–92; Avigdor W. G. Posèq, "Michelangelo's Self-Portrait on the Flayed Skin of St. Bartholomew," *Gazette des Beaux-Arts* 124 (1994): 1–14; Bernadine Barnes, *Michelangelo's Last Judgment: The Renaissance Response* (Berkeley and Los Angeles: University of California Press, 1998), 105–7; Nagel, *Michelangelo,* 195–97.

89. Reproduced and discussed in Steinberg, "Line of Fate," 100–120.

90. Rosand, "Raphael's *School of Athens,*" 223–25, reads the presence of Michelangelo in Raphael's fresco in a more symbolic way.

91. The picture has been in its current location, the Archbishop's Palace of Kromeríz, Czech Republic, since the eighteenth century. See Falomir, *Tiziano,* 414. Most scholars had not seen the painting until its London exhibition in 1983.

92. Neumann, *Titian,* n.p.

93. Goffen, *Titian's Women,* 285; Gentili, *Da Tiziano a Tiziano,* 240; D'Elia, *Poetics of Titian's Religious Paintings,* 82–83.

94. Sidney J. Freedberg, "Titian and Marsyas," *FMR* (1986): 54.

95. On exegesis and devotional images, see Paolo Berdini, *The Religious Art of Jacopo Bassano: Painting as Visual Exegesis* (Cambridge: Cambridge University Press, 1997).

96. Klibansky, Panofsky, and Saxl, *Saturn and Melancholy,* 317–66; Panofsky, *Life and Art of Albrecht Dürer,* 157–70; Charles de Tolnay, *The Sistine Ceiling* (Princeton: Princeton University Press, 1949), 149.

97. Tolnay, *Sistine Ceiling,* 149; Rosand, "Raphael's *School of Athens,*" 225; Maria Ruvoldt, *The Italian Renaissance Imagery of Inspiration* (Cambridge: Cambridge University Press, 2004), 54–56.

98. For a review of earlier interpretations, see Peter-Klaus Schuster, *Melancolia I: Dürers Denkbild* (Berlin: Mann, 1991). Still the most influential interpretation is that offered by Panofsky, *Life and Art of Albrecht Dürer,* 156–71. See, more recently, the discussion by Koerner, *Moment of Self-Portraiture,* 20–27.

99. For the modern identification as Michelangelo, see D. Redig de Campos, "Il 'Pensieroso' della Segnatura," in *Michelangiolo Buonarroti nel IV centenario del "Giudizio universale"* (Florence: G. C. Sansoni, 1942), 205–19. For further discussion, consult Hall's introduction to *Raphael's "School of Athens,"*

38–39; David Summers, *Michelangelo and the Language of Art* (Princeton: Princeton University Press, 1981), 116–17; Rosand, "Raphael's *School of Athens,*" 222–28; Rona Goffen, *Renaissance Rivals: Michelangelo, Leonardo, Raphael, Titian* (New Haven: Yale University Press, 2002), 222–26.

100. Redig de Campos, "Il 'Pensieroso,'" 205–19; Rosand, "Raphael's *School of Athens,*" 223–24. Bellori singles out for discussion the isolated figure: "[We] recognize the meditation of another philosopher, who sits and leans on his elbow, with one hand under his cheek, the other holding a pen over the page, and as he meditates he gazes fixedly at the ground and manifests his inner thoughts as he resolves the reasoning of his doctrine. He wears a sagum, with his boot tops turned down from his bare knees; in this abbreviated costume he differs from the other cloaked figures in the *Gymnasium.*" Cited from the English translation given by Alice Sedgwick Wohl in Hall, *Raphael's "School of Athens,"* 52.

101. Panofsky, *Life and Art of Albrecht Dürer,* 170–71; Koerner, *Moment of Self-Portraiture,* 20–27. Rosand ("Raphael's *School of Athens,*" 228n40) echoes these readings.

102. Consider the isolated figures of *Melancholia I,* Jeremiah, and Heraclitus.

103. *Holy Family,* ca. 1492–93, pen and ink (Kupferstichkabinett, Staatliche Museen Preußischer Kulturbesitz, Berlin). Reproduced and discussed in Koerner, *Moment of Self-Portraiture,* 17–21. On the outsider status of Joseph, his relegation to the periphery, and his absence through sleep, see Carolyn C. Wilson, *St. Joseph in Italian Renaissance Society and Art* (Philadelphia: St. Joseph's University Press, 2001).

104. On disfiguration as rhetorical subversion, see Paul De Man, "Shelley Disfigured," in *Rhetoric of Romanticism,* 99–101. Koerner, *Moment of Self-Portraiture,* 272, discusses the literal and figurative disfiguration in the work of Hans Baldung Grien.

105. Miserliness was a symptom of *avaritiosa melancholia.* Dürer's figure holds a purse, and Cesare Ripa's personification holds a moneybag. Consult Klibansky, Panofsky, and Saxl, *Saturn and Melancholy,* 284; Panofsky, *Life and Art of Albrecht Dürer,* 164, and "The Neoplatonic Movement and Michelangelo," in *Studies in Iconology* (New York: Oxford University Press, 1939), 210–11. Scholars oftentimes associate the avarice of Midas with that reported for Titian. For the painter's miserliness, see Wittkower and Wittkower, *Born Under Saturn,* 265–70.

106. "Ma vile rimase e rozzo ingegno, e gli occhi del giudicio infermi e loschi, benche havesse ogni dì molti favori dal boschareccio Pan Dio di Pastori" (Dolce, *Le trasformationi,* 109v).

107. Benedetto Varchi responded to this criticism of sculpture in his *Della maggioranza delle arti—Disputa II.* For the entire text, see *Trattati d'arte del Cinquecento fra manierismo e Controriforma,* ed. Paola Barocchi (Bari: G. Laterza, 1960–62), vol. 1, esp. 43.

108. Klibansky, Panofsky, and Saxl, *Saturn and Melancholy,* 218.

109. For a helpful description of the pastoral as a subject for painting and its complexities, see Jonathan Unglaub, "The *Concert Champêtre:* The Crises of History and the Limits of Pastoral," *Arion* 5, no. 1 (1997): 46–96.

110. Panofsky, *Problems in Titian,* 168, advances the Vienna picture as a farewell to the pastoral tradition. See also Wethey, *Paintings of Titian,* 3.166–67, cat. 27; Gentili, *Da Tiziano a Tiziano,* 225–40.

111. Klibansky, Panofsky, and Saxl, *Saturn and Melancholy,* 288.

112. John Shearman, "Cristofano Allori's 'Judith,'" *Burlington Magazine* 121 (1979): 3–10; Koerner, *Moment of Self-Portraiture,* 524n14; Wittkower, *Born Under Saturn,* 160.

113. Shearman, "Cristofano Allori's 'Judith,'" 3–10. According to a 1650 inventory, Caravaggio depicted himself as Goliath in his Borghese painting of *David and Goliath.* See Walter Friedlaender, *Caravaggio Studies* (Princeton: Princeton University Press, 1955), 202–3. The bibliography on Caravaggio's painting is too extensive to be cited here. Most interpretations of the picture find it expressive of the personal tensions in Caravaggio's later years. Representative of this approach are the following: C. L. Frommel, "Caravaggio und seine Modelle," *Castrum Peregrini* 96 (1971): 52; Herwarth Röttgen, *Il Caravaggio: Ricerche e interpretazioni* (Rome: Bulzoni Editore, 1974), 202–7; Laurie Schneider, "Donatello and Caravaggio: The Iconography of Decapitation," *American Imago* 33 (1976): 76–91; and Howard Hibbard, *Caravaggio* (New York: Harper and Row, 1983), 264–67. For interpretations that address subjectivity and decapitation, see Louis Marin, *To Destroy Painting,* trans. Mette Hjort (Chicago: University of Chicago Press, 1995); and Leo Bersani and Ulysse Dutoit, *Caravaggio's Secrets* (Cambridge, Mass.: MIT Press, 1998), 87–99.

114. The inventory entry reads: "Ritratto di Zorzon di sua man fatto

per david e Golia" (BAV, MS Rossiano 1179, fol. 1v; P. Paschini, "Le collezioni archeologiche dei Grimani," *Rendiconti della pontificia academia romana di archeologia* 5 (1928): 149ff., no. 18). Vasari identifies David as a self-portrait of Giorgione. See Vasari, *Le vite,* 4:43. Most scholars accept this identification and the resemblance to the head of Holofernes in Giorgione's *Judith.* For relevant bibliography and a review of interpretations, see Jaynie Anderson, *Giorgione: The Painter of Poetic Brevity* (Paris: Flammarion, 1997), 196–206, and "From Likeness to Allegory," in *Giorgione: Atti del convegno internazionale di studi per il V centenario della nascita* (Castelfranco Veneto: Banca popolare di Asolo e Montebelluna, 1979), 153–58. John Shearman suggests that Giorgione represented himself as Goliath in *Only Connect . . . : Art and the Spectator in the Italian Renaissance* (Princeton: Princeton University Press, 1992), 23–26.

115. Shearman, "Cristofano Allori's 'Judith,'" 9.

116. Sigmund Freud, "Medusa's Head," in *Standard Edition of the Complete Psychological Works of Sigmund Freud,* trans. and ed. James Strachey (London: Hogarth Press, 1955), 18:273.

117. Shearman, *Only Connect,* 26.

118. *Petrarch's Lyric Poems: The "Rime sparse" and Other Lyrics,* ed. and trans. Robert M. Durling (Cambridge, Mass., 1995), 110–11.

119. "Davitte colla fromba e io coll'arco. / Michelagnolo." *The Poetry of Michelangelo: An Annotated Translation,* ed. and trans. James M. Saslow (New Haven: Yale University Press, 1991), 504. Marcel Brion first suggested the interpretation of the "arco" as the bowed drill used by sculptors. *Michelangelo* (New York: Greystone Press, 1940), 102. "Arco" also could refer to the compass. See Charles Seymour Jr., *Michelangelo's David: A Search for Identity* (Pittsburgh: University of Pittsburgh Press, 1967), 3–14; Irving Lavin, "David's Sling and Michelangelo's Bow," in *Die Kunstler über Sich in seinem Werk,* ed. Matthias Winner (Weinheim: VCH, Acta Humaniora, 1992), 161–90.

120. Most scholars emphasize the mind as David's virtue. See Lavin, "David's Sling," 162–63; and in comparison to Bernini's Borghese *David,* see Cole, *Cellini,* 157.

121. Michelangelo interweaves metaphors of art into his poetic rumination on love, mortality, and selfhood. In one madrigal for Vittoria Colonna (no. 153), he compares himself to a broken mold for bronze casting: "It's not only the mold that, empty of finished work, waits to be filled with fired silver or gold, and which these can only be drawn from when it's shattered. I, too, with the fire of love refill the inner void of my desire for infinite beauty, for her whom I adore, the soul and the heart of my fragile life. But this noble and welcome lady pours down into me through such narrow spaces that to draw her out I must be torn and broken" ["Non pur d'argento o d'oro / vinto dal foco esser po'piena aspetta, / vota d'opra prefetta, / la forma, che sol fratta il tragge fora; / tal io, col foco ancora / d'amor dentro ristoro / il desir voto di beltà infinita, / di coste' ch'i' adoro, / anima e cor della mie fragil vita. / Alta donna e gradita / in me discende per sì brevi spazi, / c'a trarla fuor convien mi rompa e strazi"] (*Poetry of Michelangelo,* 306). See also the discussion in Saslow, "Themes and Content," 33–38.

122. "Rott'è l'alta colonna e 'l verde lauro" (Saslow, *Poetry of Michelangelo,* 504). Lavin does not find a close relationship between these two inscriptions, except for the possible allusion of "colonna" to the column of marble used for the sculpture; whereas Seymour (*Michelangelo's David,* 6) finds a reference to Lorenzo de' Medici.

123. *Petrarch's Lyric Poems,* 442.

124. Leonardo disparaged sculpture because of the sweat and dust involved. See his comments (from Codex Urbinas latinus 1270, fols. 20ff.), collected in *Scritti d'arte del Cinquecento,* ed. Paola Barocchi (Milan: Riccardo Ricciardi Editore, 1971), 1:475–88. See also Cole, *Cellini,* 1–3. On the personification of labor, consult Kristina Herrmann-Fiore, "Il tema 'Labor' nella creazione artistica del Rinascimento," in *Die Kunstler über Sich in seinem Werk,* 245–92.

125. Dolce wrote that "è arte a nasconder l'arte." *Dialogo della pittura,* 90–91, 176–77. Although the most direct source for Dolce's concept was Ovid ("Ars est celare artem," *Ars amatoria* 2.313), the intermediary for this idea was most likely Castiglione. See David Rosand, "Una linea sola non stentata: Castiglione, Raphael and the Aesthetics of Grace," in *Reading Medieval Culture: Essays in Honor of Robert W. Hanning,* ed. Robert M. Stein and Sandra Pierson Prior (Notre Dame: University of Notre Dame Press, 2005), 464.

126. Michelangelo expresses the neo-Platonic artistic theory in one of his best-known sonnets, which inspired the first *Lezzione* given by Benedetto Varchi to the Florentine Academy in March 1547. The sculptor wrote: "Not even the best of artists has any conception that a single marble block does not contain within its excess, and *that* is only attained by the hand that obeys the intellect" ["Non ha l'ottimo

artista alcun concetto / c'un marmo solo in sé non circonscriva / col suo superchio, e solo a quello arriva / la man che ubbidisce all'intelletto"] (*Poetry of Michelangelo,* 302).

127. *Poetry of Michelangelo,* 70. In this poem Michelangelo connects his deformed judgment to the fact that he must bend his body like a bow. See Lavin, "David's Sling," 161–90; and Cole, *Cellini,* 135.

128. Cranston, *Poetics of Portraiture,* 98–126.

129. Ibid. For the Berlin *Self-Portrait,* see Woods-Marsden, *Renaissance Self-Portraiture,* 160–65; Freedman, *Titian's Independent Self-Portraits,* 73–83, and *Titian's Portraits Through Aretino's Lens* (University Park: Pennsylvania State University Press, 1995); *Tiziano* (1990), 326; Ballarin, *Le siècle de Titien,* cat. 265, pp. 623–25. On the *Allegory of Prudence,* see Erwin Panofsky, "Titian's *Allegory of Prudence:* A Postscript," in *Meaning in the Visual Arts* (Garden City, N.Y.: Doubleday, 1955), 146–68.

130. Goffen (*Titian's Women,* 212) refers to Titian's late brushwork as defining and undermining bodily structure.

Chapter 3

1. Still the foundational study of the half-length narrative image is Sixten Ringbom, *Icon to Narrative: The Rise of the Dramatic Close-up in Fifteenth-Century Devotional Painting* (Doornspijk: Davaco, 1984). For the half-length narrative in the work of northern Italian painters, see Rona Goffen, *Giovanni Bellini* (New Haven: Yale University Press, 1989), 23–118; and Jaynie Anderson, *Giorgione: Painter of "Poetic Brevity"* (New York: Flammarion, 1997), 17–49, who notes that the half-length narrative type occurs most often as scenes of education in Giorgione's oeuvre.

2. The sources of these pictorial traditions are Leon Battista Alberti, *On Painting,* ed. and trans. Cecil Grayson (London: Penguin, 1991); Leonardo da Vinci, *Treatise on Painting,* trans. A. Philip McMahon (Princeton: Princeton University Press, 1956). I discuss several of these traditions in my book *The Poetics of Portraiture in the Italian Renaissance* (Cambridge: Cambridge University Press, 2000).

3. On the interest of Venetian painting in central Italian practice, and the regional differences, see David Rosand, *Painting in Sixteenth-Century Venice: Titian, Veronese, Tintoretto* (Cambridge: Cambridge University Press, 1997), 1–34.

4. The *Mellon Venus* also deviates from the expectations of the "woman at her toilette" type. As we discussed in chapter 2, this deviation detached desire from illusionism and reconfigured desire as an embodied experience. The pictures considered in the present chapter perform a similar operation with a similar result, except that they undermine different mimetic and thematic structures and explicitly explore the relationship between violence and materiality that the *Mellon Venus* only implied through the physicality of love.

5. *Problems in Titian, Mostly Iconographic* (New York: New York University Press, 1969), 25.

6. Gridley McKim-Smith, Greta Andersen-Bergdoll, and Richard Newman, *Examining Velázquez* (New Haven: Yale University Press, 1988).

7. For the intellectual biography of Malvezzi, see Philip L. Sohm, *Pittoresco: Marco Boschini, His Critics, and Their Critiques of Painterly Brushwork in Seventeenth- and Eighteenth-Century Italy* (Cambridge: Cambridge University Press, 1991), 58–60, and "Gendered Style in Italian Art Criticism from Michelangelo to Malvasia," *Renaissance Quarterly* 48 (1995): 796–98. Malvezzi might have been interested in characterizing different styles because of the work of his fellow Bolognese painters, the Carracci. Charles Dempsey interprets the significance of these stylistic variations. "The Carracci and the Devout Style in Emilia," in *Emilian Painting of the Sixteenth and Seventeenth Centuries* (Bologna: Nuova Alfa Editoriale, 1987), 75–87.

8. Virgilio Malvezzi, preface to *Considerationi con occasione d'alcuni luoghi delle vite d'Alcibiade e di Coriolano* (Bologna, 1648), n.p.: "Titiano forse il più famoso Pittore, e senza forse fra più famosi, tal'hora dipinte con tante, e così diligenti pennellate, che parve quasi volesse far numerabili i capelli: e tal'hora si contentò grossamente le pitture di pocchi, e rozzissimi colpi figurare. Spettatore intelligente da così diversa maniera nell'una riconoscerà il vago della femina, nell'altra il robusto maschile; Quella passarà con lode, in questa si fermarà con ammiratione, sentirassi dalla delicate soavemente inclinare, dalla rozza violentemente rapire." Cited and translated in Sohm, "Gendered Style," 797. Malvezzi's text was almost immediately published in an English translation. See, for example, the translation by Robert Gentilis published in London in 1650.

9. Translation based on Gentilis's text (1650), 179.

10. Ibid., 180–81.

11. Sohm, "Gendered Style," 759–808.

12. Ibid., 797.

13. When differentiating between the rough and smooth styles, Cicero (*Orator,* 6.20ff.; *De Oratore,* 3.7.25ff.) acknowledges the varying effects on the listeners of the oration, but without the extreme emotional responses outlined by Malvezzi. See also Sohm, "Gendered Style," 797–98.

14. Alberti, *On Painting,* ¶41, pp. 76–77.

15. "Painting possesses a truly divine power in that not only does it make the absent present (as they say of friendship), but it also represents the dead to the living"; "I used to tell my friends that the inventor of painting, according to the poets, was Narcissus" (ibid., ¶¶25–26, pp. 60–61). For a discussion of these two passages and the relationship to Renaissance visual traditions, see Cranston, *Poetics,* 62–78, 127–33.

16. "Questo è, che bisogna, che le figure movano gli animi de' riguardanti, alcune turbandogli, altri rallegrandogli, altri sospingedoli a pietà, & altri a sdegno, secondo la qualità della historia. . . . Ne puo movere il Pittore, se prima nel far delle figure non sente nel suo animo quelle passioni, o diciamo affetti, che vuole imprimere in quello d'altrui." See Mark W. Roskill, ed. and trans., *Dolce's "Aretino" and Venetian Art Theory of the Cinquecento* (New York: New York University Press, 1968), 156–57.

17. "I [fanciulli] talhor veggendo qualche imagine dipinta, la dimostrano quasi sempre col ditto: e pare, che tutti s'ingombrino di dolcezza i lor pargoletti cuori" (ibid., 114–15, 182–83).

18. Elizabeth Cropper, "The Place of Beauty in the High Renaissance and Its Displacement in the History of Art," in *Place and Displacement in the Renaissance,* ed. Alvin Vos (Binghamton, N.Y.: Medieval and Renaissance Texts and Studies, 1995), 159–205.

19. Alberti, *On Painting,* ¶42, pp. 77–78.

20. Vasari, *Le vite de' più eccellenti pittori, scultori, ed architettori: Nelle redazioni 1550 e 1568,* ed. Paola Barocchi, 6 vols. (Florence: Sansoni, 1966–69 [vols. 1–3, 5, 6]; Florence: Studi per edizione scelte, 1967 [vol. 4]), 6:166. For a more contemporary development of Vasari's idea, see also E. H. Gombrich, *Art and Illusion: A Study in the Psychology of Pictorial Representation* (Princeton: Princeton University Press, 1989), 181–202.

21. David Rosand, *Titian* (New York: H. N. Abrams, 1978), 150; Harold E. Wethey, *The Paintings of Titian* (London: Phaidon, 1969–75), 1.83, cat. 27. Carlo Ridolfi first mentions Tintoretto's acquisition of the picture. See Carlo Ridolfi, *Le meraviglie dell'arte* (Venice, 1648), ed. Detlev von Hadeln (Berlin: G. Grote, 1914–24), 1:207. Marco Boschini mentions the painting as passing into Tintoretto's possession after Titian's death: "Veramente vidi nella Casa del Tintoretto, vivendo Dominico il Figlio, un abbozzo di Tiziano, che già sino il Padre ebbe dall'Auttore, ed era un quadro di forma assai grande e di figure al naturale, dove eravi rappresentato Cristo Redentore, mentre quei ribaldi Ebrei gli ponevano la Corona di spine in capo, il qual poi lo stesso Dominico Tintoretto vendé a gran prezzo ad un Oltramontano indendente." Marco Boschini, "Breve instruzione," in *La carta del navegar pitoresco: Edizione critica con la "Breve instruzione" premessa alle "Ricche minere della pittura veneziana,"* ed. Anna Pallucchini (Venice: Istituto per la collaborazione culturale, 1966), 712. Boschini's use of the word "abbozzo" and the obvious compositional similarities with the earlier Louvre painting of the same subject have led many scholars to suggest that this is a modello; however, there are others who argue that the large size of the canvas (2.8 x 1.8 m) undermines the claim of a sketch. For a review of these arguments, see Wethey, *Paintings of Titian,* 1.83–84. Later contributors to this debate include Charles Hope, who considers the painting to be unfinished. *Titian* (New York: Harper and Row, 1980), 164.

22. Wethey, *Paintings of Titian,* 1.90–92, 122–23, cats. 37, 38, 86.

23. See, for example, the reading given to the *Saint Sebastian* (Hermitage) by Irina Artemieva in *Tiziano,* exh. cat. (Venice: Marsilio Editore, 1990), 368.

24. Alberti, *On Painting,* ¶42, p. 77.

25. The fresco dates to 1426–27, based on circumstantial documents. On this issue: James Beck and Gino Corti, *Masaccio: The Documents* (Locust Valley, N.Y.: J. J. Augustin, 1978), 27, 54–60, docs. 20–23; Paul Joannides, *Masaccio and Masolino: A Complete Catalogue* (New York: H. N. Abrams, 1993), 321–22; Rona Goffen, ed., *Masaccio's "Trinity"* (Cambridge: Cambridge University Press, 1998), 12.

26. Alberti, *On Painting,* ¶42, pp. 77–78.

27. See Rosand, *Painting in Sixteenth-Century Venice,* 45–51; *Tiziano,* 194–96; Wethey, *Paintings of Titian,* 1.79–80, 101–3, cats. 21, 55.

28. David Rosand notes the role of animals as Albertian interlocutors in Titian's paintings in "*Cave canem:* On Titian's Albertian Beasts," paper delivered at the 2004 annual

meeting of the Renaissance Society of America, New York.

29. A. Bartlett Giamatti, "Sfrenatura: Restraint and Release in the *Orlando Furioso*," in *Ariosto 1974 in America: Atti del congresso ariostesco,* ed. Aldo Scaglione (Ravenna: Longo, 1976), 31–39.

30. Fehl ("Realism and Classicism," 1387) thinks that the satirino is weeping.

31. This operation describes a central feature of deconstruction. See Jonathan Culler, *On Deconstruction: Theory and Criticism After Structuralism* (Ithaca: Cornell University Press, 1982), 85–179. The simultaneous adherence to and deviance from quattrocento visual traditions and Titian's continued interest in the isolation of the human figure distinguishes these later pictures from the emptying of contemporary structures of meaning and introduction of new compositional types in contemporary mannerist paintings. See Marcia B. Hall, *After Raphael: Painting in Central Italy in the Sixteenth* Century (Cambridge: Cambridge University Press, 1999).

32. Wethey, *Paintings of Titian, I,* 1.140–41, cat. 115.

33. This acknowledgment of the viewer is absent from Titian's earlier version of the story in the Gesuiti in Venice.

34. For a more detailed discussion of these paintings, including their significance within the larger cycle for the Scuola di San Marco, consult David Rosand, *Painting in Sixteenth-Century Venice,* 139–44; Rodolfo Pallucchini and Paola Rossi, *Tintoretto: Le opera sacre e profane* (Milan: Electa, 1982), cat. nos. 243, 244; Rosalba Tardito, *Il Ritrovamento del Corpo di San Marco del Tintoretto: Vicènde e restauri* (Florence: Cantini, 1990); Sergio Marinelli, *Il Ritrovamento del corpo di San Marco di Jacopo Tintoretto* (Milan: TEA, 1996); Tom Nichols, *Tintoretto: Tradition and Identity* (London: Reaktion Books, 1999), 137–47.

35. Barocchi, *Trattati d'arte del Cinquecento,* 2:521–43; Anton W. A. Boschloo, *Annibale Carracci in Bologna: Visible Reality in Art After the Council of Trent* (New York: Abner Schram, 1974), 85–155; Anthony Blunt, *Artistic Theory in Italy, 1450–1600* (Oxford: Clarendon Press, 1940), 102–36.

36. The specific relationship of the Counter-Reformation to Titian's work will be discussed later in this chapter. The most important study of the Counter-Reformation and art remains Émile Mâle, *L'art religieux après le Concile de Trente* (Paris: Librairie Armand Colin, 1932). For this suggestion that art expressed religious ideas that were circulating well before the Council of Trent formulated the position of the Catholic Church and, therefore, had a relatively flexible and even creative relationship to Church dogma than is oftentimes asserted, see Marcia B. Hall, *Renovation and Counter-Reformation: Vasari and Duke Cosimo in Sta. Maria Novella and Sta. Croce, 1565–1577* (New York: Oxford University Press, 1979); and Nagel, *Michelangelo and the Reform of Art.*

37. Federico Zeri, *Pittura e controriforma: L'arte senza tempo di Scipione da Gaeta* (Turin: Einaudi, 1957); Stuart Lingo, "The Capuchins and the Art of History: Retrospection and Reform in the Arts in Late Renaissance Italy" (Ph.D. diss., Harvard University, 1998); Nagel, *Michelangelo,* 13.

38. The *Beneficio di Cristo* (1543), written by Benedetto da Mantova, exemplifies this Italian reform emphasis on faith in Christ crucified.

39. "Molto più mostrerebbe il pittore la forza de l'arte in farlo afflitto, sanguinoso, pieno di sputi, depelato, piagato, difformato, livido e brutto, di maniera che non avesse forma d'uomo." Gilio, *Dialogo,* in Barocchi, *Trattati d'arte del Cinquecento,* 2:40.

40. "Mostrarlo sanguinoso, brutto, difformato, afflitto, consumato e morto" (ibid., 40).

41. "A fermarsi con maraviglia a contemplare la bassezza" (ibid., 41). On Gilio and decorum, see D'Elia, *Poetics of Titian's Religious Paintings,* 54–55; and Nagel, *Michelangelo and the Reform of Art,* 14–15, 50–51. Contemporary sermons emphasize the torturers' interest in the body of Christ. See Paolo Berdini, *The Religious Art of Jacopo Bassano: Painting as Visual Exegesis* (Cambridge: Cambridge University Press, 1997), 113–14.

42. "Il sentire narrare il martirio d'un santo, il zelo e costanza d'una vergine, la passione dello stesso Cristo, sono cose che toccano dentro di vero; ma l'esserci con vivi colori qua posto sotto gli occhi il santo martirizzato, cola la vergine combattuta e nell'altro lato Cristo inchiodato, egli e pur vero che tanto accresce la divozione e compugne le viscere, che chi non lo conosce è di legno o di marmo." Gabriele Paleotti, *Discorso intorno alle immagini sacre e profane* (1582), in Barocchi, *Trattati d'arte del Cinquecento,* 2:171–72, 2:228. See also the more recent publication of Paleotti's *Discorso* (Vatican City: Libreria Editrice Vaticana; Milan: Cad and Wellness, 2002).

43. "Onde, se tanta efficacia hanno le parole, che si odono o leggono, di tramutare i sensi nostri, con molta maggiore violenza penetreranno dentro di noi quelle figure, dalle quali si vedrà spirare pietà, modestia, santità e divozione,

dicendo S. Gregorio. . . . Essendo donque la imaginativa nostra così atta a ricevere tali impressioni, non è dubbio non ci essere istrumento più forte o più efficace a ciò delle imagini fatte al vivo, che quasi violentano i sensi incauti" (Paleotti, *Discorso,* 228–30).

44. Boschloo, *Annibale Carracci,* 126.

45. Una Roman D'Elia, "Drawing Christ's Blood: Michelangelo, Vittoria Colonna, and the Aesthetics of Reform," *Renaissance Quarterly* 59 (2006): 90–129.

46. Translation in ibid., 96. "Con divine parole il bel dissegno / fece Ei del viver vero, e poi colore / gli die' col sangue, l'intelletto / di luce appaghi, e con questa e con quella / erga e rinforzi il purgato desire; / vengano a mille in me calde quadrella / da l'aspre piaghe, ond'io con vero effetto / prenda vita immortal dal Suo morire." Vittoria Colonna, *Rime,* ed. Alan Bullock (Rome: Bari, 1982), 88.

47. Francisco de Hollanda, *Three Dialogues on Painting* (1540), in *Michael Angelo Buonarroti, with Translations of the Life of the Master by His Scholar, Ascanio Condivi, and Three Dialogues from the Portuguese by Francisco Hollanda,* by Charles Holroyd (London: Duckworth, 1911), 240. See also David Summers, *Michelangelo and the Language of Art* (Princeton: Princeton University Press, 1981), 332ff.

48. Translation in D'Elia, "Drawing Christ's Blood," 110. "Quando in se stesso il pensier nostro riede / e poi sopra di sè s'erge la mente, / sì che d'altra virtù fatta possente / vivo ne l'aspra croce il Signor vede, / sale a cotanto ardir che non pur crede / esser Suo caro membro, anzi alor sente / le spine, i chiodi, il fele e quella ardente / Sua fiamma in parte sol per viva fede" (Colonna, *Rime,* 105).

49. Other scholars have drawn attention to the similarities between the style of Titian and Tintoretto and that of Aretino. See Christopher Cairns, *Pietro Aretino and the Republic of Venice: Researches on Aretino and His Circle in Venice, 1527–1556* (Florence: Leo S. Olschki Editore, 1985), 70; Paul Larivaille, "Gli scritti religiosi," in *Pietro Aretino fra Rinascimento e Manierismo* (Rome: Bulzoni, 1980), 229–73.

50. D'Elia (*Poetics of Titian's Religious Paintings,* 107–14) describes this as indicative of the epic mode.

51. Georges Didi-Huberman describes a similar operation for the stigmata in Fra Angelico's *Noli me tangere* (ca. 1438–50; Florence, convent of San Marco, cell I). See his *Fra Angelico: Dissemblance and Figuration,* trans. Jane Marie Todd (Chicago: University of Chicago Press, 1995), 13–34. Originally published as *Fra Angelico: Dissemblance et figuration* (Paris: Flammarion, 1990).

52. Berdini (*Religious Art of Jacopo Bassano,* 113–14) connects the rapid and aggressive brushwork in Bassano's *Christ Crowned with Thorns* (Rome, private collection) to the violence of the physical attack.

53. Miguel Falomir, *Tiziano,* exh. cat. (Museo Nacional del Prado, 2003), 286.

54. Berdini (*Religious Art of Jacopo Bassano,* 34–35, 114) considers Jacopo Bassano's *tocco,* that selective brushstroke in contrast to the random *macchia,* as an activation of the "exegetical trajectory from narrative to sacrament." In another context, Jeffrey Hamburger discusses a similar operation: an "incarnational aesthetic" exemplified by the insertion of Veronica images in manuscripts and how these attached images assert a presence associated with a relic and the consecrated host. See *The Visual and the Visionary: Art and Female Spirituality in Late Medieval Germany* (Cambridge, Mass.: Zone Books, 1998), 331–32. Daniela Bohde connects Titian's materiality to incarnation in his San Salvatore *Annunciation. Haut, Fleisch und Farbe* (Emsdetten: Edition Imorde, 2002), 25–60.

55. Crowe and Cavalcaselle's description of Titian's *Pietà* reflects this: "No injury produced by centuries of neglect and destructive agencies can conceal from us the purpose of a modeling carried out with abundant impast, or hide the searching after form in primaries kneaded into shape like the clay under the tool of a sculptor" (*Life and Times of Titian,* 413).

56. The *impresa* dates to at least 1562 and alludes to the Virgilian motif of licking poetry into shape. See David Rosand, "Titian and the Critical Tradition," in *Titian: His World and His Legacy,* ed. David Rosand (New York: Columbia University Press, 1982), 16, 36n16; and Mary D. Garrard, "'Art More Powerful than Nature'? Titian's Motto Reconsidered," in *The Cambridge Companion to Titian,* ed. Patricia Meilman (Cambridge: Cambridge University Press, 2004), 241–61.

57. See the collection of *paragone* literature in Paola Barocchi, ed., *Scritti d'arte del Cinquecento* (Milan: Riccardo Ricciardi Editore, 1971), 1:465–711.

58. Joseph Leo Koerner, "Factura," *Res* 36 (1999): 5–19.

59. The Dutch sculptor Adrien de Vries left sprues in his sculptures as an indication of his working process

and knowledge of natural materials. Pamela H. Smith, *The Body of the Artisan: Art and Experience in the Scientific Revolution* (Chicago: University of Chicago Press, 2004), 107–8. Benvenuto Cellini describes these ideas—particularly in relationship to the representation of flowing blood in his *Perseus*—in his *Autobiography.* See Michael Cole, "Cellini's Blood," *Art Bulletin* 81 (1999): 215–35, and *Cellini and the Principles of Sculpture* (Cambridge: Cambridge University Press, 2002), 43–78.

60. On the problems of dating the statue, see John Pope-Hennessy, *Italian Renaissance Sculpture: An Introduction to Italian Sculpture* (New York: Vintage, 1985), 263–64. See also H. W. Janson, *The Sculpture of Donatello* (Princeton: Princeton University Press, 1963), 77–86; Sarah Blake McHam, "Donatello's Bronze *David* and *Judith* as Metaphor of Medici Rule in Florence," *Art Bulletin* 83 (2001): 44n15; Adrian Randolph, *Engaging Symbols: Gender, Politics, and Public Art in Fifteenth-Century Florence* (New Haven: Yale University Press, 2002), 140–41.

61. John Shearman, *Only Connect . . . : Art and the Spectator in the Italian Renaissance* (Princeton: Princeton University Press, 1992), 17–27.

62. Ibid., 17–27; Randolph, *Engaging Symbols,* 139–92.

63. Freud explored the relationship between aggression, death, and sexuality in, among other essays, "Beyond the Pleasure Principle" (1920), in *The Standard Edition of the Complete Psychological Works of Sigmund Freud,* trans. James Strachey (London: Hogarth Press, 1968), 18:7–66. See also Georges Bataille, *Erotism: Death and Sensuality,* trans. Mary Dalwood (San Francisco: City Lights Books, 1986); Leo Bersani, *The Freudian Body: Psychoanalysis and Art* (New York: Columbia University Press, 1986). René Girard approaches the relationship from an anthropological viewpoint in his *Violence and the Sacred,* trans. Patrick Gregory (Baltimore: Johns Hopkins University Press, 1977).

64. The earliest known location (although not necessarily the original one) of *Judith* was in the garden of the Palazzo Medici. Its position in a garden perhaps explains the attention to all sides of the sculpture. See Janson, *Sculpture of Donatello,* 200–205; Francis Ames-Lewis, "Donatello's Bronze *David* and the Palazzo Medici Courtyard," *Renaissance Studies* 3 (1989): 235–51; Christine M. Sperling, "Donatello's Bronze 'David' and the Demands of Medici Politics," *Burlington Magazine* 134 (1992): 218–24; McHam, "Donatello's Bronze *David,*" 32.

65. Ascanio Condivi asserts in his *Life of Michelangelo* that Donatello lacked patience in polishing the *David:* "ch'egli non aveva pacienza in repulir le sue opere, di sorte che, riuscendo mirabili a vista lontana, da presso perdevono riputazione." *Vita di Michelagnolo Buonarroti,* ed. Giovanni Nencioni (Florence: Studio per edizioni scelti, 1998), 22. An anonymous reader later added in a marginal note that good sculptures do not require much polishing: "Errò d[illegible] a Judetta e Oloferne; e che quando son buone non ci occorre tanti pulimenti" (xxi). For the English translation, see *The Life of Michelangelo,* 2nd ed., ed. Helmut Wohl, trans. Alice Sedgwick Wohl (University Park: Pennsylvania State University Press, 2003), 28, 129n38.

66. There is some question as to whether these were originally intended to adorn pulpits. See Pope-Hennessy, *Italian Renaissance Sculpture,* 266–68. On the chronology and style of the reliefs, see Giovanni Previtali, "Una data per il problema dei pulpiti di S. Lorenzo," *Paragone* 133 (1961): 48–56; Norbert Huse, "Beiträge zum Spätwerk Donatellos," *Jahrbuch der Berliner Museen* 10 (1968): 48–56; Irving Lavin, "The Sources of Donatello's Pulpits in San Lorenzo: Revival and Freedom of Choice in the Renaissance," *Art Bulletin* 41 (1959): 21–38; H. W. Janson, "Donatello and the Antique," in *Donatello e il suo tempo* (Florence: Istituto nazionale di studi sul Rinascimento, 1968), 77–96.

67. Baccio Bandinelli wrote of the aging sculptor's work in a letter dated December 7, 1547, to Cosimo I: "Donato fece per il vecchio Cosimo li pergami e le porte di bronzo in S. Lorenzo tanto vecchio che la vista non lo servi a giudicarle, né a dar loro bella fine, e ancoraché siano buona invenzione, Donato non fé mai la più brutta opera" [When he did the pulpits and doors of bronze in San Lorenzo for Cosimo Il Vecchio, Donatello was so old that his eyesight no longer permitted him to judge them properly and to give them a beautiful finish; and although their conception is good, Donatello never did coarser work]. Cited in Hans Semper, *Donatello: seine Zeit und Schule* (Vienna: Wilhelm Braumüller, 1875), 315; translation in Janson, *Sculpture of Donatello,* 209.

68. Herbert von Einem, "Zur Deutung des Altersstiles in der Kunstgeschichte," in *Album Amicorum J. G. van Gelder,* ed. J. Bruyn, J. A. Emmons, E. de Jongh, and D. P. Snoep (The Hague: Martinus Nijhoff, 1973), 88–92; Hans Ost, *Tizian-Studien* (Cologne: Böhlau, 1992), 1–29, esp. 8–9.

69. Vasari closed his life of Donatello with a translation of a motto created by Vincenzio Borghini: "O lo spirito di Donato opera nel Buonarroto o quello di Buonarroto anticipò in Donato." Cited in *Le vite de' più eccellenti pittori, scultori e architettori,* ed. Paola Barocchi (Florence: Sansoni Editore, 1971), 3:226. On the relationship between Donatello's sculpture and Michelangelo's approach to the art, see Summers, *Michelangelo and the Language of Art,* 144–48.

70. James M. Saslow, "Michelangelo: Sculpture, Sex, and Gender," in *Looking at Italian Renaissance Sculpture,* ed. Sarah Blake McHam (Cambridge: Cambridge University Press, 1998), 223–45; Fredrika H. Jacobs, "Aretino and Michelangelo, Dolce and Titian: *Femmina, Mascolo, Grazia,*" *Art Bulletin* 82 (2000): 51–67.

71. Saslow, "Sculpture, Sex, and Gender," 223–45. See also James M. Saslow, "Themes and Content," in *The Poetry of Michelangelo: An Annotated Translation,* ed. and trans. James M. Saslow (New Haven: Yale University Press, 1991), 23–38.

72. Donatello's sculptures were among the earliest free-standing statues. See McHam, "Donatello's Bronze *David,*" 32. His *Judith,* with its triangular base, was the first multifigure sculpture that acknowledged a spectator in motion. Other sculptures were carved in the round, but tended to be single figures in a nonnarrative context. Later cinquecento sculptures more frequently explored this device, such as Giambologna's *Sabine Women* (1581–82; Loggia dei Lanzi, Florence). Shearman (*Only Connect,* 11–33) discusses an early quattrocento interest in dynamic space and its shaping of the viewer's relationship to the work of art (especially sculpture), but his analysis and supportive examples of sculpture involve more of the temporal, rather than spatial, dimension of viewing, in which the work of art acknowledges (and therefore fixes the position of) the beholder.

73. Rosalind E. Krauss, *Passages in Modern Sculpture* (New York: Viking Press, 1977).

74. This interpretation forms a secular corollary to Nagel's interpretation (*Michelangelo and the Reform of Art,* 188–215) of roughness of execution in Michelangelo's *Pietà* sculptures as a metaphor for excavation, recovery, stripping, and digging.

75. "Però no mi destar: deh, parla basso." Michelangelo's sonnet is in response to one written by Giovanni Battista Strozzi. For the earliest record of the exchange, see Vasari, *Le vite,*6:58–59. See also Leonard Barkan, *Unearthing the Past: Archaeology and Aesthetics in the Making of Renaissance Culture* (New Haven: Yale University Press, 1999), 243–44; Cranston, "Touch of the Blind Man," 239.

76. The Renaissance sources for the melancholic sculptor remain his own poetry and letters. For his poetry, see Michelangelo Buonarroti, *Poetry of Michelangelo,* esp. nos. 21–23; for his letters, see Michelangelo, *Il Carteggio di Michelangelo,* ed. Paola Barocchi (Florence: Studio per edizioni scelti, 1988). Raphael included in his *School of Athens* sometime after its completion a portrait of Michelangelo as the melancholic philosopher Heraclitus. See above, chapter 2. Hibbard discusses Michelangelo's personal frustration and its surfacing in his carving. *Michelangelo* (New York: Harper and Row, 1974), 25.

77. Peter Stallybrass, "Patriarchal Territories: The Body Enclosed," in *Rewriting the Renaissance: The Discourses of Sexual Difference in Early Modern Europe,* ed. Margaret W. Ferguson, Maureen Quilligan, and Nancy J. Vickers (Chicago: University of Chicago Press, 1986), 123–42.

78. "All signs of its [classic body's] unfinished character, of its growth and proliferation were eliminated; its protuberances and offshoots were removed, its convexities . . . smoothed out, its apertures closed. The ever unfinished nature of the body was hidden, kept secret; conception, pregnancy, childbirth, death throes, were almost never shown. . . . The accent was placed on the completed, self-sufficient individuality of the given body. M. M. Bakhtin, *Rabelais and His World,* trans. Helene Iswolsky (Cambridge, Mass.: MIT Press, 1968), 24; 29.

79. Cynthia Marshall, *The Shattering of the Self: Violence, Subjectivity, and Early Modern Texts* (Baltimore: Johns Hopkins University Press, 2002), 1–55.

80. Cranston, *Poetics of Portraiture,* esp. 62–72.

81. The dissolution of the division between subject and object, self and other, can be understood as the extension of the structure of violence. Drawing upon psychoanalytic literature, Cynthia Marshall (*Shattering of the Self,* esp. 10–11) advances this idea of the destruction of selfhood through her consideration of pain and pleasure in Petrarchan poetry, martyrologies, and tragic drama. Whether employing a language of violence or representing violent scenes, these texts present and depend on a "shattered self," one that is fluid and unstable and finds pleasure in pain.

82. The generally accepted date of the mid-1540s, postdating the death of Gritti in 1538, comes from the Michelangesque *terribilità* of the depicted doge. Typically official portraits of the doge were not posthumously executed, leading many scholars to give the earlier date of 1535–38. For a discussion of the dating and for a wider bibliography, see Sylvia Ferino-Pagden, ed., *L'ultimo Tiziano e la sensualità della pittura* (Venice: Marsilio Editori, 2008), 155–57; *Tiziano,* 252–54; Wethey, *Paintings of Titian,* 1.108–9, cat. 50.

83. Wethey, *Paintings of Titian,* 2.23–24, 108–9; Pallucchini, *Tiziano,* 103–4, 282.

84. Wilhelm Suida proposes that Titian knew of the *Moses* through a small copy in Jacopo Sansovino's possession. *Titien* (Paris: A. Weber, 1975), 83. See also *Tiziano* (1990), 254.

85. Michael Fried articulates a similar attention to the edge of some of Courbet's paintings that he interprets as a mode of the artist's self-presence. See Fried, *Courbet's Realism* (Chicago: University of Chicago Press, 1990).

86. Rona Goffen, "Icon and Vision: Giovanni Bellini's Half-Length Madonnas," *Art Bulletin* 57 (1975): 487–518.

87. Alberti, *On Painting,* ¶25, p. 60. Alberti repeats Plutarch's story of Cassandrus, who trembled when seeing the portrait of the deceased Alexander.

88. Julia Kristeva, *Powers of Horror: An Essay on Abjection,* trans. Louis S. Roudiez (New York: Columbia University Press, 1982); Joseph Leo Koerner, "The Abject of Art History," *Res* 31 (Spring 1997): 5–9.

89. *Tiziano,* 252; Wethey, *Paintings of Titian,* 1.95, cat. 44; Paul Joannides, "Titian's *Judith* and Its Context: The Iconography of Decapitation," *Apollo* 361 (1992): 163–70.

90. The apocryphal story of Judith is found in the Book of Judith in the Latin Vulgate of Saint Jerome. This and other apocrypha were sanctioned by the Council of Trent in 1546. For the history and iconography of the story, see Mary Garrard, *Artemesia Gentileschi: The Image of the Female Hero in Italian Baroque Art* (Princeton: Princeton University Press, 1989), 278–336.

91. Pallucchini, *Tiziano,* 176.

92. Wethey, *Paintings of Titian,* 1.120–21, cat. 84; *Tiziano,* 255–58; Pallucchini, *Tiziano,* 94, 279.

93. Erika Tietze-Conrat, "Titian's Workshop in His Late Years," *Art Bulletin* 28 (1946): 76–88; Rosand, *Titian,* 44; Miguel Falomir, "Titian's Replicas," in Falomir, *Tiziano,* 326–32.

94. Falomir, *Tiziano,* 414.

95. Sohm ("Gendering Style," 797–98) offers this reading of the passage because of Malvezzi's use of "tal'hora."

96. Jacques Derrida refers to this as "differance." *De la grammatologie* (Paris: Minuit, 1967), 237; see Culler, *On Deconstruction,* 95–97.

97. Wethey, *Paintings of Titian,* vol. 1, 95, cat. 44, suggests that the restorer tampered with Judith's head in order to make the canvas appealing to potential buyers.

98. Ibid., 1.83–84, cat. 28; Falomir, *Tiziano,* 414–16; Ferino-Pagden, *L'ultimo Tiziano,* 295–96.

99. Hope, *Titian,* 161.

100. Cicero, *Orator,* 14.43ff.

101. Some scholars think of retrospectiveness as one of the chief markers of old-age style. This "late return of the early" ("späte Wiederkehr des Frühen"), as one Rembrandt scholar termed the phenomenon, afforded aging painters the opportunity to find new solutions and arrangements for earlier compositions. On Rembrandt, see Wilhelm Pinder, *Rembrandts Selbstbildnisse* (Leipzig: K. R. Langewiesche, 1943), 106. See also Einem, "Zur Deutung des Altersstiles," 91; and Ost, *Tizian-Studien,* 7.

102. Cranston, *Poetics of Portraiture,* 98–126.

103. Falomir (*Tiziano,* 402) notes the rarity of the multifigured narrative close-up in Titian's oeuvre. Titian turned to the single half-length figure of Christ for his *Ecce Homo* for Charles V, and perhaps as early as 1535 when he painted a now-lost Christ for Federico Gonzaga. The surviving images show the beaten Christ as a variant of the frontal, bust-length iconic type by presenting him in three-quarter length and in an angled pose. See Falomir, *Tiziano,* 224. After Titian, the half-length narrative type continued in seventeenth-century painting, especially for so-called genre scenes. For the origin and development of the half-length narrative, see Ringbom, *Icon to Narrative,* 1–71.

104. Wethey, *The Paintings of Titian,*vol. 1, cat. 22, p. 80.

105. Ibid., cat. 147, pp. 163–64.

106. Ibid., cat. x-33, pp. 219–20. Wethey attributes the painting to Palma il Vecchio.

107. Ringbom, *Icon to Narrative,* 52.

108. Rona Goffen, "Icon and Vision," 487–518; Ringbom, *Icon to Narrative,* 52ff. The fictive stone

parapet recalls the sculpted, memorial origins of the half-length.

109. On the "semi-industrial" production of half-length images in the latter half of the fifteenth century, see Ringbom, *Icon to Narrative,* 37.

110. Alexander Nagel and Christopher S. Wood, "Interventions: Toward a New Model of Renaissance Anachronism" and "The Authors Reply," *Art Bulletin* 87, no. 3 (2005): 430–32.

111. Nagel and Wood, "Interventions," 408–13. Nagel and Wood develop the idea of figural temporality principally from Aby Warburg's concept of *Nachleben* as distilled by Georges Didi-Huberman in *L'image survivante: Histoire de l'art et temps des fantômes selon Aby Warburg* (Paris: Minuit, 2002).

112. Titian's return to the half-length dates to 1557, when he sent to Philip II a *Deposition* with half-length figures that was lost in transit. See Falomir, *Tiziano,* 260, who deduces this from a letter from García Hernández to Philip II.

113. In addition to the work of Alexander Nagel (*Michelangelo and the Reform of Art*) and his coauthored article with Christopher S. Wood, recent contributions to the field include Stuart Lingo, "The Capuchins and the Art of History: Retrospection and Reform in the Arts in Late Renaissance Italy" (Ph.D. diss., Harvard University, 1998). Unlike Michelangelo, Titian stood as neither the specific subject nor the explicit target of reformatory writings. His residency in Venice, rather than in Rome, removed him from the active center of reformatory controversies and debates. Venice, despite its peripheral and diasporal participation in religious discussions, especially those involving Rome, was not completely unaffected by the upheavals in the Church: local Church officials—including priests—made efforts to reform the Church and frequently issued warnings against Lutheran teachings. On the Counter-Reformation and Venice, consult John Martin, "Spiritual Journeys and the Fashioning of Religious Identity in Renaissance Venice," *Renaissance Studies* 10 (1996): 358–70; Richard Cocke, "Exemplary Lives: Veronese's Representations of Martyrdom and the Council of Trent," *Renaissance Studies* 10 (1996): 388–404; and Anthony Wright, "Republican Tradition and the Maintenance of 'National' Religious Traditions in Venice," *Renaissance Studies* 10 (1996): 405–16; Meilman, *Titian and the Altarpiece,* 144. Numerous Venetian altarpieces apparently responded to Tridentine reforms by increasingly featuring in their central panel a narrative event from the life or death of the titular saint, of Christ, or of the Virgin. Martyrdoms, according to reformatory decrees, instructed and taught the devout and inspired these beholders to imitate the lives of the depicted saints. Correspondingly, altars dedicated to the sacrament and altarpieces with eucharistic subjects also increased after the close of the Tridentine decrees in 1563. See Peter Humfrey, "Altarpieces and Altar Dedications in Counter-Reformation and the Veneto," *Renaissance Studies* 10 (1996): 377–79; Meilman, *Titian and the Altarpiece,* 158. Although several cinquecento Venetian painters appear to have followed these recommendations in their devotional painting, the impact of reform on Titian's painting remains ambiguous—or at least debatable. His admired *Saint Peter Martyr Altarpiece,* which depicted the martyrdom of the saint, pre-dated Tridentine reforms but inspired later scenes of martyrdom by offering a heroic focus on the exemplary body, a focus that deviated from the northern reformatory emphasis on the gruesome. See Humfrey, "Altarpieces," 374; Meilman, *Titian and the Altarpiece,* 150–58; D'Elia, *Poetics of Titian's Religious Paintings,* 56–83. On the other hand, many of Titian's post-1550 altarpieces depict subjects relating to incarnation and a loose brushwork that could be interpreted as emphasizing the corporeality and the violence done to the body. See Bohde, *Haut, Fleisch und Farbe,* 25–60. For a different interpretation of Titian's later style as both evading reformatory dicta through suggestion and evoking the visionary experience of Catholic reformers and Counter-Reformation saints, see D'Elia, *Poetics of Titian's Religious Paintings,* 131. Both the *Pietà* and the *Flaying* demonstrate an interest in the frontal *sacra conversazione,* a type that increasingly in the mid-cinquecento was outpaced by narrative compositions. As a scene of mythological martyrdom, the *Flaying* presents, in my opinion, the most serious challenge to any claims of strict reformatory influence on Titian's later work. If anything, the painting advances a creative interpretation of the ideas circulating in post-Tridentine art—martyrdom, corporeality, violence done to the body, a return to the directness of earlier religious art—without situating these ideas in an expected or even appropriate context. Nagel (*Michelangelo and the Reform of Art,* 18) describes an analogous situation of Michelangelo's return to bacchanalia in an effort to restore the spirituality of Christian art.

114. Falomir, *Tiziano,* 402–3, 414–16; Cocke, "Exemplary Lives," 394–95; Alain Saint-Saëns, *Art and Faith in Tridentine Spain, 1545–1690* (New York: Peter Lang, 1995), 13–35.

115. Max J. Friedländer, *Quentin Massys,* trans. Heinz Norden, Early Netherlandish Painting 7 (Leiden: A. W. Sijthoff, 1971), plate 17; Falomir, *Tiziano,* 413.

116. Joseph Leo Koerner, *The Moment of Self-Portraiture in German Renaissance Art* (Chicago: University of Chicago Press, 1993), 80–126.

117. Hans Belting, "In Search of Christ's Body: Image or Imprint?" in *The Holy Face and the Paradox of Representation* (Bologna: Nuova Alfa Editoriale, 1998), 1–11. Joseph Leo Koerner addresses the relationship between the divine and the abject in "The Icon as Iconoclasm," in *Iconoclash,* ed. Bruno Latour and Peter Weibel (Cambridge, Mass.: MIT Press, 2002), 190–92: "The aesthetics of the ugly, whether Christian or modern, are a provisional, deceptive stage in a larger movement at the end of which truth, beauty, and power stand revealed. . . . True picture of his father, Christ could therefore be pictured, indeed produced pictures of himself miraculously. . . . Betrayed, humiliated, tortured, and crucified, however, Christ was also concealed in his visibility, God's perfect likeness transformed into the ugliest of things" (191–92).

118. Belting ("In Search of Christ's Body," 1–11) associates the *vera icon* with an aesthetic. See also Koerner (*Moment of Self-Portraiture,* 90–92), who observes the similarity between an imprint of the *vera icon* in a woodcut and the miraculous impression of the source. Bohde links incarnation to materiality. See her *Haut, Fleisch und Farbe,* 25–60, and "Titian's Three-Altar Project in the Venetian Church of San Salvador: Strategies of Self-Representation by Members of the Scuola Grande di San Rocco," *Renaissance Studies* 15 (2001): 450–72.

119. Koerner (*Moment of Self-Portraiture,* 83) describes a simultaneity of past and present for the *acheiropoetos.* The indexical status of the brushstroke could also be linked to the temporality ascribed to signatures by Jacques Derrida: the signature "marks and retains his [the signer's] having-been present in a past now, which will remain a future now, and therefore in a now in general, in the transcendent form of nowness." "Signature, Event, Context," in *Margins of Philosophy,* trans. Alan Bass (Chicago: University of Chicago Press, 1982), 328. This is also, in a sense, the "faciebat" of the inscription of Giovanni Bellini's *Woman Before a Mirror* (Vienna, Kunsthistorisches Museum). See Goffen, "Bellini's *Nude with Mirror,*" 185–99.

120. Goffen, *Giovanni Bellini,* 70–73; Hans Belting, *Giovanni Bellini, Pietà: Ikone und Bilderzählung in der venezianischen Malerei* (Frankfurt am Main: Fischer Taschenbuch, 1985); Ringbom, *Icon to Narrative,* 107–16.

121. A few of the many examples are cited in Mary Rogers, "Sonnets on Female Portraits from Renaissance North Italy," *Word and Image* 2 (1986): 291–305.

122. Sigüenza states that "at night the devout King Philip would spend lengthy periods [looking at *Christ on the Way to Calvary* in his private oratory], meditating on how much he owed to Christ who bore such a heavy weight on his shoulders for the sins of man and his sin" ["en los noches pasaba allí el pío Rey don Felipe buenos ratos, contemplando lo mucho que devía al Señor que tan pesada carga llevaba sobre sus hombros por los pecados de los hombres y los suyos"]. In Falomir, *Tiziano,* 268, 403.

123. John 19:13–15; Luke 23:13–22. Wethey (*Paintings of Titian,* 1.83–84, cat. 28) notes the awkwardness of the figure with his back to the viewer and its suggestion of studio involvement.

124. Wethey, *Paintings of Titian, I,* 1.79–80, cat. 21; Ferino-Pagden, *L'ultimo Tiziano,* 246.

125. Ringbom, *Icon to Narrative,* 125; David Ekserdjian, *Correggio* (New Haven: Yale University Press, 1997), 163–66.

126. Dempsey ("Carracci," 86–87) describes the retrospectiveness in the style of the Carracci as a reflection on the history of art.

127. Panofsky, *Problems in Titian,* 168.

SELECTED BIBLIOGRAPHY

Alberti, Leon Battista. *On Painting.* Edited and translated by Cecil Grayson. London: Penguin, 1991.

Alpers, Svetlana. *Rembrandt's Enterprise: The Studio and the Market.* Chicago: University of Chicago Press, 1988.

Ames-Lewis, Francis. "Donatello's Bronze *David* and the Palazzo Medici Courtyard." *Renaissance Studies* 3 (1989): 235–51.

Anderson, Jaynie. *Giorgione: The Painter of "Poetic Brevity."* New York: Flammarion, 1997.

Arasse, Daniel. "The 'Venus of Urbino,' or the Archetype of a Glance." In *Titian's "Venus of Urbino,"* edited by Rona Goffen, 91–107. Cambridge: Cambridge University Press, 1997.

Aretino, Pietro. *Lettere sull'arte di Pietro Aretino.* Edited by Fidenzio Pertile and Ettore Camesasca. Milan: Edizione del Milone, 1957.

———. *I quattro libri de la humanita di Christo.* Venice, 1539.

Armstrong, Carol. *Manet Manette.* New Haven: Yale University Press, 2002.

Bakhtin, M. M. *Rabelais and His World.* Translated by Helene Iswolsky. Cambridge, Mass.: MIT Press, 1968.

Barkan, Leonard. *Unearthing the Past: Archaeology and Aesthetics in the Making of Renaissance Culture.* New Haven: Yale University Press, 1999.

Bataille, Georges. *Erotism: Death and Sensuality.* Translated by Mary Dalwood. San Francisco: City Lights Books, 1986.

Belting, Hans. "In Search of Christ's Body: Image or Imprint?" In *The Holy Face and the Paradox of Representation,* 1–11. Bologna: Nuova Alfa Editoriale, 1998.

———. *Likeness and Presence: A History of the Image Before the Era of Art.* Translated by Edmund Jephcott. Chicago: University of Chicago Press, 1994.

Bembo, Pietro. *Gli Asolani.* Translated by Rudolf B. Gottfried. Freeport, N.Y.: Books for Libraries Press, 1971.

Berdini, Paolo. *The Religious Art of Jacopo Bassano: Painting as Visual Exegesis.* Cambridge: Cambridge University Press, 1997.

Bersani, Leo. *The Freudian Body: Psychoanalysis and Art.* New York: Columbia University Press, 1986.

Bersani, Leo, and Ulysse Dutoit. *Caravaggio's Secrets.* Cambridge, Mass.: MIT Press, 1998.

———. *Forms of Violence: Narrative in Assyrian Art and Modern Culture.* New York: Schocken Books, 1985.

Blunt, Anthony. *Artistic Theory in Italy,* 1450–1600. Oxford: Clarendon Press, 1940.

Bohde, Daniela. *Haut, Fleisch, und Farbe: Körperlichkeit und Materialität in den Gemälden Tizians.* Berlin: Emsdetten, 2002.

———. "Skin and the Search for the Interior: The Representation of Flaying in the Art and Anatomy of the Cinquecento." In *Bodily Extremities: Preoccupations with the Human Body in Early Modern Culture,* edited by Florike Egmond and Robert Zwijnenberg, 10–47. Aldershot: Ashgate, 2003.

———. "Titian's Three-Altar Project in the Venetian Church of San Salvador: Strategies of Self-Representation by Members of the Scuola Grande di San Rocco." *Renaissance Studies* 15 (2001): 450–72.

Bois, Yve-Alain, and Rosalind Krauss. *Formless: A User's Guide.* New York: Zone Books, 1997.

———. *Painting as Model.* Cambridge, Mass.: MIT Press, 1990.

Boschini, Marco. *La carta del navegar pitoresco: Edizione critica con la "Breve instruzione" premessa alle "Ricche Minere della pittura veneziana."* Edited by Anna Pallucchini. Venice: Istituto per la collaborazione culturale, 1966.

Boschloo, Anton W. A. *Annibale Carracci in Bologna: Visible Reality in Art After the Council of Trent.* New York: Abner Schram, 1974.

Braunfels, Wolfgang. "I quadri di Tiziano nello studio a Biri Grande (1530–76)." In *Tiziano e Venezia: Convegno internazionale di studi, Venezia,* 1976, 407–10. Vicenza: N. Pozza, 1980.

Brown, Katharine T. *The Painter's Reflection: Self-Portraiture in Venice,* 1458–1625. Florence: Leo S. Olschki Editore, 2000.

Buonarroti, Michelangelo. *Il Carteggio di Michelangelo.* Edited by Paola Barocchi. Florence: Studio per edizioni scelti, 1988.

Butler, Judith. *Bodies That Matter: On the Discursive Limits of "Sex."* New York: Routledge, 1993.

Bynum, Caroline Walker. "Why All the Fuss About the Body? A Medievalist's Perspective." *Critical Inquiry* 22 (1995): 1–33.

Cairns, Christopher. *Pietro Aretino and the Republic of Venice: Researches on Aretino and His Circle in Venice,* 1527–1556. Florence: Leo S. Olschki Editore, 1985.

Campbell, Stephen J. "*Fare una cosa morta parer viva:* Michelangelo, Rosso, and the (Un)divinity of Art." *Art Bulletin* 84 (2002): 596–620.

Carabell, Paula. "*Finito* and *Non-finito* in Titian's Last Paintings." *Res* 28 (1995): 79–93.

Carlino, Andrea. *Books of the Body: Anatomical Ritual and Renaissance Learning.* Translated by John Tedeschi and Anne C. Tedeschi. Chicago: University of Chicago Press, 1999.

Castiglione, Baldassare. *The Book of the Courtier.* Translated by Charles S. Singleton. London: Doubleday, 1959.

Clay, Jean. "Ointments, Makeup, Pollen." *October* 27 (1983): 3–44.

Cole, Michael. *Cellini and the Principles of Sculpture.* Cambridge: Cambridge University Press, 2002.

Condivi, Ascanio. *The Life of Michelangelo.* Translated by Alice Sedgwick Wohl. Edited by Helmut Wohl. University Park: Pennsylvania State University Press, 2003.

Cranston, Jodi. "Desire and Gravitas in the Portraits of Bindo Altoviti." In *Raphael, Cellini, and a Renaissance Banker: The Patronage of Bindo Altoviti,* edited by Alan Chong, 115–31. Boston: Isabella Stewart Gardner Museum, 2003.

———. *The Poetics of Portraiture in the Italian Renaissance.* Cambridge: Cambridge University Press, 2000.

———. "Theorising Materiality: Titian's *Flaying of Marysas.*" In *Titian: Materiality, Likeness, Istoria,* edited by Joanna Woods-Marsden, 5–18. Turnhout: Brepols, 2007.

———. "The Touch of the Blind Man: The Phenomenology of Vividness in Italian Renaissance Art." In *Sensible Flesh: On Touch in Early Modern Culture,* edited by Elizabeth D. Harvey, 224–42. Philadelphia: University of Pennsylvania Press, 2003.

———. "Tropes of Revelation in Raphael's *Transfiguration.*" *Renaissance Quarterly* 56 (2003): 1–25.

Cropper, Elizabeth. "The Beauty of Woman: Problems in the Rhetoric of Renaissance Portraiture." In *Rewriting the Renaissance: The Discourses of Sexual Difference in Early Modern Europe,* edited by Margaret W. Ferguson, Maureen Quilligan, and Nancy J. Vickers, 175–90. Chicago: University of Chicago Press, 1986.

———. "The Place of Beauty in the High Renaissance and Its Displacement in the History of Art." In *Place and Displacement in the Renaissance,* edited by Alvin Vos, 159–205. Binghamton, N.Y.: Medieval and Renaissance Texts and Studies, 1995.

Crowe, J. A., and J. B. Cavalcaselle. *The Life and Times of Titian.* London: John Murray, 1881.

Culler, Jonathan. *On Deconstruction: Theory and Criticism After Structuralism.* Ithaca: Cornell University Press, 1982.

Damisch, Hubert. *A Theory of /Cloud/: Toward a History of Painting.* Translated by Janet Lloyd. Stanford: Stanford University Press, 2002.

D'Elia, Una Roman. "Drawing Christ's Blood: Michelangelo, Vittoria Colonna, and the Aesthetics of Reform." *Renaissance Quarterly* 59 (2006): 90–129.

———. *The Poetics of Titian's Religious Paintings.* Cambridge: Cambridge University Press, 2005.

De Man, Paul. "Autobiography as De-Facement." In *The Rhetoric of Romanticism,* 67–81. New York: Columbia University Press, 1984.

De Marco, Nicholas. "Titian's *Pietà:* The Living Stone." *Venezia Cinquecento* 2 (1992): 55–92.

Dempsey, Charles. "The Carracci and the Devout Style in Emilia." In *Emilian Painting of the Sixteenth and Seventeenth Centuries,* 75–87. Bologna: Nuova Alfa Editoriale, 1987.

Derrida, Jacques. *Margins of Philosophy.* Translated by Alan Bass. Chicago: University of Chicago Press, 1982.

Didi-Huberman, Georges. *Fra Angelico: Dissemblance and Figuration.* Translated by Jane Marie Todd. Chicago: University of Chicago Press, 1995.

———. *L'image survivante: Histoire de l'art et temps des fantômes selon Aby Warburg.* Paris: Minuit, 2002.

———. "The Imaginary Breeze: Remarks on the Air of the Quattrocento." *Journal of Visual Culture* 2 (2003): 275–89.

———. "The Index of the Absent Wound (Monograph on a Stain)." *October* 29 (1984): 63–81.

Dolce, Lodovico. *Dialogo della pittura.* 1557. In *Dolce's "Aretino" and Venetian Art Theory of the Cinquecento,* by Mark W. Roskill. New York: New York University Press, 1968.

———. *Le trasformationi.* Venice: F. Sansovino, 1568.

Dorment, K. "Tomb and Testament: Architectural Significance in Titian's *Pietà."* *Art Quarterly* 35 (1972): 399–418.

Einem, Herbert von. "Zur Deutung des Altersstils in der Kunstgeschichte." In *Album Amicorum J. G. van Gelder,* edited by J. Bruyn, J. A. Emmons, E. de Jongh, and D. P. Snoep, 88–92. The Hague: Martinus Nijhoff, 1973.

Ekserdjian, David. *Correggio.* New Haven: Yale University Press, 1997.

Elkins, James."Marks, Traces, *Traits,* Contours, *Orli,* and *Splendores:* Nonsemiotic Elements in Pictures." *Critical Inquiry* 21 (1995): 822–60.

———. *Pictures of the Body: Pain and Metamorphosis.* Stanford: Stanford University Press, 1999.

Emison, Patricia A. *Creating the "Divine" Artist: From Dante to Michelangelo.* Leiden: E. J. Brill, 2004.

Enterline, Lynn. *The Rhetoric of the Body from Ovid to Shakespeare.* Cambridge: Cambridge University Press, 2000.

Falomir, Miguel, ed. *Tiziano.* Madrid: Museo Nacional del Prado, 2003.

Fehl, Philipp P. "Realism and Classicism in the Representation of a Painful Scene: Titian's 'Flaying of Marysas' at the Archiepiscopal Palace at Kromeríz." In *Czechoslovakia Past and Present,* edited by Miloslav Rechcígl, vol. 2, 1387–1415. The Hague: Mouton, 1968.

Ferino-Pagden, Sylvia, ed. *L'ultimo Tiziano e la sensualità della pittura.* Venice: Marsilio Editori, 2008.

Ferrarino, Luigi. *Tiziano e la corte di Spagna nei documenti dell'Archivio Generale di Simancas.* Madrid: Istituto italiano di cultura, 1975.

Formicova, Tamara. "Lo sviluppo compositivo della 'Venere allo specchio con due amorini' nell'opera di Tiziano e la copia dell'Ermitage." *Arte Veneta* 31 (1977): 195–99.

Foster, Hal. "The Expressive Fallacy." *Art in America* (January 1983): 80–83, 137.

Freedman, Luba. *The Revival of the Olympian Gods in Renaissance Art.* Cambridge: Cambridge University Press, 2003.

———. *Titian's Independent Self-Portraits.* Florence: Leo S. Olschki Editore, 1990.

Freud, Sigmund. "Beyond the Pleasure Principle." 1920. In *The Standard Edition of the Complete Psychological Works of Sigmund Freud,* translated by James Strachey, vol. 18, 7–66. London: Hogarth Press, 1968.

———. "Medusa's Head." 1940. In *The Standard Edition of the Complete Psychological Works of Sigmund Freud,* translated by James Strachey, vol. 18, 273–74. London: Hogarth Press, 1968.

Fried, Michael. "Art and Objecthood." *Art Forum* 5 (June 1967), 12–23.

———. *Courbet's Realism.* Chicago: University of Chicago Press, 1990.

Garrard, Mary. *Artemesia Gentileschi: The Image of the Female Hero in Italian Baroque Art.* Princeton: Princeton University Press, 1989.

Gentili, Augusto. *Da Tiziano a Tiziano: Mito e allegoria nella cultura veneziana del Cinquecento.* Milan: Feltrinelli, 1980.

———. "Tiziano e il non finito." *Venezia Cinquecento* 2 (1992): 93–127.

Gilio, Giovanni Andrea. *Dialogo nel quale si ragiona degli errori e degli abusi dei pittori circa l'istorie.* 1564. In *Trattati d'arte del Cinquecento fra manierismo e Controriforma,* edited by Paola Barocchi, vol. 2, 1–115. Bari: G. Laterza, 1961.

Gilmore, Jonathan. *The Life of a Style: Beginnings and Endings in the Narrative History of Art.* Ithaca: Cornell University Press,

Girard, René. *Violence and the Sacred.* Translated by Patrick Gregory. Baltimore: Johns Hopkins University Press, 1977.

Goffen, Rona. "Bellini's *Nude with Mirror.*" *Venezia Cinquecento* 1 (1991): 185–99.

———. *Giovanni Bellini.* New Haven: Yale University Press, 1989.

———. "Icon and Vision: Giovanni Bellini's Half-Length Madonnas." *Art Bulletin* 57 (1975): 487–514.

———. *Renaissance Rivals: Michelangelo, Leonardo, Raphael, Titian.* New Haven: Yale University Press, 2002.

———. "Signatures: Inscribing Identity in Italian Renaissance Art." *Viator* 32 (2001): 303–70.

———. *Titian's Women.* New Haven: Yale University Press, 1997.

Gombrich, E. H. *Art and Illusion: A Study in the Psychology of Pictorial Representation.* Princeton: Princeton University Press, 1989.

Goodman-Soellner, Elise. "Poetic Interpretations of the 'Lady at Her Toilette' Theme in Sixteenth-Century Painting." *Sixteenth-Century Journal* 14 (1983): 426–42.

Hall, Marcia B. *After Raphael: Painting in Central Italy in the Sixteenth Century.* Cambridge: Cambridge University Press, 1999.

Heckscher, William S. *Rembrandt's "Anatomy of Dr. Nicolaas Tulp."* New York: New York University Press, 1958.

Hetzer, Theodor. *Tizian: Geschichte seiner Farbe.* Frankfurt am Main: V. Klostermann, 1935.

Hills, Paul. *Venetian Colour: Marble, Mosaic, Painting and Glass, 1250–1550.* New Haven: Yale University Press, 1999.

Hodges, Devon L. *Renaissance Fictions of Anatomy.* Amherst, Mass.: University of Massachusetts Press, 1985.

Hollanda, Francisco de. *Three Dialogues on Painting.* 1540. In *Michael Angelo Buonarroti, with Translations of the Life of the Master by His Scholar, Ascanio Condivi, and Three Dialogues from the Portuguese by Francisco Hollanda,* by Charles Holroyd. 2nd ed. London: Duckworth, 1911.

Hope, Charles. *Titian.* New York: Harper and Row, 1980.

Humfrey, Peter. *The Altarpiece in Renaissance Venice.* New Haven: Yale University Press, 1993.

Huse, Norbert. "Beiträge zum Spätwerk Donatellos." *Jahrbuch der Berliner Museen* 10 (1968): 48–56.

Jacobs, Fredrika H. "Aretino and Michelangelo, Dolce and Titian: *Femmina, Mascolo, Grazia.*" *Art Bulletin* 82 (2000): 51–67.

———. *Defining the Renaissance Virtuosa: Women Artists and the Language of Art History and Criticism.* Cambridge: Cambridge University Press, 1997.

———. *The Living Image in Renaissance Art.* Cambridge: Cambridge University Press, 2005.

Jaffé, Michael. *Titian.* London: National Gallery, 2003.

Janson, H. W. "Donatello and the Antique." In *Donatello e il suo tempo,* 77–96. Florence: Istituto nazionale di studi sul Rinascimento, 1968.

———. "The 'Image Made by Chance' in Renaissance Thought." In *De Artibus Opuscula XL: Essays in Honor of Erwin Panofsky,* edited by Millard Meiss, 254–66. New York: New York University Press, 1961.

———. *The Sculpture of Donatello.* Princeton: Princeton University Press, 1963.

Joannides, Paul. "Titian's *Judith* and Its Context: The Iconography of Decapitation." *Apollo* 361 (1992):163–70.

Junkerman, Anne Christine. "*Bellissima donna:* An Interdisciplinary Study of Venetian Sensuous Half-Length Images of the Early Sixteenth Century." Ph.D. diss., University of California, Berkeley, 1988.

Kemp, Martin. "The 'Super-Artist' as Genius: The Sixteenth-Century View." In *Genius: The History of an Idea,* edited by Penelope Murray, 32–53. Oxford: Basil Blackwell, 1989.

Koerner, Joseph Leo. "The Abject of Art History." *Res* 31 (Spring 1997): 5–9.

———. "Factura." *Res* 36 (1999): 5–19.

———. *The Moment of Self-Portraiture in German Renaissance Art.* Chicago: University of Chicago Press, 1993.

Krauss, Rosalind E. *The Originality of the Avant-Garde and Other Modernist Myths.* Cambridge, Mass.: MIT Press, 1985.

———. *Passages in Modern Sculpture.* New York: Viking Press, 1977.

Kris, Ernst, and Otto Kurz. *Legend, Myth, and Magic in the Image of the Artist: A Historical Experiment.* New Haven: Yale University Press, 1979.

Kristeva, Julia. *Powers of Horror: An Essay on Abjection.* Translated by Louis S. Roudiez. New York: Columbia University Press, 1982.

Larivaille, Paul. *Pietro Aretino fra Rinascimento e manierismo.* Rome: Bulzoni, 1980.

Lavin, Irving. "The Sources of Donatello's Pulpits in San Lorenzo: Revival and Freedom of Choice in the Renaissance." *Art Bulletin* 41 (1959): 21–38.

Lawrence, Sarah. "*Conversazioni profane:* In Dialogue with Pagan Gods." Ph.D. diss., Columbia University, 1994.

Leja, Michael. *Reframing Abstract Expressionism: Subjectivity and Painting in the 1940s.* New Haven: Yale University Press, 1993.

Leonardo da Vinci. *Libro di pittura.* 2 vols. Edited by Carlo Pedretti. Florence: Giunti Gruppo Editoriale, 1995.

———. *The Literary Works of Leonardo da Vinci.* Edited and translated by Jean Paul Richter. London: Phaidon, 1970.

———. *Treatise on Painting.* Translated by A. Philip McMahon. Princeton: Princeton University Press, 1956.

Lichtenstein, Jacqueline. *The Eloquence of Color: Rhetoric and Painting in the French Classical Age.* Translated by Emily McVarish. Berkeley and Los Angeles: University of California Press, 1993.

Lingo, Stuart. "The Capuchins and the Art of History: Retrospection and Reform in the Arts in Late Renaissance Italy." Ph.D. diss., Harvard University, 1998.

Malvezzi, Virgilio. *Considerationi con occasione d'alcuni luoghi delle vite d'Alcibiade e di Coriolano.* Bologna, 1648.

Mancini, Matteo. *Tiziano e le corti d'Asburgo nei documenti degli archivi spagnoli.* Venice: Istituto Veneto di scienze, lettere ed arti, 1998.

Marin, Louis. *To Destroy Painting.* Translated by Mette Hjort. Chicago: University of Chicago Press, 1995.

Marshall, Cynthia. *The Shattering of the Self: Violence, Subjectivity, and Early Modern Texts.* Baltimore: Johns Hopkins University Press, 2002.

Martin, John. "Spiritual Journeys and the Fashioning of Religious Identity in Renaissance Venice." *Renaissance Studies* 10 (1996): 358–70.

Matthew, Louisa C. "The Painter's Presence: Signatures in Venetian Renaissance Pictures." *Art Bulletin* 80 (1998): 616–47.

McHam, Sarah Blake. "Donatello's Bronze *David* and *Judith* as Metaphor of Medici Rule in Florence." *Art Bulletin* 83 (2001): 32–47.

McKim-Smith, Gridley, Greta Andersen-Bergdoll, and Richard Newman. *Examining Velázquez.* New Haven: Yale University Press, 1988.

Meilman, Patricia. *Titian and the Altarpiece in Renaissance Venice.* Cambridge: Cambridge University Press, 2000.

Merleau-Ponty, Maurice. *The Merleau-Ponty Aesthetics Reader.* Edited and translated by Michael B. Smith. Evanston: Northwestern University Press, 1993.

———. *The Visible and the Invisible.* Edited by Claude Lefort. Translated by Alphonso Lingus. Evanston: Northwestern University Press, 1968.

Nagel, Alexander. *Michelangelo and the Reform of Art.* Cambridge: Cambridge University Press, 2000.

Nagel, Alexander, and Christopher S. Wood. "Interventions: Toward a New Model of Renaissance Anachronism." *Art Bulletin* 87 (2005): 403–32.

Nash, Jane C. *Titian's "Poesie" for Philip II.* Baltimore: Johns Hopkins University Press, 1980.

Nelson, Charles. *Renaissance Theory of Love: The Context of Giordano Bruno's "Eroici Furori."* New York: Columbia University Press, 1958.

Neumann, Jaromir. *Titian: The Flaying of Marsyas.* Translated by Till Gottheiner. London: Spring Books, 1962.

Niero, A. "Pietà liturgica e pietà popolare nel 'Vesperbild' di Tiziano." In *Interpretazioni veneziane: Studi in storia dell'arte in onore di Michelangelo Muraro,* edited by David Rosand, 323–29. Venice: Arsenale Editrice, 1984.

Ost, Hans. *Tizian-Studien.* Cologne: Böhlau, 1992.

Paleotti, Gabriele. *Discorso intorno alle immagini sacre e profane.* 1582. In *Trattati d'arte del Cinquecento fra manierismo e Controriforma,* edited by Paola Barocchi, vol. 2, 117–509. Bari: G. Laterza, 1961.

Pallucchini, Rodolfo. *Tiziano.* Florence: G. C. Sansoni, 1969.

Panofsky, Erwin. *Idea: A Concept in Art Theory.* Columbia: University of South Carolina Press, 1968.

———. *Problems in Titian, Mostly Iconographic.* New York: New York University Press, 1969.

———. *Studies in Iconology: Humanistic Themes in the Art of the Renaissance.* New York: Harper and Row, 1962.

Pardo, Mary. "Artifice as Seduction in Titian." In *Sexuality and Gender in Early Modern Europe: Institutions, Texts, Images,* edited by James Grantham Turner, 55–89. Cambridge: Cambridge University Press, 1993.

———. "The Subject of Savoldo's *Magdalene*." *Art Bulletin* 71 (1989): 67–91.

———. "Veiling the V*enus of Urbino*." In *Titian's "Venus of Urbino,"* edited by Rona Goffen, 108–28. Cambridge: Cambridge University Press, 1997.

Park, Katharine. "The Criminal and the Saintly Body: Autopsy and Dissection in Renaissance Italy." *Renaissance Quarterly* 47 (1994): 1–33.

Pino, Paolo. *Dialogo di pittura.* 1548. In *Trattati d'arte del Cinquecento fra manierismo e Controriforma,* edited by Paola Barocchi, vol. 1, 93–139. Bari: G. Laterza, 1960.

Podro, Michael. *Depiction.* New Haven: Yale University Press, 1998.

———. "Fiction and Reality in Painting." In *Funktionen des Fiktiven,* edited by Dieter Henrich and Wolfgang Iser, 225–37. Poetik und Hermeneutik 10. Munich: Wilhelm Fink, 1983.

Poglayen-Neuwall, Stephan. "Titian's Pictures of the Toilet of Venus and Their Copies." *Art Bulletin* 16 (1934): 358–84.

Pope-Hennessy, John. *Italian Renaissance Sculpture: An Introduction to Italian Sculpture.* New York: Vintage, 1985.

———. *The Portrait in the Renaissance.* New York: Pantheon, 1966.

Potts, Alex. *The Sculptural Imagination: Figurative, Modernist, Minimalist.* New Haven: Yale University Press, 2000.

Prater, Andreas. *Venus at Her Mirror: Velásquez and the Art of Nude Painting.* Munich: Prestel, 2002.

Previtali, Giovanni. "Una data per il problema dei pulpiti di S. Lorenzo." *Paragone* 133 (1961): 48–56.

Puttfarken, Thomas. *Titian and Tragic Painting. Aristotle's Poetics and the Rise of the Modern Artist.* New Haven: Yale University Press, 2005.

Randolph, Adrian. *Engaging Symbols: Gender, Politics, and Public Art in Fifteenth-Century Florence.* New Haven: Yale University Press, 2002.

Rapp, J. "Tizians Marsyas in Kremsier: Ein neu-platonisch-orphisches Mysterium vom Leiden des Menschen und seiner Erlösung." *Pantheon* 45 (1987): 70–89.

Reilly, Patricia L. "The Taming of the Blue: Writing out Color in Italian Renaissance Theory." In *The Expanding Discourse: Feminism and Art History,* edited by Norma Broude and Mary D. Garrard, 87–99. New York: Icon Editions, 1992.

Ridolfi, Carlo. *Le meraviglie dell'arte.* 1648. Edited by Detlev von Hadeln. Berlin: G. Grote, 1914–24.

Ringbom, Sixten. *Icon to Narrative: The Rise of the Dramatic Close-up in Fifteenth-Century Devotional Painting.* Doornspijk: Davaco, 1984

Rogers, Mary. "Sonnets on Female Portraits from Renaissance North Italy." *Word and Image* 2 (1986): 291–305.

Rosand, David. *Drawing Acts: Studies in Graphic Expression and Representation.* Cambridge: Cambridge University Press, 2002.

———. "*Ermeneutica amorosa:* Observations on the Interpretation of Titian's Venuses." In *Tiziano e Venezia: Convegno internazionale di studi, Venezia,* 1976, 375–81. Vicenza: N. Pozza, 1980.

———. "La mano di Tiziano." In *Tiziano: Técnicas y restauraciones, Actas del Simposium Internacional celebrado en el Museo nacional del Prado,* 127–38. Madrid: Museo nacional del Prado, 1999.

———. *The Meaning of the Mark: Leonardo and Titian.* Lawrence: Spencer Museum of Art, University of Kansas, 1988.

———. *Painting in Sixteenth-Century Venice: Titian, Veronese, Tintoretto.* Cambridge: Cambridge University Press, 1997.

———. "Raphael's *School of Athens* and the Artist of the Modern Manner." In *The World of Savonarola: Italian Elites and Perceptions of Crisis,* edited by Stella Fletcher and Christine Shaw, 212–32. Aldershot: Ashgate, 2000.

———. "So-and-So Reclining on Her Couch." In *Titian* 500, edited by Joseph Manca, 101–19. Studies in the History of Art 45. Washington: National Gallery of Art, 1993.

———. *Titian.* New York: H. N. Abrams, 1978.

———. "Titian and the Critical Tradition." In *Titian: His World and His Legacy,* edited by David Rosand, 1–39. New York: Columbia University Press, 1982.

———. "*Ut Pictor Poeta:* Meaning in Titian's *Poesie*." *New Literary History* 3 (1971–72): 527–46.

Rosen, Valeska von. *Mimesis und Selbstbezüglichkeit in Werken Tizians.* Emsdetten: Edition Imorde, 2001.

Roskill, Mark W., ed. and trans. *Dolce's "Aretino" and Venetian Art Theory of the Cinquecento.* New York: New York University Press, 1968.

Rubin, Patricia Lee. *Giorgio Vasari: Art and History.* New Haven: Yale University Press, 1995.

Ruvoldt, Maria. *The Italian Renaissance Imagery of Inspiration: Metaphors of Sex, Sleep, and Dreams.* Cambridge: Cambridge University Press, 2004.

Saint-Saëns, Alain. *Art and Faith in Tridentine Spain, 1545–1690.* New York: Peter Lang, 1995.

Saslow, James M. "Michelangelo: Sculpture, Sex, and Gender." In *Looking at Italian Renaissance Sculpture,* edited by Sarah Blake McHam, 223–45. Cambridge: Cambridge University Press, 1998.

———. *The Poetry of Michelangelo. An Annotated Translation.* New Haven: Yale University Press, 1991.

Sawday, Jonathan. *The Body Emblazoned: Dissection and the Human Body in Renaissance Culture.* London: Routledge, 1995.

Scarry, Elaine. *The Body in Pain: The Making and Unmaking of the World.* Oxford: Oxford University Press, 1985.

Schäpers, Petra. *Die junge Frau bei der Toilette.* Frankfurt am Main: Peter Lang, 1997.

Schleif, Corine. "Nicodemus and Sculptors: Self-Reflexivity in Works by Adam Kraft and Tilman Riemenschneider." *Art Bulletin* 75 (1993): 599–626.

Shapley, Fern Rusk. "Titian's *Venus with a Mirror.*" *Studies in the History of Art* 4–5 (1971–72): 93–105.

Shearman, John. "Cristofano Allori's 'Judith.'" *The Burlington Magazine* 121 (1979): 3–10.

———. *Only Connect . . . : Art and the Spectator in the Italian Renaissance.* Princeton: Princeton University Press, 1992.

Smith, Pamela H. *The Body of the Artisan: Art and Experience in the Scientific Revolution.* Chicago: University of Chicago Press, 2004.

Snow, Edward. "Theorizing the Male Gaze: Some Problems." *Representations* 25 (1989): 30–41.

Sohm, Philip L. *The Artist Grows Old: The Aging of Art and Artists in Italy,* 1500–1800. New Haven: Yale University Press, 2007.

———. "Gendered Style in Italian Art Criticism from Michelangelo to Malvasia." *Renaissance Quarterly* 48 (1995): 759–808.

———. *Pittoresco: Marco Boschini, His Critics, and Their Critiques of Painterly Brushwork in Seventeenth- and Eighteenth-Century Italy.* Cambridge: Cambridge University Press, 1991.

———. *Style in the Art Theory of Early Modern Italy.* Cambridge: Cambridge University Press, 2001.

Sperling, Christine M. "Donatello's Bronze 'David' and the Demands of Medici Politics." *Burlington Magazine* 134 (1992): 218–24.

Stafford, Barbara Maria. *Body Criticism: Imagining the Unseen in Enlightenment Art and Medicine.* Cambridge, Mass.: MIT Press, 1991.

Stallybrass, Peter. "Patriarchal Territories: The Body Enclosed." In *Rewriting the Renaissance: The Discourses of Sexual Difference in Early Modern Europe,* edited by Margaret W. Ferguson, Maureen Quilligan, and Nancy J. Vickers, 123–42. Chicago: University of Chicago Press, 1986.

Stechow, Wolfgang. "Joseph of Arimathea or Nicodemus." In *Studien zur Toskanischen Kunst: Festschrift für Ludwig Heinrich Heydenreich,* edited by Wolfgang Lotz and Lise Lotte Möller, 289–302. Munich: Prestel, 1964.

Steinberg, Leo. "The Line of Fate in Michelangelo's Painting." In *The Language of Images,* edited by W. T. J. Mitchell, 95–110. Chicago: University of Chicago Press, 1980.

———. *Michelangelo's Last Paintings.* New York: Oxford University Press, 1975.

Stoichita, Victor I. *The Self-Aware Image: An Insight into Early-Modern Meta-Painting.* Translated by Anne-Marie Glasheen. Cambridge: Cambridge University Press, 1997.

Suida, Wilhelm. *Le Titien.* Paris: A. Weber, 1975.

Summers, David. "Aria II: The Union of Image and Artist as an Aesthetic Ideal in Renaissance Art." *Artibus et Historiae* 20 (1989): 15–31.

———. "Form and Gender." *New Literary History* 24 (1993): 243–71.

———. *The Judgment of Sense: Renaissance Naturalism and the Rise of Aesthetics.* Cambridge: Cambridge University Press, 1987.

———. *Michelangelo and the Language of Art.* Princeton: Princeton University Press, 1981.

Tietze, Hans. "An Early Version of Titian's *Danaë:* An Analysis of Titian's Replicas." *Arte Veneta* 8 (1954): 199–208.

———. *Leben und Werk.* 2 vols. Vienna: Phaidon, 1936.

Tietze-Conrat, Erika. "Titian's Workshop in His Late Years." *Art Bulletin* 28 (1946):76–88.

Tiziano. Exh. cat. Venice: Marsilio Editore, 1990.

Valcanover, Francesco. *Tutta la pittura di Tiziano.* 2 vols. Milan: Rizzoli, 1960.

Varchi, Benedetto. *Della maggioranza delle arti—Disputa II.* In *Trattati d'arte del Cinquecento fra manierismo e Controriforma,* edited by Paola Barocchi, vol. 1, 34–52. Bari: G. Laterza, 1960.

Vasari, Giorgio. *Le vite de' più eccellenti pittori, scultori, ed architettori: Nelle redazioni* 1550 *e* 1568. Edited by Paola Barocchi, 6 vols. Florence: Sansoni, 1966–69 (vols. 1–3, 5, 6); Florence: Studi per edizione scelte, 1967 (vol. 4).

Warburg, Aby. *The Renewal of Pagan Antiquity.* Translated by David Britt. Los Angeles: Getty Research Institute for the History of Art and the Humanities, 1999.

Wethey, Harold E. The *Paintings of Titian.* 3 vols. London: Phaidon, 1969–75.

Wollheim, Richard. *Painting as an Art.* Princeton: Princeton University Press, 1987.

Woods-Marsden, Joanna. *Renaissance Self-Portraiture: The Visual Construction of Identity and the Social Status of the Artist.* New Haven: Yale University Press, 1998.

______, ed. *Titian: Materiality, Likeness, Istoria.* Turnhout: Brepols, 2007.

Wright, Anthony. "Republican Tradition and the Maintenance of 'National' Religious Traditions in Venice." *Renaissance Studies* 10 (1996): 405–16.

Wyss, Edith. *The Myth of Apollo and Marsyas in the Art of the Italian Renaissance: An Inquiry into the Meaning of Images.* Newark: University of Delaware Press, 1996.

Zeri, Federico. *Pittura e controriforma: L'arte senza tempo di Scipione da Gaeta.* Turin: Giulio Einaudi, 1957.

Zorach, Rebecca. *Blood, Milk, Ink, Gold: Abundance and Excess in the French Renaissance.* Chicago: University of Chicago Press, 2005.

———. "Despoiled at the Source." *Art History* 22 (1999): 244–69.

INDEX